Where the Magic Happens

How a Young Family Changed Their Lives and Sailed Around the World

CASPAR CRAVEN

ADLARD COLES NAUTICAL

BLOOMSBURY

LONDON · OXFORD · NEW YORK · NEW DELHI · SYDNEY

ADLARD COLES
Bloomsbury Publishing Plc

50 Bedford Square, London, WC1B 3DP, UK

BLOOMSBURY, ADLARD COLES and the Adlard Coles logo are
trademarks of Bloomsbury Publishing Plc

First published in Great Britain 2018

A catalogue record for this book is available from the British Library
Library of Congress Cataloguing-in-Publication data has been applied for

ISBN: HB: 978-1-4729-4991-2
eBook: 978-1-4729-4992-9
ePDF: 978-1-4729-4990-5

2 4 6 8 10 9 7 5 3 1

Typeset in Celeste by Deanta Global Publishing Services, Chennai, India
Printed and bound in USA by Berryville Graphics Inc., Berryville, Virginia

Bloomsbury Publishing Plc makes every effort to ensure that the papers used in
the manufacture of our books are natural, recyclable products made from wood
grown in well-managed forests. Our manufacturing processes conform to
the environmental regulations of the country of origin.

To find out more about our authors and books visit www.bloomsbury.com
and sign up for our newsletters

Contents

CONTENTS

Foreword

"Fortune favors the brave"

Terence 190–159 BC

I use this quote in my book *My Heroes: Extraordinary Courage, Exceptional People* to describe people who can take on a challenge, survive, have the ability to react with speed not haste when things go wrong, and thrive. Although the quote was penned over 2,000 years ago, it is as appropriate today as it has ever been. The world is changing and we need to be brave and nurture and cherish these skills in our society.

How refreshing then, at a time when these qualities of bravery need to be developed, to find a young husband and wife team in Caspar and Nichola Craven. A team who took on multiple challenges once they had decided to change their lives and sail around the world: the not-insignificant challenge of raising the money to make their expedition happen; the challenge of navigating the highs and lows of a marital relationship; and the challenge of building and leading a team of their three young children, ready to explore the world's oceans together and really test their limits.

For all those wanting more from life, Caspar's message is incredibly motivating, providing plain-speaking practical guidance mixed with an exhilarating tale of adventure. The book goes behind the scenes of how exactly the Craven family made their magical plan happen, and gives clear advice on how we can follow in their footsteps, before taking us on a fantastic voyage around the world in their boat *Aretha*.

Fortune really does favor the brave.

Ranulph Fiennes

2018

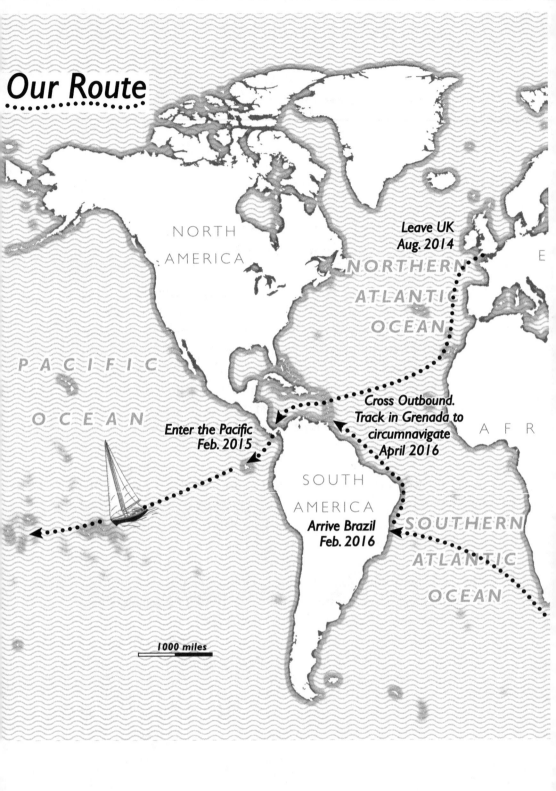

Our Route

Leave UK
Aug. 2014

NORTH
AMERICA

NORTHERN
ATLANTIC
OCEAN

PACIFIC

OCEAN

Enter the Pacific
Feb. 2015

Cross Outbound.
Track in Grenada to
circumnavigate
April 2016

A F R

SOUTH
AMERICA

Arrive Brazil
Feb. 2016

SOUTHERN
ATLANTIC
OCEAN

1000 miles

Prologue

It's pitch black. My hands, the saloon, the cockpit—everything reeks of diesel. The wind is howling outside and we are being thrown around as *Aretha*, our 53-foot sailboat, slides off one wave into the next, whitewater crashing over the lifelines, filling the cockpit. We are drifting sideways.

Aretha is hove-to, slowed down in a sailing maneuver that lessens the boat's motions while we figure things out. The sails are set one on each side of the boat and the steering wheel is lashed down on one side. Nichola and I are physically exhausted. Every 20 minutes one of us wakes and wearily climbs up on deck to make sure no boats are bearing down on us.

We have experienced a power failure. We can't start our generator or engine. And while *Aretha* is a sailboat, we nevertheless have no electronic navigation, no autopilot to steer the boat, no communications, no navigation lights, no lights down below (except our flashlights), no stove, no marine toilets, no way to pump water from our water tanks.

We are, as they say, dead in the water.

Nichola and I are wearing our foul-weather gear, sleeping in the saloon instead of our bunks. Our three children are in our cabin at the stern where there is less movement with the rise and fall of each wave, and where they will get the most sleep.

The saloon, a space smaller than your average kitchen, looks like it has been ravaged by an intruder. The floorboards are up, tools and spare engine parts are everywhere, and Nichola and I are covered in grease and grime from wrestling with the engine. We still can't determine the cause of our power failure.

We are in one of the remotest parts of the world, deep in the Pacific Ocean, more than 500 miles from the nearest piece of land, which itself is a tiny rock in the vast Pacific. There are no rescue services out here. We truly are on our own. There are three other boats within 100 miles but there's not much they can do to help. It's pretty unfeasible for them to sail 100 miles and come alongside in 30-foot seas. We feel extremely isolated. We have to figure out the solution ourselves.

It's just the five of us: Nichola, my wife, age 43, our three young children—ages 9, 7, and 2—and me, age 42.

Introduction

How did our young family arrive mid-Pacific aboard *Aretha*, wave-tossed, without navigation instruments or power?

When we planned to sail around the world with our three children to create magical life-changing experiences, this wasn't quite what we had in mind. We had imagined deserted tropical islands and snorkeling beautiful reefs. We had experienced all of that, true enough, and it was magical. What we would discover, though, is that the true "magic" happens on a much deeper level. We learned in our moments of adversity the power of working together as a team. Our toughest times became some of our most defining moments. We used the skills and tools I'll share with you in these pages when the going got rough. Magic happens when you decide to step beyond your comfort zone—when you challenge your beliefs, decide what you want, and make it happen by following through with resolute determination.

On that dark Pacific night, we worked together to solve a vexing problem that two years earlier would have frightened and panicked us. Instead we had settled the boat, settled our selves, and were working through the issues. We figured out how to survive and thrive in the face of adversity—a skill we all need for dealing with life. The seeds for how we survived were sown five years earlier. This power loss would eventually become one of our proudest experiences working together as a family team.

Along with challenging moments in mountainous seas and wild storms, our journey was filled with countless magical, shared experiences of the world: we explored and delighted in the Galapagos Islands, climbed the Mount Yasur volcano, swam with sharks in the Tuamoto Islands, brought humanitarian aid to a disaster zone in Vanuatu, and were entranced by warm welcomes the world over.

Many people assume you need to be wealthy before you can live your dream. We did it the other way around. We made the decision to put our dream first and then created the wealth to make it happen. The reality is that to live your dreams—whatever they are—you need to make a committed decision, be extremely resourceful, and then, go make things happen.

Where the Magic Happens tells how the spark of an idea developed into a decision that created a full-blown, life-changing adventure that transformed our lives, our relationships, and our fortunes. Nichola and I stepped out of our suburban commuter lifestyle, way beyond our comfort zones, undertaking something that challenged each of us, forcing us to grow in ways that we never imagined. In Part One we chart our course for making the change; in Part Two we take readers around the world with us, sharing a glimpse of the magic we experienced.

The Seeds Are Sown

Fifteen years prior to finding ourselves sea-tossed in the Pacific, back in 2000/2001, I'd been fortunate enough to sail around the world for my first time as part of the BT Global Challenge, known as the world's toughest yacht race. As part of the selection process for the race, I was interviewed by its founder, Sir Chay Blyth, who said something that has stayed with me ever since:

"Caspar—there will come a day, a day when you are lying down looking at your toes. As you draw your final breath, you'll ask yourself, have I done everything I want to do in life? If the answer is no, you're going to be pretty brassed off. So stop messing around, work out what you want to do, and get on with it!"

It's been my guiding force ever since.

This plan to sail around the world with our family was more than simply an adventure. Nichola and I had both had adventures before. Adventures are temporary. At some point with an adventure, you return to the life you had before. This was about lasting change.

There's an abundance of advice on how to get more out of life—to live your dreams and to live before you die. Plenty of people would like to break out and live life to the full. Here are the three hurdles where many people get stuck: their partners, children, and money. It can be uncertain and tricky to navigate these obstacles, to embrace a shared dream to make it happen. Yet, it is all doable. In *Where the Magic Happens* we show how we followed our path.

Our story is about creating major life changes together. Creating the family team. Creating the bonds. Creating relationships to last a lifetime. This is the story of the Craven Family. It covers the sacrifices that Caspar, Nichola, Bluebell, Columbus, and Willow made so we could transform our lives. It's also about dealing with adversity and challenging conventional thinking.

We were nothing special. What Nichola and I did was make a committed joint decision (1) and we spent time truly understanding our purpose (2) and why that decision was so important to both of us. We created a plan that we pursued with relentless and unstoppable action (3). When one approach didn't work, we were flexible and adapted our plans (4) until we finally achieved the reality that we had spent so much time imagining.

Those four elements enabled us to pull it off. However, we had to work it out as we went; there was no guidebook to help us. Our aim for *Where the Magic Happens* is to combine inspiration with practical guidance so you, too, can live your dreams.

Four Elements for Family Life Change

1. Committed joint decision—dream together and create a shared picture and story around the future.
2. Understand your purpose—why your decision is a "must have" rather than a "nice to have."
3. Make a plan together and get into relentless action to bring that plan to life.
4. Be flexible and keep adapting your approach until you achieve the future you imagined.

PART ONE

Dreaming, Planning, and Making the Plan Happen

Chapter 1

Creating a Vision of the Future
(Five Years Before Our Departure)

Birth of an Idea

There are moments in life when everything changes.

You're not always aware of them at the time, but when you look back you realize you've experienced a transformational moment—life was never the same again. I can remember only three or four such moments. Those are the big days—the instinctive decisions that you make in a heartbeat—without any real thought—because you just know. They just feel right.

It was June 13, 2009. Imagine a warm, early summer's day in the garden of the leafy commuter village of Shipborne in Kent, southeast England. A buffet lunch on the patio, children running around playing, laughter and fun filling the air. We were living a typical family life in suburban London and celebrating my sister Pippa's birthday. I was 37; Nichola, my wife, was 38.

Our Life Together—The Early Years

We'd met in our early twenties at a friend's house party in London. I was fresh out of university and training as a chartered accountant, while Nichola was training as an attorney. I distinctly remember seeing Nichola across the room. I was captivated in a moment. She was talking to a friend of mine and I jumped straight into the conversation without hesitation. We talked and then two weeks later we met again at a housewarming party Nichola was hosting. I asked for her number, and said I'd like to take her out on a date but that it wouldn't be for two months as I was in the middle of my accountancy exams. She was curious and amused at my admission. When I phoned her two months later, I'm certain she wasn't expecting it. We ended up chatting for an hour.

We just connected and, buoyed by the flowing conversation, we ended by making a date for the following week. I arranged for us to go to the Jazz Cafe in Camden in North London. Only when we got there did we discover it was closed; Nichola clearly got the message that I needed an organizer in my life. Despite the change in plans we had a magical romantic evening at a piano-bar restaurant, Kettners in central London, and then walked the banks of the Thames under the stars. When she arrived home, Nichola told her brother that she'd met the person she was going to spend the rest of her life with.

Our relationship blossomed quickly. After three months Nichola's mom suggested we move in together as we spent all our time at each other's places—so why pay double rent? She had a good point.

I spent the first nine years of my career climbing the corporate ladder. I didn't particularly enjoy it and don't think I was very good at it. So by 2002 I'd made the break to run my own business. By then I'd launched at least five different ventures. None were as successful as I wanted at this point; I'd have earned more stacking shelves at a supermarket. Nichola, meanwhile, worked as a criminal attorney and we lived a typical city lifestyle: we worked hard, enjoyed our time with friends, and loved spending time together.

In 2004, when we were in our early thirties, we got married and decided to have children. Bluebell—our energetic, larger-than-life baby girl—came first. Nichola paused her legal career: the stresses of being a full-time attorney and a full-time mom just didn't work. Less than two years later Columbus arrived; we had the perfect set—one boy, one girl. Life was full. Life was busy. Life wasn't particularly fulfilling. We looked like any other family trying to make their way in the world, clattering in a haze from one week to the next, one month to the next, year to year.

The Daily Routine: The Way We Were

Life rolled forward and by 2009 we were both in our late thirties. I was the co-founder of an early stage consultancy business and Nichola had returned to work part-time in her father's company.

Our routine had become entrenched: life patterns we followed unconsciously because we'd done it for so long, because everyone around us had done it for so long. Rise at 6am, breakfast, cycle to the station, get a coffee, jostle along with all the other commuters. Stand at the same spot on the platform; the same faces always looking down—at the ground, at their coffee, at their iPhones—rarely looking up. Variety entails choosing a different location on the platform. Board the train, look for a seat—squeeze in if it's full and start reading the news, or catching up on Facebook. Arrive at London Waterloo and join the river of commuters flowing through the station in waves as train after train empties its load. The connecting train and the walk to work, a full day at the office—meetings, calls, ideas, plans—and before I knew it, it was 6.30pm, time to head home.

Arriving home by 8pm, I was lucky if I'd catch ten minutes with the children, and, if I still had the energy, perhaps I'd read them a story. Watch some TV, spend time with Nichola, and by 11pm it was time to sleep. Nichola the night owl would stay up later—after her day working and spending time with the children, the late evenings were her time to herself. Come the weekend, I was shattered. I'd spend a little time with the children, go for a run, undertake the weekly food shopping, and spend time with friends. And so the weeks rolled from one to the next, with me barely seeing the children—most of their time taken up with school and mine with work.

Was this the life we had consciously chosen? Nichola and I had each other. We had our children. But we had little time to appreciate each other or the children, to live life, to enjoy life. Life was dominated by work. The signs of pressure showed: a strained relationship, arguments, not really seeing eye to eye, and knowing that nothing new was going to happen that would fundamentally change that. I knew that there was more to life. There had to be more.

The typical scheme of things is: get educated, get a job, get married, have kids, work until you retire, and maybe then have some adventures once you've got a little money together. Sure, pack in a few holidays a year—maybe even two weeks away if you are lucky. Who defined this pattern? Why should we have to follow this route? Maybe, just maybe, there was another way. There was a whole world out there to explore and we had the feeling that we were racing through our lives with things that in reality weren't all that important. This was an itch that had to be scratched. I know many people have a similar itch—if you are reading this I suspect you do, too—a yearning for something more.

The Day Life Changed

Our life was about to change. As we chatted over lunch in my sister's garden that June day, my brother-in-law, James, shared a story he'd read about a family who had decided to break from normal life and sail around the world. Nichola and I both shared an interest in traveling and this topic, being different from the usual garden-party-type conversation, piqued Nichola's interest and she wanted to know more. The conversation ended with James concluding that the family was crazy and so the topic was closed. Talk returned to the more usual conversational topics of work, kids, and the week ahead.

I thought no more about it. That afternoon, as we got back into our family car and reversed out of the drive, waving our goodbyes to head back to Surrey, something was different. Nichola turned to me and asked:

"Shall we do it?"

"Do what?" I said.

"Take a year out and go sailing with the children?"

One look at her and I knew she was serious. I couldn't hide my excitement—I needed no encouragement for an adventure. I was excited because I knew that if Nichola was on board as well, we were going to do this together.

The seed was planted. All it needed now was sunshine and water to grow. The most dangerous time for any idea is when it's just been hatched; we all have so many ideas and yet so few are ever acted on. But we gently nurtured the idea over the months that followed.

Nichola's initial thought was for us to take a year on a classics tour of the Mediterranean via sailboat. We'd done two flotilla sailing holidays there before we'd had children.

"What about the ARC?" I mused out loud. Nichola looked blank. "The Atlantic Rally for Cruisers—where 200–300 yachts every year sail the Atlantic in convoy, crossing from the Canary Islands to St. Lucia in the Caribbean."

"Oh. Well, that sounds safe enough," said Nichola. "We'd be in the company of lots of other yachts."

I pressed on. "And once we've sailed the Atlantic, why not keep going—through the Panama Canal, across the Pacific to Australia, and then back via the Indian Ocean and up the Atlantic again?"

And so the idea developed.

Turning an Idea into a Vision—Brainstorming and Planning

The following Saturday, once the children had gone to bed, we sat on our living room floor with sheets of paper and a blue felt-tip pen. We brainstormed anything and everything. The ideas flowed effortlessly and fast.

We wanted to sail around the world with our children—for two years, we'd decided. We jotted down all the countries we wanted to visit, and the festivals we wanted to attend, such as Carnival in Brazil. This suddenly put anchor dates into our two-year time slot. We wrote down our thoughts, feelings, what we wanted, and how we wanted our life to be different. We wrote down anything and everything that came into our heads connected with this idea. Then, faced with several sheets of paper covered in blue felt-tip, we put the plan into some sort of order.

First of all, we had to map out a route. Then we had to work out a timeline—how long were we going to spend in each place, how long would it take us to sail across each ocean? We quickly realized that two years might seem a long time, but we were planning on getting the

11

whole way round the world in this time and we would have to plan passages based on global weather systems.

We discussed what we were both looking for from this experience. Partly, it was about wanting an adventure, but we were going to be traveling with children who were still fairly young. The aim was to create life-changing experiences for all of us—not scare them and us. This type of decision helped us map out a route—we would not be going around Cape Horn but rather through the Panama Canal. We would not be sailing into the Southern Ocean but keeping as far north as the current and weather would allow. We would be sailing across the Indian Ocean from Australia to South Africa, keeping sufficiently south and offshore so as to avoid pirates. We also decided that we would join the ARC to sail the Atlantic, our first ocean in company.

Skill Assessment—The Good, the Bad, and the Ugly of Where You Start Out

We were realistic about the skills we possessed and the ones we lacked. The most obvious one for Nichola was that she had no sailing background. Not only that, she suffered from seasickness. For her, the excitement would come from traveling the world and traveling with our children. She figured the trade-off of being seasick would be worth the payout.

For me, having grown up near the water, the sea was the attraction and to be able to share this magic with my children while they were young was a dream. But neither of us were medics or mechanics and we lacked any experience should any of us be ill offshore or if the boat needed repairs. There was a big skills gap between what we had and what we would need.

We continued our discussions, being absolutely and totally realistic about what skills we possessed. Being an attorney and an accountant seemed less relevant when it came to what we wanted to do. We were planning on taking our children sailing for two years, and they would need schooling. Neither of us were teachers—how would that work?

We also started thinking about how much money we'd need to make this all happen. Honestly, at this stage we did not have a clue, we just knew that it was a lot of money and certainly way more than we had.

Yet we were undeterred; in fact, we were both vibrating with excitement—maybe, just maybe, this could happen.

We continued writing it all down—the good, the bad, and the ugly. We didn't let any of it put us off. Our notes had a single aim—assessing what we would need to make this happen. From there we could analyze which skills we didn't have, and then work out how to fill them.

Our Sailing Experience

I'd been on boats all my life. I learned to sail dinghies with my mom around the Devon coast and later progressed to sailing on friends' yachts. I started a fishing business at the age of 14, and by 17 was running a commercial fishing boat exporting ½ ton of crabs a week to Spain. Understanding the sea was part of my DNA.

Back in 2000/2001 when I joined the BT Global Challenge, described as the "World's Toughest Yacht Race," I had sailed around the world on a crewed boat. After our boat won the first leg into Boston I was made a watch leader, running one of the two watches.

When I returned at the age of 28, I took all the exams to be a Yacht Master and continued sailing around the Mediterranean as well as taking part in a race around Britain and Ireland.

Nichola had sailed less—her only experience was two flotilla holidays we did together around the Mediterranean.

Setting a Date on the Calendar

By now it was 2009, and Bluebell was four and Columbus was two. Our idea was to set sail and return before Bluebell started secondary school at the age of eleven, which would be September 2016. Allowing two years for a circumnavigation, we planned to set off in the summer of 2014 after the children had finished that school year, leaving as soon as possible after the summer term finished. The ARC left Las Palmas in the

Canaries at the end of November each year. This meant that we had to leave the UK and arrive in Las Palmas by the end of October to be in time for the start of the ARC. We put a departure date on our family calendar: August 1, 2014. We then mapped out a timeline for the advance work. It was the summer of 2009, which gave us five years to prepare. That felt like an eternity to get our lives in order and do whatever we needed to make the plan happen.

To nurture the idea, we had to keep it in the forefront of our minds. We talked about it whenever we got the opportunity. At this stage it was just a conversation between the two of us. Importantly, though, we kept adding more and more detail—where we'd go, what we would do, what we would like to see and experience. We wrote it all down. Still with no idea of cost we created a financial target.

We worked out what would be the ideal boat we wanted and how much that would cost us to buy new. Then we guesstimated how much money we would need to live with complete financial freedom (the number we came up with was $7.5m or £5m!). Our number was so huge compared to where we were, so far away as to be laughable. It did not deter us. We had created a big goal and we were going for it.

Marital Teamwork

The quality of our relationship back in 2009 was fairly typical. Both of us were working long hours and neither of us were particularly fulfilled by what we were doing. Like so many relationships, we felt the life pressures and yet we communicated about needs and wants differently. I've always been someone who likes to get things out in the open and discuss them; Nichola prefers to quietly resolve things in her own mind. This setup doesn't make for harmonious living. We had at various times sought help to get us communicating and appreciating our different styles, as well as the strengths that each of us brought to our family team. Yet we'd fallen into a pattern where the same arguments circled round and round. Finally, after working with a counselor, we began to learn how to break the cycle. We became more conscious of our emotions—witnessing what triggered each of us and how we'd spiral into anger or resentment or silence or blame—and then developed skills for breaking those patterns. In our culture there is a stigma around getting relationship help—which really just amounts to self-awareness and learning communication skills. This lack of awareness results in a missed opportunity, as this is a fundamental component of being human.

Our plans now meant that Nichola and I really had to get on the same page and work as a team. We had spent most of our lives working independently. My work was in finance, at large companies that hosted countless training courses on working in teams, bringing other people along with you. Nichola's career as an attorney was vastly different—you work independently—working as part of a team wasn't part of her working culture. To make our big dream happen we realized we would have to come together—there was no way to achieve it if we worked independently. Despite our lack of sailing trip planning experience, we both had valuable skills and talents: now we had to unlock them and work together.

I lost count of the number of planning sessions. We had a formula: arrange childcare, or wait until the children were asleep, or get up at 5am to work on the plans; get a pile of blank paper and some pens; find the earlier notes and plans; put the coffee pot on and sit at the kitchen table discussing and moving things forward. Sometimes it was dark and cold and we'd drag ourselves out of our warm bed, often short of sleep, having gone to bed only four hours earlier. We'd leave parties and friends' houses early because we wanted to get up early; we'd pass on events and outings. Our vision of sailing around the world had become our top priority.

The Power of a Committed Joint Decision—Your Reason Why

Making a committed decision to what we were embarking on was everything. There were times during the planning years when nothing seemed to work and we were driving each other mad, frustrated that we weren't making meaningful progress. If we hadn't been crystal clear on our decision and our motivations—why we wanted this so badly—then I can guarantee we'd have given up. The difference was we were clear and unified on our vision and goals from the start.

We'd both set unsuccessful goals in the past and knew only too well the truth that if you have a goal, you'll either achieve it or you'll find an excuse as to why you haven't. "Oh I don't want it that badly—this other outcome isn't so bad..." We didn't want to settle for anything less than our world sailing vision.

What was so powerful that this vision would be worth the sacrifices? We created the time and space to really think deeply about the plan. We knew that our "Reason Why" had to be strong enough to stand up to the challenges we'd inevitably face from family, friends, and even our own inner doubts that were certain to creep in from time to time.

There was a story that resonated with us. Imagine an island surrounded by shark-infested waters. On that island there is a castle surrounded by barbed wire and armed guards. Now, inside that castle there is a room. Inside that room is a $10 bill. If someone suggested that you swim through the sharks, and climb the walls past the barbed wire, and get around the armed guards, I can't imagine many people risking that for $10. Imagine, however, that your children are being held in there and you have to save them. Not much will stand in your way—you will find a way to storm the castle to save them. If you have a strong reason why you want to do something (like save your children), you will go and make it happen because it's truly important.

Your Reason Why—your motivation—matters. It really matters. There are a million reasons why you shouldn't do something, but we decided that we really just needed one good Reason Why we should take the family sailing around the world. We focused our energy on what our powerful reason was, crafting it together. We asked a lot of hard questions of ourselves and over the course of many weeks we revisited this subject, debating it late into the evening. Why exactly did we want to do this? What was it that we wanted to achieve for each other, for our children, for us as a family? It was largely the same for both of us. Really, it all boiled down to one thing. It was way deeper than just going sailing for two years.

Our Reason Why was to create magical, life-changing experiences for us and our family.

Not only that, but the prospect of spending time together as a family, seeing our children grow, daily, in front of our eyes—to experience the world with them and to teach them what was important—was too big an opportunity for us to pass up. We wanted to create a different kind of life with them. We wanted to experience the wonder of the world together, broadening our horizons beyond normal everyday suburban life.

The vision was in many ways the easy part. We'd painted a picture of what we wanted. The hard work had to begin now: drilling down into the details, creating a workable plan that we could focus and take action on so we could actually bring our vision to life.

Commit Your Vision to Paper and Make It Public

Early on, in addition to committing all our ideas to paper, Nichola and I took a first pass at writing a shared vision statement, blending elements of what we both wanted to accomplish. We kept going back to it, refining it, and editing it. Importantly, all of this was written out on paper with a pen, no computer. It was all handwritten and got scribbled on and edited and brought to life. Finally, when we were happy with the final version, we both signed it and posted it on the wall. We had publicly committed to it. We came back to it a few weeks later and refined it and rewrote it—then reposted it on the wall.

Drafting a Vision Statement: Mumbo Jumbo?

Investing the time to create a shared vision felt like a strange activity at home. I remember being scornful of this sort of thing in my corporate days, thinking it was just wishy-washy words, mumbo jumbo. But having lived through our experience, I know there is nothing wishy-washy about creating a big, compelling vision that both partners—and then the rest of the family—buy into. It is specific, engaging, and life-changing to produce this vision. Spending the quality time exploring what that vision means for each of you—really getting underneath the surface of the words—strengthens the vision, forcing stronger articulation, making a firm foundation for the planning and execution stages.

This final, one page, sail-around-the-world vision was tacked to our kitchen wall, deliberately in full view of house visitors (see plate section, image 1). In addition we bought a huge map of the world and stuck this up alongside our vision statement. The map, with our route traced along it, could not be missed when you came into our kitchen. It invited conversation. Why was this important? Because the more we talked about our vision with each other and our family and friends, the more answers we came up with to all the questions.

We read our vision statement day and night and it didn't take long for me to be able to recite it word for word without looking at it. It became our burning ambition—our focus. First thing in the morning in my mind's eye, I'd see us sitting on our sailboat leaving the shores of England, heading out to the open ocean, sailing down to the Canary Islands—I could hear the flags fluttering in the wind in my imagination—on through the Panama Canal, across the Pacific, sailing into Cape Town. It became so real; I could feel it already.

Make the Magic Happen: Creating a Vision of the Future—Your Actions

Time Required
Several uninterrupted evenings

Tools Required
Blank sheets of paper
Colored felt pens
A clear space to work
A bottle of wine and glasses (optional)

1. Create Your Vision
   This is the exciting part. At this stage do not give any thought to the detail of how you are actually going to achieve your vision. The "how" stage comes later. For now you need a vision that excites both of you enough to rise early in the morning, keep you working late at night, and gets you dreaming and thinking whenever you have a spare moment. Don't give any thought to whether it sounds laughable or

---

ridiculous. If it's your passion or dream, write it down, share it, get it out there. This is not the place to be shy—you need to speak up and spell it out.

Both partners need to share what is truly important to them. You need to listen and understand what is truly important to your partner.

It's highly unlikely you'll have perfectly matching visions. The key is to focus on what you have in common rather than what is different. It's really hard to build on conflict. It's infinitely easier to build on what you share. What we experienced is that the magic happened when we only focused on the elements we shared.

Take this common ground and create a narrative or a story around it. What could a story look like that encompasses what is important to both of you? Enjoy debating the ideas and coming up with different versions of what a compelling shared story could look like.

It may be that there are things important to you individually that you have to let go of and that you just focus on what you have in common. What we found remarkable is that when we started to fill in a shared exciting picture we also created energy and momentum that then expanded the whole vision to include more and more things.

The magic is where you are creating a shared vision for the future.

2. Keep Revisiting Your Vision

This is the start of a conversation, not a one-time conversation. Keep having that conversation and keep listening and exploring to create your shared picture that excites both of you.

3. Commit Your Shared Vision to Paper

OK, so you have a vision: it's shared, it's exciting, it's madness. Write down the final draft on one piece of paper with a pen. Provide a deadline by when it will happen. Nothing happens without a deadline. Make it colorful, make it bold, make it a physical thing. Sign it jointly and date it with today's date.

4. Make Your Vision Public

Pin this piece of paper up in your home. Do not hide it in a room that nobody goes in. Put your colorful, signed, shared vision statement in the most public place you can think of—you want your family and friends to see it and to ask about it. We put ours in the kitchen in full view of everyone who visited our home.

5. Read It

Read your shared vision to yourself and out loud every day so that it becomes second nature. You want it to feel natural. The more natural it feels to you, the more natural it will feel to your family and friends. Also, the more natural the vision, the greater the likelihood the idea will move from what feels fanciful to something actual. Once it feels real, your energy will be concentrated on steps to make the vision happen, not whether you can make it happen.

Life-Changing Possibilities

Traveling the Americas by Camper

Paul and Rebecca were your typical American parents with two children aged 13 and 11. Life was a full schedule of work, school, and sports. They wanted to enjoy more of life together and set off in a camper to explore Mexico and Central America for a year. For them, this wasn't simply an adventure —it was the stepping-stone to a new life. They now live in Mexico.

Selling Up and Moving to Greece

Laura and Euan and their 2-year-old daughter, Sophie, moved from London to Greece in 2016. After 10 years living in London, they made plans for a different type of life where they could spend time together as a family and follow their passions—things that were truly important to them. They now live a few minutes from a Greek beach.

Redundancy Forces the Issue

Jo and her husband were in their late 30s. They had both experienced layoffs, which gave them the catalyst to start a new life. They moved to the southwest of England and bought a small plot of land, which they are developing into a vineyard—they are on their way to becoming winemakers.

Backpacking Around the World

Family of four, Tim, Julie, Tyler, and Kara, left their home in Virginia for a 13-month adventure around the world in 2014. They traveled 87,000 miles with backpacks when the children were 11 and 9. Rather than just being a one-off adventure, their lives are now centered around exploring, traveling to far-flung places around the world. They've now made a business out of sharing their experiences and helping others travel the world.

Life Change in France

Tracey and her husband lived a typical London suburban life with their three children aged 7, 5, and 2. In search of a better quality of life, they packed up and moved to a small village in France. Their children are now enrolled in French schools while they run their business between the UK and France.

Chapter 2

Show Me the Money

(Four Years Before Our Departure)

More than any other reason so many people claim they can't follow their own adventure—no matter how big or small—is that they don't have the money. Well, here's the thing: we didn't have the money either. When we made our decision to sail around the world, the idea that Nichola and I could afford an offshore sailboat and fund two years of life-changing adventures was utterly laughable.

How Much Money Did We Need?

Without a doubt this was, so to speak, the 64 million dollar question. It was the question everyone asked us when we started sharing our plans. It was also the question we constantly asked ourselves.

Truthfully, other than we knew it was going to be expensive, we had no idea what our sailing plan would cost. The reality is the cost will depend entirely on what it is you want to do. I suspect that only a small proportion of people will want to sail around the world. If your dream does happen to be sailing, your costs will depend on the kind of sailing experience you want: how you want to travel, how much luxury, what size boat, how much safety you want, how much boat work you can do yourself, how much of the world you want to see, how quickly you want to travel, whether you will work as you go, or whether you want to have the money sorted before you leave. We asked lots of people we thought might know and we read everything we could find but no definitive answer was forthcoming on how much it would cost.

The key for us was this: not knowing the answer did not put us off. It was a question of mindset. There were two distinct mindsets and approaches to money available to us:

Mindset 1. Abundance—work out what we needed and wanted, then go create it.

Mindset 2. Scarcity—look at what we could afford and figure out what we can make happen for that budget.

I can guarantee that if we had taken Mindset 2, working to a budget from the start, we would never have made our plans happen, simple as that. We would have been constrained in our minds by resource limitations that dictated what we could or couldn't have.

The magic of adopting Mindset 1 is that by focusing on what we ideally wanted, i.e. to sail around the world, it literally forced us to be creative and resourceful. We didn't have the money. We had to go create it. Because we created a big goal, we had to learn more than we had ever learned before to create new businesses, finding ways to make the money.

This resourcefulness and creativity is a skill and talent that we all have. It's different to what a lot of people think of as positive thinking. It's muscle building and training your mind to work consistently in a way that is counterintuitive to our natural instincts. It needs to be worked and trained before it becomes strong. This is what we did in Part One of this book, and that training paid dividends when we were actually on our way.

It's the strength of this mindset muscle that helped us survive dangerous situations as we sailed around the world. Creativity, resourcefulness, the ability to see what is right in any particular situation, and to deal with whatever comes

Mindset and Belief

The single biggest factor in making our vision come true was our mindset and belief that we were going to make it happen. If there is something you want, you'll either find a way or make a way. The mindset of belief fosters creativity and resourcefulness, and is the single biggest habit I'd encourage you to focus on. Build that muscle—its strength is what changes your life.

up—I can think of no more valuable skill set. It's the one I'm most proud to have taught my children during our journey.

Costing it Out

We worked out how we wanted to live our lives and from there we drew up a list—not a list of things we needed, which feels hard, but rather a list of desired outcomes, which was more exciting.

- To buy the safest and best-equipped boat for round-the-world sailing
- To make this boat our home for the two years we sailed on her
- To become our own boat mechanics, riggers, navigators
- To be able to communicate with other boats and ashore while at sea
- To each be medically trained and equipped to keep ourselves and our children safe
- To educate our children in the most interesting and exciting ways possible during these two years
- To log our adventures so that we would have memories forever

Our list of objectives continued growing—we probably had about twelve of them by the time we had finished. By starting with the objectives, it was easier to compile a list of what we needed to do, to train for, to purchase, to learn.

From our list of outcomes, we started to work out what we would need to do in a logical order. (In Appendix 1, you'll find a section called "By the Numbers" that has some of our headline costs and a suggestion of additional resources concerning the costs of this kind of trip.)

Once we had our list, we could work out the various costs so that we knew how much money was needed to get us to the starting line. We had in mind to spend up to $750,000 on a sailboat. We could have planned to spend a lot less or a lot more, but that was what we figured would be right for us when we really got into the details. You can get an ocean-going sailboat for in the region of $100,000 right up into the millions of dollars.

We then began to work out the monthly costs of the boat (fuel, maintenance, provisioning, entertainment, communication, dockage or moorings, emergencies). We worked out what we thought it would cost us on a monthly basis to live and travel the way we wanted to. We considered that the greatest cost would be boat maintenance; we didn't plan on using too much fuel.

Boat life is much simpler than land life: we wanted to see as much of the world as possible; no car to run, no after-school clubs. We would have some entertainment in various countries but while at sea, entertainment was us. Provisioning would be simple food and we planned on eating on the boat as much as possible while in port since we had young children.

So from our calculations we came up with a figure that we would need upfront to get us to the starting line and a monthly income thereafter to make it around the world.

Getting the Money Together—What We Started With

So now we knew what we needed, how on earth would we be able to get ourselves in a position where we could do this? At that point, we had no idea. What we did have was a decision that we were going to sail our family around the world, and a departure date. It wasn't wishful thinking, it wasn't "someday I'd like to do this." It was a decision we were committed to, come hell or high water, within a fixed timescale. Nothing in this world focuses things like a deadline and a solid decision.

Our Day Jobs

When we came up with our plan, I co-owned a consultancy business called Trovus. I'd started it with my friend Ed in 2006 as a means to shaping our own destiny and creating our own wealth. We threw our heart and soul into running our small business. Before that, I'd worked for large corporations for ten years and never found life particularly fulfilling as an employee. Ed and I quickly discovered that running your own business is tough and has its own challenges. At the time Nichola and I had our idea to sail the world, we still hadn't worked out the formula to create a profitable and successful business.

We'd launched Trovus by selling consultancy—our expertise and time—to help companies understand the power of online communities, largely based on what I'd learned from building them in a consumer world at my previous start-up businesses. I'd launched two websites and learned about online marketing; although neither had been a financial success, the knowledge I'd acquired was valuable. Our idea was to take these concepts from a B2C world (businesses selling to consumers) into a B2B world (businesses selling to businesses). We started by running small seminars and workshops, presenting and sharing our ideas. On the back of our ideas, we started to pick up clients who wanted to use the power of communities to grow their business. Within three months, we landed one of our largest clients, Hewlett Packard, and we were off and running.

Our business grew as we developed a full-scale product with large clients like IBM, the *Financial Times*, Cisco, top-tier law firms, and a few banks. Despite our powerful client list, running a small business was tough. In the startup years we didn't take a living wage. As the business grew, we paid ourselves more, but it was much less than we had been making back in the corporate world. They were hard days but I loved it. We worked well as a team, we were learning, we were winning clients, and delivering innovative work that our clients appreciated. Ed and I were the heartbeat of the business and managed to attract great people to come work with us.

Yet, with four years to go until our departure date, we were making sales of less than $500,000 per year and losing money. Like many entrepreneurs, we put on a brave face every day, went out into battle, and worked incredibly hard for our meager rewards. We worked from month to month, day to day, to make sure we could meet payroll and live to fight another day.

Nichola, meanwhile, had a job as an HR Manager at her father's business and when not working was looking after the children as well as running our home. We had two salaries and some small savings, but it would be a drop in the ocean compared to funding what we had in mind. We spent hours going over our finances and our options. What could we do, what did we have that could make some inroads into what we needed?

Other Sources of Income: Rentals

We owned our home, which we knew we could rent out. Interest rates were at an all-time low and although we had a large mortgage there was a small amount of profit between the rental income and mortgage. It would be nowhere near enough, though, for what we needed, so we decided early on that we preferred not to rent our home. Instead we'd create enough income so that would be unnecessary.

Growing the Business

Funding our adventure was going to be challenging. We were forced to dig deep, to be creative in our approach, invest in learning and growth, and never give up. Our financial situation was the one thing that put the most strain on the whole plan. It caused the most arguments, and was also the catalyst to us learning a huge amount about how to launch and successfully create profitable businesses.

Sharing our plans with Ed, my business partner, and charting a route to successfully realizing value from Trovus was a critical part of the overall plan. Our partnership was such an integral part of the business that without a strong succession plan we risked everything we'd worked for. The flip side was that I knew that this had the potential to drive through change and make good things happen for both Ed and me. Everything in life has two sides to it and there are many times when you need to embrace uncertainty to make things happen.

Plan A (and my ideal outcome) was for us to aggressively grow the business so we could sell it, preferably before I left, possibly the dream of every entrepreneur when they begin. The percentage of people who actually achieve this outcome is minuscule. The odds weren't in our favor.

Ed and I talked about the future we both wanted—personally and for the business. I knew that all things start with a vision; the next step is to assess the current situation and take steps to close the gap between the two. We came up with the 8-2 plan: to develop Trovus by creating specialist software applications, our own products, with a goal of creating a business making £8 million in sales and £2 million in profit.

As they say, if you want to make God laugh, tell him your plans. We had a lot to do. On the other hand, I fully bought into the belief that the purpose of a target is not necessarily to hit the target, but to take the actions and develop the business so that it becomes capable of hitting the target. The question I asked myself every moment was: "How can I make things better?" I started to seek out new ideas to generate growth. Ed and I had used business coaches during our early days and had been exposed to numerous ideas.

We needed to go back to learn more. Unlocking new ideas was the key and we realized we needed to do something different, both in Trovus and in our overall family financial plans. It wasn't enough now to tick along and grow steadily. We needed rapid acceleration to make our targets. Nichola and I adopted a philosophy, an approach to getting the money together. It boiled down to a pretty simple five-step formula.

The Five-Step Formula for Achieving Anything

1. Visualize Your Outcome
   We had a crystal clear, burning vision of what we wanted to achieve. We put as much specific detail and clarity into this as possible.
2. Know Your Reason Why
   There were times—many more than I care to remember— when everything was failing all around us, when nothing seemed to work, and all was black. Our Reason Why was the antidote. So many times we came back to that and our Reason Why refocused events, giving us energy and drive to pick ourselves up and keep going on.
3. Take Relentless Action
   Our dreams—going sailing around the world, growing the business—wouldn't happen by wishing them. They happened by doing. In growing the business we became relentless in our pursuit of different approaches and different ideas.

4. Notice What's Working

My mantra was simple—let's try lots of different approaches. We had plenty of ideas but no certainty which would work. So we tried lots of things to find out. If it worked, we did more of it. If it didn't, we stopped doing it. We embraced failure and learned from what didn't work. We measured results. We figured out which activities were moving us measurably closer to our goal.

5. Keep Changing the Approach Until You Reach Your Goal

Once we stopped doing things that weren't working, we brainstormed to find new ideas. What else could we do? What was working? We did more of that. We kept trying other things.

Ed and I met weekly to discuss progress. We had strong energy to start with but it became apparent that what we were doing was just small scale and wasn't having the impact we needed. We repeatedly referred back to Step 4 of the Five-Step Formula: notice what's working and if it's not working, try something different.

We had a lot to do and we were just at the beginning of the journey to answer the challenging question of "How do we get the money together for this?" We had our mindset in place, but many highs and lows were to come in the months and years that followed.

Make the Magic Happen: Show Me the Money—Your Actions

Make a list of the nonfinancial goals that will shape your plan. It's very hard to start with only a financial goal and then set out to achieve it. It's not inspiring and you will lose heart quickly. Better to work out what you want to achieve, making your goals as exciting as possible. Do you want to be world-class adventurers, first-class inspirers, educators of your children, and ace photographers with an amazing photographic record of your experiences? Whatever it is, work out the goals because from there it will be clear where your priorities are and from that you will work out the costs. Also define the amount you are willing to involve yourself in the areas you need to cover. Are you self-sufficient or will you need to buy the expertise of others?

Consider your mindset. Are you operating from abundance or scarcity? Start to get resourceful and creative about what your dream looks like. Remember that resourcefulness is a muscle that needs to be trained, developed, and strengthened. Adopt the mindset that you will either find a way or make a way.

From your goals, work out what you need and the learning gaps you need to fill. Find out what training you can get and its cost. Find out what equipment you need.

Now, from this list, budget for getting to the start line and what you will need to cover monthly expenses. Look realistically at the resources you have already—current employment, current assets and skills, existing liabilities.

Finally, you can now see the gap between what you have and what you will need. Now you know what money you have to find.

Chapter 3

Involving the Children
(Three to Four Years Before Our Departure Date)

In many ways the most controversial aspect of our idea was that we planned to travel with young children. When we first came up with our sailing vision, we had two children; by the time we left we had three—aged nine, seven, and two.

Traveling with our young children was an intentional decision—we wanted to see the world with them while they were young enough to want to spend time with us, yet old enough to hopefully learn from, and enjoy, the experience. This decision, so deliberate for us, was also the most contentious for others—concerns ranged from the two eldest getting pulled out of school to the potential dangers of offshore sailing and health risks. Many parents also joked that they could not imagine being in a confined space with their children for such a long period of time.

We were not naïve—we appreciated the pros and cons—and we realized including children required an extra level of preparation. Not just the usual work of boat checks and buying equipment, but the larger effort to become a cohesive family team—we needed to work together whatever the circumstances.

We would need to create a strong family vision, excite the children with our idea, and communicate it to them in a way that they'd understand. This would be a challenge. In addition, Nichola and I both had different experiences of traveling in our childhoods, and working as a family team. We would need to merge our past experiences while building our sail-around-the-world vision.

My Own Traveling Experiences from Childhood Onward

The seeds for family adventure and travel were planted in me at an early age. Before I was born, my mother and father, together with my older sister, Pippa, traveled around Europe in a VW Dormobile camper van for three months. My dad had been running his own law practice and had gotten to a point where he wasn't satisfied with life and wanted to do something different. My parents decided time away to travel and explore was the perfect way to think and reflect. As a child, I remember hearing the stories and seeing the photos from this trip.

Pippa and I grew up in the southwest of England, spending our time between Bristol and Devon with long summers playing on the beaches of South Devon, always in and out of the sea. It was the perfect start in life. Everything changed when my parents divorced when I was nine.

The split was difficult although Mom worked hard to shield me from the arguments and unhappiness that can accompany divorce. Pippa, three years older than me, has stronger and less happy memories of that time than I do. We were living in an apartment in the center of Bristol and I was teed up to sit the entrance exam for one of the best schools in the area. I passed and was all set to attend. Yet Mom decided we'd be better off farther away from Bristol so we moved to South Devon to the tiny village of Hallsands where we had a small bungalow that my dad had built before I was born. Both Mom and Dad wanted the bungalow so we ended up with a concrete wall in the middle splitting it in two—one half for Mom and us and one half for Dad.

Post divorce, financially times were tough. I have strong memories of Mom going without, working hard to make ends meet so that she could provide for my sister and me as well as ensuring that we had a strong, stable, and loving home and family life.

I remember consciously deciding back then that I'd never be in a position of financial hardship and knew that I'd always find a way to create my own certainty and make money. My first job was fruit picking at the age of 11. I was pretty lousy at it and I think an afternoon's work yielded around $3. I went on to start my first business catching and selling crabs and lobsters at the age of 14.

We attended the local comprehensive (high) school in Kingsbridge, walking the 1 mile up the steep hill to Bickerton Top in the morning to catch the bus. On weekends and evenings I began my love affair with the sea, spending hours on the beach, fishing and exploring the coastline and bays around where we lived. I loved it—the beach and sea was my playground.

The original village of Hallsands was built on cliffs that seem to cling to the coastline. In the early 20th century, Start Bay was heavily dredged to provide the shingle needed for the building of the dockyards in Devonport, changing the ecosystem, making the bay much more susceptible to storms. After two major storms the village was largely washed away and had to be relocated a half mile farther inland, where the fishermen and their families rebuilt their homes and livelihoods. I've always identified with the resilience of these tough fishermen who refused to yield to misfortune and carried on with life and thrived.

Pippa and I spent summer and winter holidays and the occasional weekend with Dad. He remarried and went on to have a second family of five children; we got to know them well, moving past the distinction of "step," and simply became brothers and sisters. It's testament to these deep bonds we formed that my brother Max joined us for over three months on our sailing adventure.

My dad loved to travel. We always used to joke that I'd see far more of him when I was traveling since he'd just pop up wherever I was in the world. On my first trip around the world by plane at the age of 24, we met up in Western Australia. When I raced around the world at age 28 on the BT Global Challenge, he and his third wife, Sharon, came to meet me in Boston, Buenos Aires, Sydney, Cape Town, and La Rochelle. He and Sharon had a white camper van they traveled the world in. Though inside it was kitted out to their specification, its appearance meant they could park in any city in the world—to any outsider it looked like a delivery van.

Dad was a larger-than-life character. He lived life on his own terms. He had made a career in the law of knowing the rules and then finding ways to avoid them. He loved taking on officialdom—burying administrators with endless letters and points that were impossible to answer or to deal with, pressing them until they got frustrated, gave up, and moved on. Life for him was at its best when it was at its simplest: spending time with his family, fishing, laughing, talking, and sharing stories at the pub; cooking and enjoying good food washed down with a pint or two of beer. Ever the raconteur, he had a story for every occasion.

My dad was my closest friend. When I was 13 I won a scholarship to attend a boarding school in Plymouth. It took me a while to adjust and when I was having a tough time I'd phone him most days to talk. I wouldn't talk about what was happening to me—we'd just chat about things that were happening in the world or plans for fishing or what I'd been learning. He was always there with a story or a quote to share. Through my adult life we'd speak less often but when we did the conversations—at the pub over a few beers—were always easy, ranging from business ideas, to traveling, and life plans.

Nichola's Traveling Experiences

Nichola had not traveled as much as I had as a child, but she still had much experience. Growing up, her family lived in the Middle East so there were visits to see them and family holidays together. While in college Nichola traveled around Europe by train in the summer, and after working and saving for a year backpacked around the world. Inevitably, studies, work, and children curbed her traveling, although not the desire. When Nichola had a bad day while working as an attorney she'd seek solace by buying a travel guide and planning a trip somewhere as a form of escapism.

Family Feedback

My dad didn't really say much about our vision to sail around the world—just a raised eyebrow and some supportive words, "Let's see what happens." The father of many children, he was used to hearing ideas and plans and waiting to see what evolved. The idea appealed to his love of travel, as did the prospect of visiting ports around the world to meet us.

Mom didn't really say anything at first. My mom generally likes to keep quiet while she thinks about things, sharing her thoughts later on. She was overall very positive about the concept. Mom has always been a sailor and in fact taught me how to sail. She understood our vision and why we wanted to do it, though I'm sure like many people she didn't think it would really happen. And as moms always do, she thought about what could go wrong. Gradually, there was a steady flow of questions: Have you thought about what would happen if the engine broke? What about the children's schooling—you've got to make sure they are happy with it and they won't lose out. What if something happens to one of the children—will you know what to do?

My sister Pippa likewise kept her counsel. On the surface, she was quietly supportive of her little brother, though I feel confident in saying that on the inside she thought we were utterly nuts and she couldn't possibly think of anything she'd like to do less.

I think maybe over the years I'd conditioned my family against trying to talk me out of things.

Introducing Our Children to the Idea of Traveling

Introducing our children to our vision early in the planning process was critical. We couldn't just turn round and say, "Well, kids, we're off tomorrow to sail around the world for two years."

There was no manual for this—we had to figure it out ourselves. In 2011—three years before departure—we decided they were old enough to participate in creating the plan. Our children were still young: Bluebell was six, Columbus was four, and Willow was not yet born. We knew we had to be smart about how we introduced the concept, getting them focused on aspects that would appeal to them. We wanted to create energy and excitement for the idea. So we scheduled our first family planning session for just as long as their attention span could comfortably handle—about half an hour.

It was a quiet weekend at home and we'd just had lunch. Our living room had a large brown sofa and a large beanbag, the kind that envelops you as you settle into it. A large window flooded the room with natural light. We pulled out photos from our most recent sailing holiday. We had the children's favorite snacks and drinks at hand, wanting to stir positive emotions and associations as we talked about our plan.

Spreading ourselves out on the soft beige carpet between the beanbag and the sofa, we told the children that we were planning to take two years to sail around the world as a family, and started to explain that would mean living on a boat and experiencing new things. We showed them photos. Bluebell latched on to the idea of swimming with dolphins in warm seas, deserted tropical islands, and meeting other children. With Columbus we talked about seeing and catching big fish. They were both excited about the idea of sleeping in bunk beds on a boat.

Soon their attention wandered to the next toy or the television. How much they understood at that stage is debatable but we simply wanted it to become part of our everyday conversation. We just needed to embed the concept of sailing around the world. We knew that in the following years we needed to provide as many good experiences in and around the water as possible to develop positive thoughts of sailing. I know plenty of people who've been put off sailing for life because of a bad experience—whether it was scary because the boat was heeling or the skipper was inexperienced and shouting at them, or just feeling uncertain because of the new environment. Our goal was to carefully map out their time on the water so that they felt safe and secure. If our children were fearful and unwilling it would scupper the whole thing.

We were taking a risk, creating this huge vision for them—what if it didn't happen? But we made the choice to use the energy of the shared enthusiasm to drive us forward. It was another reason for us to be absolutely committed to the plan—to deliver to our children what we said we would.

We had a huge, vibrant, colorful painting I'd bought in South Africa many years earlier hanging center stage on our kitchen wall. When we announced our sailing plan we stuck a huge map of the world over the top of the painting and sketched out in pencil our tentative route around the world (see plate section, image 3). We scribbled in the names of places we wanted to go with dates when we wanted to be there. It made our vision much more real and visual. The map joined the vision statement that hung next to it and became a conversation centerpiece. This placed our shared vision truly in our actual vision—first thing in the morning and last thing at night. For our children it was also the introduction to their world geography lessons.

After that initial Saturday discussion, our sessions with the children became regular weekend events, usually just for 30 minutes on a Saturday morning when we would talk, draw, cut out pictures, and make collages, planning the exciting activities that sailing around the world would offer. We made it fun and lighthearted. We usually had music, treats, and best of all a small trampoline in our kitchen, allowing the kids to bounce up and down to the music while we talked.

Getting the Children (and Nichola) Aboard Sailboats

Although I had sailed extensively, Nichola by contrast had only sailed a couple of times and the children hadn't sailed at all. We knew that we had to build up sailing experience for Nichola, to create positive experiences of being on the water for the children, and to begin working together as a team on a boat. This was going to be a new experience for all of us.

We decided to begin with a week-long vacation in the summer of 2011 in the calm, sheltered waters of the Greek islands and then slowly increase the time on the water for the children. We also planned time on the water for Nichola independently of the children and me so that she could get as much training and experience as possible.

We decided not to go on other vacations and prioritized sailing time. We initially went for one week at a time and then for two weeks at a time as experience and confidence grew. Coming from England, sailing vacations in Greece cost us in the region of $3,000 to $4,000 for a week for the four of us. At the same time Nichola was working to gain both her competent crew and day skipper sailing qualifications.

Sharing the Idea Beyond the Family to Make it Stronger

Alongside our preparation with the children, Nichola and I gradually fleshed out more details of our plan. We debated, compromised, and then we both bought into our shared plans 100 percent.

As the months rolled on, we continued to mention our plans to our friends and family, making our goals as public as we could. We wanted to make rods for our own backs—we wanted people to hold us to account on our progress or lack of progress at any point in time. It was early in the planning and easy for people to pick holes in our plans. This was all part of taking the idea and making it stronger.

Sharing our plans created unexpected magic. Help and support flowed toward us as a result of our bold plans, assistance we wouldn't have ever asked for, such as with the business or childcare. Our choice was to boldly and publicly state the life that we imagined, heading in that direction with utter conviction.

Trust in the Decision

Making a firm decision with a vivid vision enabled us to create and continuously shape our plan. We had absolute belief that we would make things happen—all our energy went toward the plan's achievement.

I love the military saying "Time spent in reconnaissance is seldom wasted." Our time planning and imagining the future as a team was worth its weight in gold. It's fascinating to reflect back now and see how much of what we planned happened. For instance, we scribbled on the world map in the kitchen that we'd be sailing through the Panama Canal on Valentine's Day 2015. In fact, we went through on February 5, nine days sooner. We made what at one time seemed impossible happen. We made the magic happen.

If we'd given way to doubt and fear and hadn't publicly declared our intent I don't believe we would have made it happen. There were leaps of faith we had to take when we simply didn't have the answers, but we knew our desired outcome. As the children got older they also started to share our plans with their friends and other adults as well.

Our Vision Book and a Family Painting

One day I was at a work conference when someone mentioned the idea of creating a "vision board"—a tangible visualization of the business or product you want to create. To aid visualization of your unique plan, they recommended cutting pictures from magazines or other sources to produce a collage representing your concept. This vision board then becomes a communication tool to share and build your ideas, strengthening them and creating a focal point for your group.

I took this idea and adapted it for our family. We decided to create a vision book. Over the course of a weekend Nichola and I gathered and illustrated the concepts that were important to us about our vision. We took a binder with plastic sleeves, inserting our vision statement as the first page. The second page was our timeline. The third was the chart of how we had to accumulate wealth each year to be able to achieve our plan.

From there we unleashed our search powers. We found all sorts of magazines: sailing, travel, health, and any others that related and began cutting out images showing what was important to both of us—places we wanted to go, activities we wanted to experience, the boat we wanted, our health and fitness goals. If it was important to either of us, it got found and included in the book. We created collages of related topics, too: catching tropical fish and exploring deserted islands. The overall effect was a vivid pictorial statement of what we wanted the future to look like—this in turn fed our joint imaginations, making the trip around the world more real.

We continued involving the children, getting them to dream and imagine their futures, too. There were valuable life lessons available for them in terms of approaching their own goals in life. So at another Saturday session, sitting on the lounge floor with magazines, scissors, paper, and glue, we outlined the vision book idea to the kids.

"Right, as you know we're going to sail around the world. You've got to find pictures you like and cut them out. Think about where you'd like to go, things you'd like to learn about, things you'd like to do. Then stick the pictures together on paper and explain them to the rest of us."

And with that, we were off. We laughed, we had fun, we took breaks, and stopped for drinks and snacks, all the while taking the time to listen to the children and what was important to them. We worked as teams—I worked with Columbus while Nichola worked with Bluebell. Columbus found fish pictures and pictures of women in bikinis, while Bluebell was more focused on places and beautiful, colorful scenes. They both took the task seriously and before long were sticking pictures on blank sheets of paper. Bluebell was incredibly neat and organized and had her pictures perfectly aligned. Both were open-minded and excited—the plan sounded like a long, fun holiday where we could do a whole bunch of cool stuff.

I remember clearly Bluebell starting to pick up the language and using the phrase "we're going to sail around the world," getting comfortable saying the words, trying the idea aloud. She was warming to the trip and all the fun activities and possibilities it would mean for her.

The final exercise of the afternoon was to give our vision book a name. After discussion we settled on "The Craven Family Winners' Bible." Not a bible in the religious sense, but in the sense of an authoritative book. We now had our reference point, a living document we'd all invested in emotionally that became another anchor that allowed our vision to grow into a reality.

This plastic binder lived on our kitchen table as a daily reminder of what we were working toward. I'd look at it most days, flicking through the pages to visualize what we were doing and why. I encouraged the rest of the family to do the same. We added to the bible as we thought of new things and we began to set monthly, quarterly, and annual goals.

We held ourselves accountable to these targets and measured how we were doing (see plate section, image 2).

Creating this book of images seemed a strange thing to do at the time and raised plenty of eyebrows. Most people just don't do this sort of thing—they don't think of themselves as a family team and imagine the future this way. For us, this vision book became a cornerstone of our planning for the entire adventure.

Imagine now the prospect of saying to the children, "I'm sorry, we can't do this. Mommy and Daddy haven't been able to get the money together and the plans are off." Mommy and Daddy now had to find a way to make it happen.

Make the Magic Happen: Involving the Children—Your Actions

- Be utterly certain about your family vision. You should by now have your exciting vision clear in your head.
- Create the time to introduce the plan to your children.
- Sit down with them when they are full of energy and you have their full attention.
- Ask your children what they think the plan might involve, and what it might look like.
- Keep the sessions short and fun. End sessions with treats (favorite snacks, drinks).
- The ages of the children will affect what specific activities you undertake: the younger children might cut out pictures from magazines while older children might draw or write their thoughts. Keep the work, make it visible, look back at it later with the children, talk about it, add to it. You are making your own family vision book—give it a name that suits your family.
- Talk to family and friends positively in front of your children to reinforce your plan. You want your children to start to believe that this is the most natural and normal idea in the

world. Stay calm, relaxed—ensure they have confidence in you as parents. Be able to answer their questions, even if the answer is "I'm not sure but I will find out."

Most importantly, enjoy this process and look forward to spending the time with your children to talk about the vision. You will be amazed how emotionally mature children can be when discussing family goals, and how much they will enjoy the sessions. They will also become excited about the plans—and their joy and enthusiasm will keep you motivated to achieve your goals.

Chapter 4

Frustration, Breakthrough Thinking, and Building Energy
(Three Years Before Our Departure Date)

We had a clear and exciting vision and we had engaged the children. Plus we had told everybody we knew that we were going to sail around the world. This was probably the point of maximum discomfort because we had deliberately made a very bold declaration to our circle of friends and family. Now we had to move from the idea to making it happen.

When It's Not Working, Go Back to the Drawing Board

Back in November 2010, as the nights were getting shorter and English winter was drawing in, our biggest issue remained growing the business. We realized that we needed to learn a lot more about making money. I was frustrated we weren't getting the breakthroughs that we needed to start making a dent in our plans. We needed to do something else. My mind was alert, open, and looking for opportunity.

I'd been online and an entrepreneurs' training course had caught my eye. So had the eye-watering price tag of $7,500 for a three-day seminar. The idea of paying this seemed utterly absurd, but nonetheless the seminar stuck in my mind. Some weeks later I was with a client and it came up in conversation that he had attended that course. This was a hard-hitting, no-nonsense business owner who ran a company providing part-time finance directors. I asked what it was like. "It was incredible," he said. "I got so much from it."

That was enough to shift my mindset. Some days later I saw an ad selling the course material from that event. The price tag was $1,500. I deliberated for half an hour and then pressed the buy button. I couldn't quite believe that I was paying $1,500 for a set of DVDs and a workbook. I couldn't quite bring myself to tell Ed and the guys at work. They'd have thought I was mad.

The DVDs arrived just before Christmas. On Boxing Day, with the children happily playing with their new toys, I locked myself in my study and broke open the cellophane. For the next three days I barely slept or spoke to anyone, coming out only for meals and to go to the bathroom. I was totally immersed and engaged. I had light-bulb moments with ideas for growing Trovus and how we might change things. I returned to work in January with more energy than I imagined possible plus pages of notes and action items that we could begin immediately to make changes. Ed was in for a shock.

I'd studied accountancy and economics at university, spent three years training as a chartered accountant and five years as an investment banker (plus another three years undergoing business coaching)—all that background and yet I learned more about how to grow a business to make money during those three days with my DVDs and workbook than I had with all my previous experience. The DVDs were cheap at the price.

I got straight into action. I put in place processes to overhaul how our business operated. I was getting a lot of ideas from the US and also borrowing ideas from the business-to-consumer sector. One of the best ways to get an edge is to take ideas from outside your sector and use them where no one else is applying them.

Ed and the team had a hard time accepting some of these ideas. We had a good number of healthy debates—frankly they thought some of the ideas were nuts. They didn't like the language or style I was using. There was some truth in what they were saying. I was challenging long-held beliefs in the company about how things should be done. There were times when I needed to listen and be flexible.

My approach was: here are some ideas, let's run with them, adapt them as needed to see what works and what doesn't. Some things bombed with no responses. Other actions brought in big clients. I loved testing and finding new ideas. I also relished the copy writing and started creating hard-copy newsletters that mailed to 1,500 people a month. I got a good amount of criticism for using paper copy when everyone else was using email and digital communications. For me, that was exactly the point. If you do the same as everyone else, the best result you can expect is the average result.

Stay Active–Keep Trying Different Things

One of the lessons I learned was this: if you want the success that other people have, watch and follow what the most successful people do. Study their patterns and behaviors, and replicate them. If you copy the ways of successful people, you're almost guaranteed to eventually get the same results they do. Making money is a learnable skill. Whether you are employed, self-employed, or unemployed, find access to the experts who can help advance your knowledge.

We couldn't win by thinking alone. We had to try lots of actions and it was certain that a number of them would fail. We learned from failures and moved on. My mantra was "get into action" and do things regularly that moved us measurably forward.

I immersed myself in study, reading as many business books as I could, and when I realized I was a slow reader I took a course in speed reading and also downloaded audiobooks. I networked like crazy and took the opportunity to ask the most successful people I knew what they had done to achieve success. I paid to get access to the experts. I recalled the maxim that you get the life of the five people that you spend most time with. I sought out and spent more time with people who were on the move and wanted to go places, people who'd go to the gym, or to conferences and training courses in the evening rather than to the pub. These were people who wanted very specific outcomes in their lives and were prepared to go to extreme lengths to achieve them.

Both Ed and I joined Mastermind groups so we could surround ourselves with other entrepreneurs keen on learning and sharing.

My group, The Supper Club, was composed of founders or CEOs of businesses with sales of more than $1.5m/year. It was inspiring to surround myself with sharp people driven to achieve extreme results. We were aiming for an extreme result.

The Importance of Daily Routines and Consistency

I also totally changed my daily routine. I'd wake up at 5am and start the day by drinking hot water and lemon juice, meditating on the outcomes I wanted for the day. I'd do some breathing exercises, then I'd jump for 10 minutes on a mini trampoline, listening to music, getting my body fired up, my cells moving and energized. Then breakfast—salad, broccoli, avocado, anything green in essence, and some nuts.

I'd hop on my bike, cycling the mile or so to the train station, board the train, plug in my headphones, and write or think. That early morning time was always my best writing time for newsletters—by the time the train pulled into the city 35 minutes later I usually had 1,000 to 2,000 words written.

When I had worked as an accountant I read three or four newspapers a day: one in the morning on the way to the office, one or two at lunchtime, and one in the evening. I thought I needed to know all that was going on in the world. But now I came to the view that reading newspapers and watching the news wasn't serving me at all. The news was unremittingly negative, largely written to sell papers rather than to educate, and I came away with a jaundiced view of things. I made the decision to stop reading the papers to see what effect it had. I went for a month. I didn't miss anything and felt I had a brighter, more positive outlook. I could devote that time to reading high-quality books and magazines. If there were events happening in the world that were important I'd hear about them through colleagues, clients, partners, and friends.

Leaving early in the morning meant avoiding rush hour, always getting a seat on the train, and not having to wade through the thronging masses when I arrived in London. I'd be in the office by 7.30. I've always been a morning person—I have the most energy first thing in the day. I'd start my office day with green tea and water, and I'd plan. I'd clump together similar activities and block them out in my diary. Time for phone calls to clients or partners, time to write, time with the team, time with Ed, time to deal with emails. I'd print off my schedule for the day and aim to follow it religiously, respecting the time that I'd carved out for each activity.

Before I got wise to managing my time, I'd work with my email inbox open and my phone switched on. That was until I began to appreciate how destructive that was to my work patterns. When doing my best work, my thoughts and ideas are in a state of "flow." I am energized, and it's in those moments that I am significantly more effective than at any other time in the working day. When you are in flow and someone distracts you, it takes you 20 minutes to get back to that flow state. That's exactly what happens when working with your email open and phone on. A new email pops in and flashes up on your screen. Your mind is taken to a different place and your flow is broken. To solve this I'd switch my email on only two or three times a day and instead worked through triaging what was urgent and needed to be dealt with, what was important, needing my best attention, and what could be rapidly deleted (or unsubscribed from).

I'd stay in the office until most of the team had left—often around 6 or 6.30—in order to allow Ed and me a chance to catch up and discuss whatever was on our minds. I'd then catch the train home, listening to business audiobooks or reading. If my mind was distracted with the events of the day, I'd write down what had gone well and what I could improve on.

Nichola being a night owl would work late into the night, often forgoing sleep. During the day she worked from home while the children were at school and for one day a week in the office with her Mom covering childcare. As the months went on, Nichola adopted many of my practices like regular exercise and a healthier diet.

Our lives were full and it's hard to imagine how we could have squeezed any more productive time out of the day. We were focused and working to our plan.

The Power of Habits

It's not what you do once in a while that makes a difference, it's what you do every day. Here are just some of the habits I cultivated:

- Read only high-quality books
- Exercise 3 or 4 times per week
- Meditate daily with additional breathing exercises
- Plan daily calendar to maximize use of time
- Switch off distractions to stay in your state of flow
- Hydrate regularly
- Live alcohol-free, and eat a low-sugar diet

Health and Fitness Goals and Changes

I scheduled a personal trainer three times a week because I realized my health and fitness were critical to performing at the highest level. I didn't have the time to work out the best diet or exercises for me and I wanted someone to push me and hold me accountable. I'd first used a personal trainer in the early years of Trovus. I remember Joe, my trainer, laughing at me on the first day as I turned up having just consumed a cooked breakfast with a large latte, and was nearly sick in the first 15 minutes. Over the coming weeks Joe asked me to keep a food diary to record every single thing I ate. After the first inspection a week in, he simply told me I had a sugar addiction and was eating all the wrong things. The rules he put in place were simple—no bread, no carbs after 6pm, alcohol only twice a week, and eat more salad and vegetables. Not rocket science. Exercising twice a week too helped me lose 20 pounds in 12 weeks. It may sound obvious but for me it was a revelation. I had more energy than I'd had in years.

Of course I could do it myself after a while—eating the right foods, running, training, and so on. However, I wanted my energies focused on building our plan, and found it easier that my health and fitness were the responsibility of my new trainer, Niki. It was her job. I told Niki that I wanted to have as much energy as possible and I wanted her to tell me what I could and couldn't eat and exactly what exercises I needed. I could ill afford a trainer and it seemed to everyone else an expensive luxury. The rewards were worth more than the cost—and if it meant eating out less, that was fine by me. It was an investment so I could focus on growing Trovus. As with my business DVD purchase, it was one of the best investments I would make.

The work required to get to our sailing start line was much more than we'd ever possibly imagined; so after several years of physical training with Niki, I encouraged Nichola to start training as well. We had changed our lifestyles totally from how we had lived through our 20s and most of our 30s. We swapped a glass of wine for a glass of lemon water, exercise increased, and we adopted healthier diets. I stopped drinking alcohol entirely and cut out all meat for one year. It was extreme but we wanted extreme results. We were now fitter and stronger than ever before, with loads of energy.

Brainstorming and Reinventing Previous Business Ideas

Some years earlier, I had set up an internet business in online social networking. It had never made a profit. When we revisited the resources available to us I looked at this business concept with fresh eyes and could see that bringing a different set of talents to it, armed with new

Training for Extreme Results

Focus on what you are brilliant at. Outsource as much of the rest as possible. For example, I made my health and fitness the responsibility of my fitness trainer. The deal was she had to specifically tell me exactly what I could and couldn't do. My part was to do it.

Be conscious of and take great care who you spend the most time with and what you allow to influence you. I sought out people who had already achieved the results that I wanted, learning from them, and looking at the behaviors they used to get successful results.

In addition to peak physical fitness, adopt an attitude of continuous learning. Always be learning. Seek out new ideas, new ways to do things, and find ways to bring those ideas into your life.

skills, strategies, and energy, could make the business successful. I was totally committed to my full-time job of making a success of Trovus, working 14-hour days with little spare capacity. Nichola and I discussed the idea of developing a new business using the new strategies we were learning.

So Nichola set up a new business and started to launch online marketing websites. It didn't take long before one of these was making a healthy profit. She launched some more and within six months she had 13 sites, and we were finally making money.

We speculated. If one site could make us $3,000 profit a year, then 500 sites would give us $1,500,000 a year in profit. The logic felt compelling. We knew we had to make big bold moves to achieve our goals and we weren't going to make it happen by just wishing it. Fortune favors the brave, we told ourselves, and steeled ourselves.

We decided to roll the dice and roll out the 500 sites. I sold the shares I'd accumulated over the years for the investment needed. Nichola recruited a team of developers and a right-hand person to help manage the process. Her talents as someone who gets right into the details are second to none: she is organized, determined, and thorough. Over the coming months the portfolio expanded and Nichola had a full-time job staying on top of all the details. Gradually we brought Morna in to run the internet businesses. Morna had skills that perfectly complemented ours and quickly became an integral part of the team.

Some of the sites were successful and took off, and some were complete clunkers that bombed. What worked well one year didn't work well the next year, as things change. Could we have picked out which of those sites would have been high performing? No. We relied on the process of test and measure. Try lots of things—some will work, some won't. We were both fully in our stride, striving to make magic things happen with every ounce of energy we had.

Make the Magic Happen: Frustration, Breakthrough Thinking, and Building Energy—Your Actions

1. Assess realistically where you are currently and where you have to get to according to your vision.
2. Go back to basics—look at how you are doing things—be honest with yourself, could you benefit from changing your habits or methods, by learning from others who excel in the areas where you have weaknesses?
3. Get started—you need to get moving.
4. At regular intervals, look at the results obtained, are they good, bad, or indifferent? Work as a team with your partner, children, or whoever else is working with you on this vision.
5. Depending on your results, make changes and then start again. Keep checking where you are against your target.
6. Keep repeating steps 4 and 5.
7. Remember that unexpected things will come into your life (a new baby, death, illness all happened to us). That's just life. Accept it.
8. Embrace smart thinking with your time and resources. You will get 80 percent of your results from 20 percent of your actions, so find the most productive uses for your time and money.
9. Be consistent and move toward your goals at the same pace every day, no matter what. This is how you will achieve your goals: step by step. Disciplined activity will create your success and hopefully shield you when the unexpected hits.

Chapter 5

Closing in on the Deadline
(Two Years Before our Departure Date)

Learning from the Experts

Nichola and I looked around at the 80 or so attendees gathered for a two-day seminar arranged by the World Cruising Club. All of us had ambitions to sail either the Atlantic or around the world—but we were about 20 years younger than everyone else in the room and at this point we didn't even own a boat.

We learned a lot that weekend, including preparing the boat, electrical and mechanical systems, managing crew, weather routing, and yacht provisioning. We also met Paul and Caroline. Paul had been one of the UK's most successful investors in technology companies, running his own private equity firm, and we had many mutual acquaintances. Paul is extremely thorough, leaving no detail to chance. He is also determined and committed and at the same time very generous with his time, helping others. He shared

The World Cruising Club (WCC)

The World Cruising Club is a UK organization that arranges sailing rallies around the world. Its most popular rally is the ARC—the Atlantic Rally for Cruisers, a mass crossing of the Atlantic from the Canary Islands to the Caribbean every year. It also runs the World ARC and other rallies around Europe and North America. In order that rally participants are prepared, they also organize events and training sessions on multiple aspects of offshore sailing. (See page 292 in the Appendix for more.)

knowledge and ideas that helped us shape our plans; he intended to buy an Oyster sailboat and raved about their customer support around the world.

Paul also recommended a book that he'd found inspiring, *The Missing Centimetre* by a Swedish author, Leon Schulz, who'd taken a year to sail the Atlantic with his wife and their two young children. Back when they conceived their plan, they took a milliner's tape measure and measured out one centimeter to represent each year of their lives if they lived to the age of 80. At that time, Leon and his wife were in their early forties. They cut out the centimeter between 42 and 43, put that to one side and stuck the tape measure back together. Holding it up, the new 79cm length of tape measure looked much as it did when it was 80cm—but they now had that extra, "missing centimeter," and could do something with it. The story resonated deeply with us and the concept was an easy one to share with people as we talked about our plans.

One of the things that I was extremely mindful of, however, was that our vision wasn't simply about having an adventure and going back to what we were doing before. Years earlier when I'd sailed around the world in a competitive yacht race the focus was on the amazing experience, yet when the adventure finished and I returned to normal life—with the excitement gone, suddenly back in the same flat, the same job—it was as if I fell off a cliff. I found it terribly hard to adjust. I learned from this that it's really important to focus not just on the planned adventure, but also what happens afterward.

So this was about changing our lives. Our adventure would be the springboard for a new and exciting way of living: maybe somewhere different to live, a different business, a new project. We weren't sure what, but we knew our world would expand and we couldn't simply return to where we were before. This wasn't a temporary thing—this was about changing our world forever.

A New Arrival

In April 2012 we were thrilled when Willow, our third child, was born. It was now only a little over two years until our departure date. Many people expected us to change our plans entirely and were surprised to hear that we were still going and nothing was going to fundamentally change—just more things to think about and handle with three rather than two children on board.

Dad's Cancer

When my dad had his first bout of cancer in 1996, he had surgery and radiotherapy and made a complete recovery. He used to tell the story of how his surgeon had a photo on his desk of my dad running around a swimming pool on a cruise after his recovery as an inspiration to other patients to focus on one of the outcomes you can have after cancer.

Near the time of Willow's birth in that early spring of 2012 I had a phone call from my dad's wife, Sharon. We knew my dad had been having sinus problems. He'd been for tests and they had found that the cancer had returned in his sinuses and had developed into secondary lung cancer. Dad underwent a punishing regime of chemotherapy. I'm certain that in years to come, when better cancer treatments are discovered, we will look back on the use of chemotherapy as barbaric—literally poisoning the body to kill off this deadly disease.

My dad was a big strong man and the doctors kept upping the doses as he had the strength to take it. The treatment began to take its toll though, and over the months, propped up by morphine, he slowly found things harder and harder. Anyone who's been affected by cancer will recognize this heartbreaking picture of watching someone you love in pain.

Our consolation was to spend time with him, talking of the important things we wanted to share, enjoying a meal, sharing stories, and laughing—despite everything, we always found things to laugh about. He passed away in October 2012 surrounded by the love of his immediate family.

The Importance of Values in Achieving Your Goals

Virtually every Sunday evening for the final three years prior to departure, we'd sit down as a couple at the kitchen table with the map of the world hanging nearby to review our plans. We'd get out the vision book to look at what we'd done in the week, what was moving forward, and what we'd have to do the following week. It was relentless—we had so much to do to get ready. We had to grow and exit Trovus, we had to grow Nichola's business, we had to buy a boat, and undertake a lot of training. We'd lighten the atmosphere by playing music and watching the children jump with happiness on the small trampoline in the kitchen. Seeing Bluebell bouncing, singing, and dancing to "Gangnam Style" changed our focus from what needed to be done to what we hoped to achieve—joy in family experiences.

I was continually learning and looking for an edge in all the ventures we were running so we could create more growth. I attended one seminar in Chicago where I listened to a talk by the CEO of a large US plumbing and electrical firm. Her topic was instilling core values throughout a business. Her premise was that we all have a set of values—the beliefs that guide how we behave in the world. The challenge and the opportunity in business is to create behavior that drives the firm's goals. 1) the firm needs to create a clear vision of where it wants to go, and 2) the firm needs a clear set of values that are truly lived in the business to guide the team's actions and behavior toward reaching that vision.

In my experience, businesses usually get it wrong by underestimating people's skepticism toward the idea of imposing values from top management without engaging staff and their sense of values or core beliefs. The result is no connection or buy-in from the workers concerning the business's values.

Values at Trovus

I could see that instilling a values-driven approach had huge potential to transform our business. I introduced the concept to Trovus and predictably got a range of initial reactions including a healthy amount of skepticism. I persisted and over a period of several months collectively we developed a set of shared values. As importantly we also created concrete examples and illustrations of what our business did when we lived those values. We made the process fun and enjoyable and the entire business came on the journey.

What was critical was this wasn't just something we did once a year. It was something that we made live in the business and we made it a regular part of the conversation. On a Monday morning I'd highlight specific actions that different employees had undertaken and reward them with chocolate. Another values prize was chosen by one of the staff so that the team was actively looking for good behavior by the others. My goal was to engage as many of the team as possible.

Values for me are all about celebrating the things we do well and applauding and encouraging more of the behaviors that we want to see. That's the opposite of what we are typically hardwired to do. In life, we are taught to spot what's wrong, to call out the problems, but when it comes to relationships, people respond much better when focusing on the one or two things that are right and building on those. I can remember with great clarity times when someone has shared with me specific feedback on something I've done well. Positive, well-meaning comments and feedback can last a lifetime.

Values at Home

Nichola and I were working hard to think how we would manage life at sea with three children for weeks at a time. How would we work together in close, confined, and often frightening circumstances 24 hours a day? Encouraged by the success of the values process at Trovus, we decided to implement a values-based approach to our family. We had to start thinking and acting like a team as it would be just the five of us at sea so we'd have to figure things out together.

Bluebell and Columbus were already familiar with values from their elementary school where each month they focused on a different value, discussing what it meant, and what they could do to demonstrate it. This helped our work on family values immensely. To engage them on the values at home we turned the topic into a joint craft project. The first stage was talking, using the school values as a reference point, saying that we were going to create our own family values. (By the way, if you're thinking this sounds odd, you're not alone—many people did and still do. But the practical application was one of the most important keys to us successfully working as a team on the boat.)

Just as we'd done with our Winners' Bible, we organized a stack of magazines, just what we had in the house—sailing, beauty, and business magazines. Armed with scissors, all four of us were soon snipping, finding photos of activities that appealed to us, turning the living room into piles of paper. We then worked in teams of two to say what value each picture could represent. Was it a picture that was happy, did it show getting into action? We wanted the children to create associations with different pictures. Naturally Nichola and I were steering the conversation, but we were engaging the children while actively listening to them. The session finished with everyone pasting their favorite pictures onto a single piece of paper with value words written next to them.

We tabled the values discussion for several weeks and one Saturday afternoon revisited it, asking the children to tell us what they remembered. Then we started crafting a range of possible concepts that could become our family values, exploring what those words meant to each of us. We were just laying a foundation, planting the ideas, and creating a common language where we could say certain words and all understand what we meant by them. Many family problems exist because of misunderstandings, miscommunications—we wanted to do as much as possible to avoid that.

We came up with a set of six values that best summed up how we wanted to live our lives, how we wanted to live on the boat, and how we would behave. We then created an acronym that pulled them all together. The values were summed up by the word LAUGH. This stood for:

Love + Learn Something

Action

Understanding

Go Prepared

Happy

The Values Painting

Over the next few weeks each of us was responsible for painting a picture for each of the values. We let Bluebell and Columbus lead. Columbus drew the picture for Action, Bluebell drew the picture for Understanding. Section by section the values picture came together. We completed the picture late one afternoon, celebrating with special drinks and snacks (see plate section, image 4).

We only had one more thing to do once the painting dried. Willow was only a few months old and clearly couldn't participate in quite the same way. We wanted to find a way to make her a part of the story, so we could all own the picture. We'd deliberately left a white border all the way around the main picture. One by one we pressed our hands into different color paints so that all five of us left our handprints on the picture. We then signed our names around the edges.

As well as providing a powerful anchor for all that we would do in our adventures, this was a group family activity that the children really enjoyed. With all the preparation going on, finding time for fun group activities had been hard, so it was important for the precious time engaging with the children.

We hung our values painting prominently on the landing so we'd all walk past it many times a day, keeping it front of our minds. We discussed what it meant to live each value at its very best. We found the best values talk time was after we'd all had breakfast, while we were planning the day. When they were showing Understanding at its very best, what did that mean? Rather than telling them off and say, "You're not listening to me," we'd try to turn it around and ask the question, "What is Understanding all about, how do you show you are listening to someone? How do you demonstrate Understanding?" Or "Do you guys remember, what did we say that Understanding was all about when we did the values exercise?" We'd try to trigger their thoughts, getting the kids to answer the questions for themselves.

I'll be the first to say we got it wrong a good deal of the time, falling into the trap of telling the children what not to do, what was wrong with their behavior. What helped was that Nichola and I were on this parenting journey together—we'd support each other, commenting respectfully on what we needed to do.

Learning Relationship Lessons the Tough Way

Back in 2006, we were living in southwest London with a one-year-old Bluebell. Work was not especially satisfying and neither was our lifestyle. We were torn between working in London or living the more relaxed country life in Devon. Instead of deciding on one or the other, we made the mistake of compromising and we moved to Bristol, geographically halfway between London and Devon. We believed we would end up with the best of both worlds. We moved to Bristol and bought a house that had been empty for two years and needed renovating.

My work in London meant that I spent Monday to Friday there and only weekends in Bristol with Nichola and Bluebell. This left no time to visit Devon and also meant that Nichola was living in a building site with a toddler while pregnant with Columbus. She missed the network of friends and family back in Surrey. In reality our decision was not right for us and very nearly broke us. However, it was a decision that ended up making us stronger. How? We weren't afraid to admit our error and start again. It took time and effort but once we did this and got back on track it gave us confidence to make bold decisions knowing that if they don't work out its OK, not failure, just feedback. It's OK to go back and start again on a different path.

Feedback Rather than Failure at Trovus

I've worked to develop a mindset that there is no such thing as failure. You have an idea. You try something. You get a result, an outcome. It might not be the result you wanted, but you've learned something and can try something different next time. Life then becomes a continuous set of experiments in finding out what works for you and what doesn't. That's it. Nothing is set in stone—it's a process of learning and discovery. (Nothing, that is, except values, your core set of beliefs that stays constant and keeps you upright.) I try not to take myself too seriously when I win or when I lose. It's just that that set of actions led to that outcome.

I love the Thomas Edison quote: "10,000 failed attempts and I am not discouraged. Each failed attempt is one step closer to success."

It had become clear to Ed and me that what we were doing at Trovus wasn't making a big enough difference in our income. We needed to do more to change things. We decided we needed a single leader rather than joint chiefs for faster, more effective decision-making. I suggested that Ed take the role of CEO, leaving me to focus more on sales and marketing. It also became apparent that if we really wanted to achieve the success of our role model companies we needed to develop our own products.

We met one product developer and spent a couple of hours with him in a coffee shop. The rapport he created with Ed was amazing— they seemed to think the same way, to have similar approaches as well as skill sets. As Ed and I walked back to the office, we were thinking the same thing but it was Ed who vocalized it. Maybe we have the product developer inside the business already but in the wrong role. We needed to change our roles again. I'd take on the CEO role and steer our strategy, direction, and team; Ed would focus on product development and sales.

I started as CEO by refocusing the business with a clear set of values, and attaching greater responsibility and accountability to each staff position. I was prepared to change personnel if people weren't on board with the plan. Having a freer hand as sole CEO enabled me to make faster, sometimes, tough decisions. I also brought in HR experts, recognizing that I had several skills gaps.

I'd been coming back from visits to the US with ideas and energy, forcing them on the business. While some of the ideas worked, the ones that didn't stood out, creating tension. I clearly wasn't taking my crew along with me. Sometimes in life, lessons are hard to learn, especially concerning one's own personality and interactions with others.

I re-asked my primary question, "How can I make things better?" and took the staff's responses on the chin and worked with them. I received coaching to make sure that I was actually engaging with the team.

After our staff reshuffle, I took the opportunity to set up quarterly targets, establishing a baseline revenue goal plus a stretch target to encourage high performance. If we hit the baseline target we'd fly everyone to Amsterdam for the weekend to celebrate, and if we hit the stretch target then we'd put an additional amount of money into the pot for the team to spend as they wished. It was a big incentive and the first time we'd done this. We had to make sure we hit the target, especially on the back of all the staff changes. We had to galvanize the 15-strong team, making sure everyone was on board.

Celebrating Success

The energy in the business during that first quarter was fabulous. We exceeded our target and celebrated in style, creating many memories and deeper friendships in Amsterdam. We moved offices to a better working environment—a bright, airy space with lots of other buzzing businesses. It included a great canteen where you could connect—we felt proud to meet there with clients. We continued to set quarterly targets and rewards. Ed flourished, bringing in some big clients, signing some brilliant deals. Over the course of a year we grew faster than we had in the previous four years, making more profit than we'd made in the previous six.

All I was doing was implementing the ideas I'd been learning from others—there was no great magic. We were doing things other people had found successful. It was our team who made it happen and unlocked the growth—I got out of their way and let them get on with it. I embraced the concept of finding out what people are most passionate about, then letting them do those things that energize them. I was getting the right people in the right roles and giving them support.

I remember hearing an African proverb at the time that resonated very deeply with me and sums up the essence of building a winning team: "If you want to go fast, go alone. If you want to go far, go together."

Make the Magic Happen: Closing in on the Deadline—Your Actions

1. Values

   Sit down with your team to work out your core values. Don't
   pick too many and don't get too hung up about getting them
   perfect. The important part is to select a few values that mean
   something to you and your team and are necessary in
   succeeding in your goal. Keep them simple to remember so
   that you will actually call upon and use them when faced with
   a decision.

   Once you state those values, find a way to make them
   visible so that you see them each day. We created a painting
   that we hung in the house. Figure out what works for you.

2. Feedback

   Apply these values to your actions. You should now be getting
   feedback on your actions. Is it working? Great, do more. Or
   what—maybe more likely—is not working? Stop, adapt, and
   then move on again. It's not failure, it's feedback.

3. Celebrate

   Don't leave this out. Celebrate what works.

Chapter 6

"The problem is…"—Addressing the Problems and Solving Them

(One Year Before Departure)

Departure was now getting close and we still had much to do. The pressure on us increased and we were being pulled in many directions to manage businesses, family life, training, preparation, and of course buying a boat, which we still didn't own.

We had been looking at several different sailboats. We attended boat shows in London and Southampton, getting to know the salespeople for both new and used boats. The children loved going to the shows. When we had a tour around the Oyster boats, Bluebell and Columbus were super-excited, running from one end of the boat to the other. Trying to keep them under control was like herding cats. They loved the bunk beds and agreed between themselves who was going to get the top and bottom bunks. They could imagine what their new home would look like.

In September 2013 the World Cruising Club opened their booking slots for the 2014 ARC rally across the Atlantic. We called up, paid the deposit, and booked our place. We didn't yet have the money for our trip. We didn't yet have a boat. We hadn't done our medical, diesel, or safety trainings. Nichola still hadn't sailed out of sight of land.

The staff at the WCC were bemused. "What's the name of your boat and how long is it?" "We haven't got one yet, but we will, and we think it will be 58 feet long." They must have wondered if we were genuine or not. We checked the following day on their website. There we were,

Caspar and Nichola Craven—Yacht to Be Advised. We celebrated. It was a big milestone in our planning and our sense of belief.

We had been sharing and talking about our plans for four years. We had a large map of the world outlining our departure date and sailing route. We became known as "the family planning to sail around the world." But I think a lot of people never actually believed we would pull it off and leave. It's quite possible we were the first people to enter the ARC rally without having a boat. I'm certain there were a lot of eyebrows raised. No matter, we were committed, and were going to find a way. If you want to do something you'll either find a way or you'll find an excuse.

There was humor too. Around the same time, in the fall of 2013, we were at home when the phone rang. Nichola answered, and it was the school's admissions officer. They were planning the school trips for the following school year and were confused as Bluebell, age eight at the time, refused to put her name down and kept telling the teachers that she wouldn't be there as she would be sailing around the world. They thought she had a wild imagination. Nichola explained that she was being truthful and yes, that we were planning to sail around the world.

Assessing the Challenges

There were many practical challenges that we needed to face. We were not in the habit of being cavalier with risks and we wanted to assess each risk we could possibly encounter, do our research, and devise our own solutions.

There were plenty of possible challenges ahead. What would happen if one of us got sick? Would sailing around the world be safe for the children? How would we deal with living together 24 hours a day, 365 days a year? Friends and family offered up the reasons why we shouldn't go: you haven't got a boat and you've never owned a boat; Nichola has never sailed out of sight of land; Nichola gets seasick. You've never homeschooled before and it's dangerous out there.

What we found was useful was how we reacted to all the advice that friends and family shared with us. Rather than getting cross and pushing back against it, we took it all on board and noted it down. These were things for us to think about, to research and to come to our own conclusions. They were not reasons for us to stop following our plans.

Just about every person I ever speak to has a dream, something they'd like to do, but they also have a list of reasons why they can't do it now. The reasons most commonly include "I haven't got the money," or "I can't take the time out from my career," or "I can't imagine doing that with my children—I'll do it when the children leave home." I've heard this called "The Tyranny of How." Rather than focusing on the desired outcome and imagining a clear compelling future, people get caught up in the "How to Achieve It."

Instead, set aside your "Why Nots" and refocus on your Reason Why. Why should you do it? What's your burning reason why this dream would be so amazing? Imagine the possibilities and where your life could lead if you did live your dreams.

If we'd tried to answer all the "Hows" up front, I can categorically guarantee we would not have achieved our dream. We would have been overwhelmed. We would have gotten bogged down in details, trying to solve every challenge at once, and would never have started taking action. It would have been too daunting. Instead, we first focused our energies on creating our clear compelling vision of the future and why we wanted that. Then we focused our energies and resources on solving how to make the magic happen.

In truth, we only fully resolved many of the "How" questions later on. We had to trust that we would work things out as we went along. If we had waited for everything to be perfect, we'd never have gotten underway.

Jump

Every successful person I've ever met has at some point faced a decision that is not clear-cut and where there is a risk. They had to jump into the unknown. If we had waited until all was certain, we'd have missed the boat— literally. When you are standing there on the edge of making a choice, it's that decision of whether to jump or not that defines the outcome.

65

When we came up with our plan, we knew people were going to call us crazy and give us their Reasons Why Not. Not because they didn't care and didn't want us to live our dreams—but because they did care and wanted us to make safe, sensible choices. But, here's the thing. Anyone else can only ever give you their opinion. It might be dressed up and come across with such certainty that it sounds like a fact, but it is only ever an opinion. We knew that we were far better placed to form a view on what was sensible and what was crazy than any one else. Of course we had to remember that we were making choices for our children. We needed to make sure our planning was thorough. We formed our own views.

We took each question and worked through to what we believed was a sensible solution. We had to trust ourselves to work it out as we needed, when we needed. And that was the magic that happened.

"What Will Happen to Our Careers? Will We Be Able to Get Jobs Again?"

I vividly remember having a beer with a good friend in a quiet country bar when he commented on how brave we were. What he meant was taking time out in the middle of our careers, just when we were coming into our most productive years work-wise. It just wasn't normal. Many of our generation traveled as students or early in their careers, but pretty much all of our friends were now settled into relationships, careers, and family life. The prospect of traveling was something kicked out into the long grass—something to do when the children leave home.

Here's the thing, though, that got us. By then, sure, you've probably managed to accumulate some wealth, making it easier to travel, but a big chunk of your life has gone already. We've all had friends or family who've died too early and it's been a wake-up call. Your life is short and you have to make the most of it. We wanted to make it happen.

When we returned from the trip we'd be in our early forties. We'd be rejuvenated, recharged, full of fresh ideas and energy. From what we'd learned, most people make the big leaps in their careers in their forties—the time when people are most productive. What better time in our careers than our late thirties to go out there, get some life experiences, really get to know our children and each other, and then come back with a full tank of energy ready to have a real impact? When we returned we'd know better what problems we wanted to solve and the benefit our work could bring to the world.

When we looked at our job interruption in this light, we couldn't think of a better time to take a break. We could also see that with an online business we wouldn't be taking a massive step away—we would create work that we could carry on from anywhere in the world.

"What If Someone Gets Sick?"—Health Matters

This was a big concern, one we took seriously, particularly because we were taking our children into the unknown. We broke the health issues into two aspects—prevention and cure.

Prevention—Staying Healthy

First we prioritized our health and fitness. As mentioned above, having enough energy was critical in being able to achieve our goals. We radically changed our diet, reducing our intake of sugar, white bread, white pasta, and meat as well as dramatically reducing our consumption of alcohol and caffeine. At the same time we increased the quantity and quality of fresh foods. We also introduced exercise into our daily routine: swimming and running were the most obvious ones.

Cure—Preparing for Medical Emergencies

We also looked closely at what we could do to prepare ourselves for health issues when we were out at sea with the children, and reliant on our own skills and equipment. We were particularly interested in the extensive medical training courses available for non-medic sailors such as ourselves.

Fear of a medical emergency aboard caused the most concern. We rationalized that you could get sick anywhere, at any time—you could be knocked over by a bus walking down the street—there are so many things that can affect you but it doesn't stop you from carrying on. It is different, of course, when you're thousands of miles from anywhere, and you have to work through the crisis on your own.

When I'd sailed around the world nine years earlier as part of the BT Challenge, we had a qualified nurse on board, together with a full medical kit with every drug imaginable. During that race a sailor got airlifted off a competitor's yacht with suspected appendicitis; another sailor was swept through the steering wheel, breaking his legs and hips in many places. I broke my thumb and also needed dental treatment in the Southern Ocean. We knew that medical emergencies would happen. It's just a fact of life—whether you are on land or at sea. The only question is how you deal with them.

We had a responsibility to address this area properly both for ourselves and for the peace of mind of others. Of course, no matter where you are in the world, there will be some medical facilities, however basic, and we'd often be near other ships with doctors on board. Our time crossing oceans would be the most challenging—we would be much more isolated, for example, in the middle of the Pacific. The bottom line—we had to be confident, and fully prepared so that we could address any medical emergency.

We did our research and found the most advanced training course available was the nine-day Ship's Doctor's course—the best thing outside of actually training to become a doctor or a nurse. This is the course taken by captains of seagoing commercial vessels—a top-notch training. If you pass, your Ship's Doctor's certificate enables you to access and prescribe medications. With that comes a massive responsibility—someone's life is in your hands.

The training was expensive and it would also be hard to make the time to go, plus put childcare arrangements in place. We debated which of us should take the course. It was a big time commitment. Could we afford it? Could we afford not to take it? What would happen if the one who took the training was the one who got sick or injured at sea?

We took the view that we should both know as much as practically possible about all things. If something happened to one or other of us, the responsibility would all fall to one person. That person had to be as prepared as possible. As often happens with difficult decisions, when you look back the right thing seems so obvious. We decided the right thing was for both of us to take the training. We found a way to do it, with generous help from friends and family who juggled childcare while we attended class for ten days.

Meeting other like-minded seafarers and immersing ourselves in the sailing community at this course kept us energized. All their friends and family thought they were mad too. There is a solidarity among fellow sailors and it was good to be in such company, swapping future plans, sharing issues we all faced in the tremendous amount of preparation for offshore sailing. The course was fast paced and small— just a handful of attendees so we covered all manner of things. I recall wincing as we had to insert a catheter into plastic genitals (male and female), inserting cannulas, as well as the more usual CPR training, using a defibrillator etc. The pictures, stories, and solutions were graphic, detailed, and shocking—intentionally—so we would take these medical matters seriously. They were long days and by the time we got home in the evenings the children would be fast asleep and we'd be spent—heads fully loaded with medical know-how.

By Day 9 we were pretty shattered—the work was intense and involved serious learning on top of driving for three hours a day between home and the south coast where the course was held. Day 10 had the written exam in the morning and the practical exam in the afternoon. We all passed and were duly awarded our certificates—our license to stock up on a vast array of drugs and treatments (much to the interest of our friends). The training had been excellent, and we felt that short of training as medics we had done all that we could to prepare us and our children.

We then had to budget for the medical supplies we needed to take with us—all the time hoping that this money was spent on stuff we'd never need to use. Our medical gear would fill three large holdall bags, as much medical kit as your average doctor's office. We had every conceivable piece of equipment and drug. We also spoke to a good friend of ours, Zoe, a doctor in southwest London; we gave her a list of the drugs and supplies we had on board, and she said we could call whenever we were stuck, and she'd give us advice over the phone. Our excellent medical course trainer would also be on hand to give us advice via email if needed. We had learned a lot and had done as much as we could short of finding a doctor or nurse to actually join us on board. We now needed to move on and focus on what else we had to do.

We obtained medical insurance designed for offshore sailing. Additionally, by sailing as part of the ARC fleet we had access to the crew of other boats—including sailors who were also trained doctors— available to help us via radio at sea or on land.

Vaccinations and Other Preparations

Before we left the UK we visited our local doctor's practice and spoke with the nurse who specialized in vaccinations. When we first approached her I think she was a little horrified at the prospect of our plans. However, we left her with the long list of countries that we planned to visit and she turned out to be a total star. When we returned to see her a week later she had not only researched all the vaccinations needed—along with costs—she also gave us a timetable of when we needed to have them, in what order, as some of these we needed to have while traveling.

There are many other areas of medical preparation. See more detailed information in the resources section.

"What About the Children's Education?"

Initially we didn't have a clue about homeschooling, but we knew we'd figure this out. Others had done it before and we were confident that with the skills we had between us there was plenty we could teach. We gradually began to seek out the advice of other sailing families who'd done the same.

I made contact with Brian and Sheila who'd circumnavigated three years before us, also with three children. We met at a local bar and they invited me to join them for supper, where I met their oldest daughter who by then was 13. What struck me was how confident and engaging their daughter was—full of questions—with a social poise that placed her comfortably among adults. She was remarkable. Her parents shared that they had initially taken a tutor when they departed, but by the time they'd reached Gibraltar they'd decided that wasn't working and they parted company. From then on they didn't follow any formal schooling and just let their three children experience the world. By the time they returned two years later the children rejoined their grades and were top of their classes in no time at all. The kids hadn't skipped a beat.

Nichola and I had different yet complementary skills. I'm the ideas person, better at seeing the bigger picture. Nichola is the detail person. We get our energy in different ways but need each other. Nichola spent a lot of time researching the curriculum for each child, speaking to their teachers, and amassing a huge amount of books and educational material, as well as looking at homeschooling courses and structures. The teachers were supportive of what we were doing. Their advice was to ensure that the children read as much as possible, kept up with their mathematics, and kept writing. Other than that the consensus was good luck and don't worry, the children will thrive.

As the trip progressed we did as we were advised, teaching mathematics traditionally and having the children read as much and as widely as possible. We also insisted they kept written daily journals. On top of that the schoolwork was topic-based depending on our location so we could cover history, geography, science, languages, religion, and philosophy as well as creative subjects such as art, cooking, design, and technology—plus anything else we wanted to bring in. We taught subjects we were passionate about as well as those usually covered in school. (See the Resources Section for more on homeschooling.)

"Is Sailing Around the World Safe? What About Pirates?"

I'm pretty sure there are statistics to show that more people get killed on the roads than by sailing around the world. It is a fact of life at sea that there are pirates, but there are probably far more dangers in driving every day. Safety was a serious consideration—a thing to be watchful of, not a reason not to travel. We took the best advice we could. We'd already plotted our route to avoid the areas most plagued with modern-day pirates.

"But We Don't Have A Boat!"

Ah, yes the elephant in the room. We didn't have a boat.

But there are always a lot of boats for sale and we didn't think we'd have any difficulty finding one. In fact, this was an easy challenge. In deciding on our boat we spoke to a number of boat owners. After much deliberation we decided we would sail on an Oyster. Why? Firstly their unrivaled customer service and care—they build solid boats that sail forever. We loved the center cockpit that provided us with the extra feeling of safety given that we were sailing with young children. On a more aesthetic note, we loved the fact that below deck there was so much light in the saloon. The master cabin had proper bunks with plenty of headroom (important when you are 6' 3").

"Nichola Gets Seasick"

I knew from my first circumnavigation that it was extremely rare for someone to be seasick for more than a couple of days. That said, I'm grateful that I've never been seasick and it wasn't me who had to deal with this. Nichola knew the risk of her susceptibility and decided to deal with it. She learned to cope with it but sadly it never left her completely. Each time we set sail her seasickness returned. She never conquered it but managed to find ways to handle it.

Lack of money, uncertain medical skills, lack of boat, seasick stomach for Nichola—just issues to be dealt with, not reasons we shouldn't sail around the world. They warranted consideration and we had to decide how much weight and importance to place on each. We stayed focused on our outcome—that was our priority. We had our Reason Why we were going to make our adventure happen and every day we sought to reinforce it. We were ready to build momentum. We didn't know how we were going to do everything, but we were absolutely certain about our desired outcome.

When we would first tell people our plans, some were positive, others were horrified, troubled, and concerned. However, once they saw our commitment and had time to process what we wanted to do, virtually everyone was not only excited for us, but also willing to help in any way possible. This was common. I will never forget our vaccinations nurse—who'd been so worried about our plans initially—calling us up on the day we left the UK to wish us all the best on our travels.

Make the Magic Happen: "The problem is…"— Your Actions

1. Write down every single reason that you can come up with to not accomplish your shared vision, making sure you add in all the reasons your family and friends give you as well.
2. Group the reasons into themes—a lot will probably fit under the same umbrella, e.g., health or safety.
3. Take each reason in turn and work out the answer; there will be a creative solution for each and every one. It's certain you won't be able to resolve all of the concerns right away—that is expected and OK. Keep focusing on the outcome you want and keep working on finding your solutions. Guaranteed, the more you can identify the issues, the more you can either resolve or at least know what they are so that you can be on the lookout for them.

Chapter 7

Actually Going Ahead (or Not?)
(The Year of Departure)

The beginning of 2014 was the start of the real countdown. We were now in the same calendar year as our departure date of August 1, 2014. We had spoken about this date every day since 2009—it was now only months away. The feeling was a mixture of exhilaration and trepidation as there was still so much to do. Including perhaps the most obvious thing. We still didn't have a boat.

Time to Buy a Boat

We attended a seminar at the London Boat Show in January 2014 for offshore sailing. The first question anyone asks you at a sailing seminar is "What boat do you have?"

We still didn't have one. When we explained we were going to sail around the world in seven months' time, their reactions said it all—nobody believed we would be ready.

Many other people in our circle were asking if our plan to sail around the world was really going to happen. It's too late to get a boat now, they said; you won't have time to get properly prepared. Surely, you'd be better off delaying a year and going next year when you've had more of a chance to get the money together and get the boat you want? That may have been the reasonable thing to do. We weren't reasonable and we were set that we were leaving on August 1. Nothing ever happens without a deadline and that was our deadline.

During the five years before our departure I'd regularly look at the boats for sale in sailing magazines. Our approach to deciding on the right boat was straightforward and much in line with a mindset of abundance: use creativity and resourcefulness. We started at the end point of what we wanted: to make our adventure the safest and most fulfilling it could be. We opted to get the best possible boat for our needs and then find a way to fund it. Sailing oceans is vastly different from coastal and inland sailing. We needed a proper offshore sailboat, one that would give us and our families peace of mind about its ability to handle big seas and stronger winds than we had ever encountered. This was an area where we would not skimp: we needed the best. How we were going to afford it still wasn't answered.

Naturally, everyone has a different opinion about the best offshore boat. There are many excellent resources and books about stability and other seaworthy features needed in an offshore boat. When deciding on our boat, we spoke to people we trusted, focusing on their recommendations. What became apparent quickly was that Oyster Yachts, a British manufacturer of hand-built sailboats, was one of the leading brands of safe and solid bluewater cruising sailboats. After hearing about them from our circle we concurred that there was no better boat for handling big seas, offshore stability, and safety.

What also became apparent in our conversations was just how much work we'd have learning about the maintenance and repair of an ocean-going sailboat. This is where Oyster also stood out against the rest of the market. Their after-sales service is legendary—we heard one story after another of how they responded quickly, with first-class fix-it advice whatever problem you had, arranging for the parts to be shipped wherever you are in the world.

Given that boat maintenance wasn't yet one of our strongest skills, having the best boat-maintenance and systems support network we could was essential. Our decision was easy so we spent little time looking at other boats.

Next we debated buying a new or a used Oyster. There were pros and cons. We soon learned that whatever boat you get, things will need fixing. With a used secondhand boat, there's a good chance that many things that need to be fixed have been fixed. On the other hand, a

75

damaged boat's reputation can linger: we looked at one sailboat that had suffered hurricane damage and even though it was repaired, its history would have been at the back of our minds whenever we faced heavy weather. Peace of mind knowing you have the right sailboat for what you are tackling is paramount.

I visited the Oyster website most weeks looking at their new and used boats. For two years we had tracked every single Oyster on the market, becoming quite familiar with what was out there. We decided that with the five of us, we needed to have a 50-foot-plus boat for space, a boat that would sail fast, was solidly constructed, and safe. What also became apparent was that for maximum purchasing power for a sailboat, cash was key, as well as a motivated seller that could be flexible on pricing.

We looked at the numbers and with the budget we had in mind knew we needed even more capital, so we took out a second mortgage on our home. The conversation with the bank was interesting. What do you want a second mortgage for? Well, to buy a boat. OK, and what income will you have to pay off the mortgage? Well, we're working on that. Fortunately, we had a good relationship with the bank and managed to convince them that we had the cash flow and that we didn't present any additional risk to them. That was a lucky break—they could have said no. We'd have found another way but that would have taken more time—a commodity we had little of, with just five months to go until departure date.

We now had to step it up to find our boat. We got to know Matthew at Oyster, taking a day off to visit their headquarters in Ipswich, northeast of London. The day gave us a huge amount to consider—we left feeling both excited and daunted by how much it was going to cost—not just the purchase but the running costs too. Matthew showed us the details of three boats that could be right for us. All were in Palma de Mallorca in Spain; our friend Paul was there and invited me to stay on his yacht, *Juno*, and offered to look at them with me.

In March I flew out to spend half a day exploring the boats, talking through the true running costs. One of the boats felt like it could be right for us and I put in a speculative offer. It was promptly rejected. Back to the drawing board.

A few weeks later Nichola went on her own to the south coast of the UK and looked at four more Oysters. Each was either not quite right for us or out of our price range. It was starting to feel like an impossible mission.

We decided to go right back to the beginning and broaden the search. Had we made the right choice for an Oyster? Were there other equally good boats out there that were less expensive? We blocked out a Saturday and arranged a series of back-to-back boat viewings of 11 boats from five different boatbuilders such as Swan, Moody, Hallberg-Rassy, Discovery, and Trintella. We had the children with us and it was set to be a full day, starting with the first viewings at 9am.

As the day wore on, we hadn't found anything that felt right and the kids were getting increasingly fractious. We arrived at the final viewing of the day in the Hamble. By now Bluebell and Willow had had enough and just wanted to stay in the car. We checked the details for the final boat and how we'd get on board. The owner, David, had left the keys with the marina office and we were on our own without a salesperson or owner to show us around.

Columbus and I went on ahead to view *Aretha*, an Oyster 53. She was the nearest boat on the dock—painted in a stunning blue. She instantly stood out as a special boat. As we stepped on board, I had a feeling that this was the one. Nichola joined me and we explored down below. She was well presented and well organized with printed and laminated notes on the systems. She had four berths including a bunk cabin that would be perfect for two children. She would need some adapting and upgrades for our purposes, and some of the features like the pristine cream saloon seats weren't practical as we knew they would be magnets for Marmite-covered children's hands. But *Aretha* worked her magic as we explored. Nichola and I knew then and there that we had found our seagoing home.

It took several months to negotiate the purchase, which involved a sea trial, a detailed survey, and extensive bills for the upgrades needed to get her ready for our voyage. Things were starting to come together. We had the sixth member of the family. We completed the purchase on May 30, ten weeks before our planned departure date.

As the final pieces of the jigsaw puzzle were coming together, our friends and family finally started to appreciate and realize that this wasn't just a conversation. This was truly happening and we were going to sail around the world as a family.

The Next Stage for Trovus

In that final year before our departure, Ed wondered if I was really going to leave Trovus to go sailing. We were committed—I said yes, we were leaving on August 1, 2014. It was a testing time. Ed and I had spent the last seven years working intensely and closely, and now here I was about to change the dynamic, stepping out of the business on a sabbatical. We sought expert advice to guide us through the process and called in Margaret Meyer, a trusted advisor, to help us work through the conversation. Margaret got us to change the conversation and focus on the outcomes we both wanted and to appreciate each other's different perspectives.

Ed wasn't sure he wanted to continue the business on his own so we decided to start looking at other options. First we hired a chairman, Vic, who had grown other product companies and could be "hands on." Secondly, we also decided to look for companies that might be interested in buying Trovus. Two large global companies expressed interest, attracted by the innovative work we were doing, the client base we'd built up, and the team we'd created. We would continue to court their interest in the hope of selling Trovus, but in the meantime the business had to keep running in my absence. It would take some time, but the interest we ignited with these two global companies would come back to us in the following months.

I also had to manage my way out of Trovus. It was no small task. Ed and the team were amazing and once I started stepping away, the business with its strong culture and leadership from Ed took the reins and forged forward. I was in the office several times a week, but the business understandably was keen to press on without me and to adjust to life as it was going to be.

Around the start of the year I had decided to start training to run the London Marathon in April 2014. The long runs helped clear my mind and provided much-needed thinking time. It was painfully apparent to both Nichola and me that we were not making meaningful progress toward our financial target. No money, no adventure, was our simple reality. Our values were a strong anchor point for how we approached this situation: Learning, Getting in Action, and Understanding were key values at this point. We had to adapt our approach and keep going.

Dealing with the Reactions of Others

Over the previous couple of years we'd taken a fair bit of flak. Nichola came back from picking the kids up after school one day having been told by one mom that if we took the kids away we'd never get them back into the school system again and that life would be difficult. Nichola's reaction was: "If that's all that's keeping us here, then it's definitely time to leave." She came home in tears, though, on more than one occasion at the reactions she was getting and the lack of support she felt. We were doing every single thing in our power to make our dream happen and were stretched beyond belief. We had no spare capacity left. Nothing. To then have to deal with criticism and be told we shouldn't be doing this didn't help. This was a time when we had to stick to our guns and be resilient. We knew that people would come around—we had to get on with it, make our own choices, and live our own lives rather than the lives other people thought we should live.

When people started to believe we were actually going ahead, it brought out mixed reactions. It ranged from people who thought what we were doing was brilliant to those who thought we were utterly irresponsible. I found it helpful to have the mindset that the reactions were coming from a place of care and concern, and that people were looking out for our welfare. Some people wouldn't say things to us directly. One friend confided by saying, "I don't agree with what other people are saying, that you are mad." My mom would tell us stories about people who had drowned while sailing.

In May 2014, just four months before we were set to depart, there was a tragic incident in the mid-Atlantic when the sailboat *Cheeki Rafiki* lost her keel, overturned, and sank along with her four crew. It hit the front pages of the papers and was all over social media. The pressure on us not to go sailing stepped up several gears. We explained to our families we were leaving no stone unturned in how we approached safety. We knew there was more to this than simply buying the best boat. We were doing all we could to fully prepare.

Sailboat Safety

Sailing oceans is different from coastal sailing or inshore sailing. You need a boat built to seaworthy standards (ISO Category A in Europe), one that can take boarding seas and gale-force winds. You will need a wide range of sails aboard to cope with everything from the doldrums to 60-knot gales. The keel and rudders need to be staunch and seaworthy—able to weather cross-seas. The boat needs to be equipped with systems for long offshore passages including satellite communications, watermaker, EPIRBs (Emergency Position Indicator Radio Beacons), liferaft, and autopilot. The integrity of your boat, the safety track record of the manufacturer, and paying continuous attention to boat and rig structural integrity is critical.

We read enough sailing magazines to know that Oyster sailboats were regularly used to sail around the world. Our trusted friends let us know that Oyster boats were reputed to be among the best offshore boats on the market. Offshore sailboats have a stability rating you can research. This includes a STIX value (ISO STability IndeX) and the AVS (Angle of Vanishing Stability). For our Oyster 53, with standard 2.15m (7-foot) draft keel and alloy rig, the results showed a STIX of 41.385 and AVS of 112 degrees. To learn more about these ratings and how they apply see *The Complete Yachtmaster: Sailing, Seamanship and Navigation for the Modern Yacht Skipper* by Tom Cunliffe.

Safety on Board

I prioritized safety and made our boat rules clear to all:

- Lifejackets are to be worn at all times on deck, always clipped in to lifelines.
- No leaving the cockpit unless someone else knows what you are doing.
- Always wear shoes on deck.
- No drinking alcohol at sea and no smoking on board.
- When underway, always someone awake on watch keeping a regular lookout.
- No going on the foredeck unless someone else is on deck watching you.

Our boat rules had to be embedded as second nature from Day 1 and applied to anyone on board—adults and children. No exceptions.

Getting *Aretha* Ready for Our Voyage

Buying *Aretha* was the easy step. Now we had to commission her to be ocean-ready. The to-do list was extensive:

- Complete audit and inventory of everything on board
- Upgrade the life raft and replace safety equipment (flares, EPIRBs, and lifejackets)
- Fully service the engine, generator, and watermaker
- Service the steering
- Full rigging checks—both standing and running rigging
- Full sail service and checks
- Install satellite communications
- Service propane fittings and supply lines
- Service and test the electronics, including the navigation systems
- Service and test all winches (and windlass)
- Double-check and service anchors and rodes
- Service all the seacocks and through-hull fittings
- Service and test the fresh- and sea-water systems

Not only that, we had to learn how to drive and handle this extremely complex piece of machinery and understand its electronics. There were literally thousands of working parts. We truly had our work cut out and used the services of an extensive array of specialist suppliers to rapidly climb the learning curve. All at the same time as packing up our house, transitioning our businesses, and looking after our children and each other.

We had help from lots of friends. Paul Covell is the person I have sailed the most ocean miles with, and one of the most inspiring people I know. Two weeks after we purchased *Aretha* Paul and I spent two days doing essential work aboard, including attaching netting along the lifelines and applying nonslip paint on the cabintop aft of the mast.

In May 2014, four months before departure, I took *Aretha* on a week-long shakedown sail along the south coast of England with three trusted crew—Jani, John, and Nandi—to get to know the boat, test the systems, and see how they worked. I'd sailed with all three of these accomplished sailors before. Jani is a tough, resourceful Hungarian, and a brilliant chef who makes an amazing goulash—that alone would put him high on my crew list. Add to that, he's a first-class mechanic and engineer. John is an experienced sailor with a dry sense of humor, always ready to join in any banter. Nandi was Jani's nephew—a powerful young man always willing to lend a hand. They were the perfect crew for getting to know our boat as we navigated along the south coast. Nichola stayed at home on this occasion, but she had been working her way through the sailing courses over the previous five years to build her experience.

Aretha performed magnificently. I, on the other hand, did not.

I had completed the London Marathon in April, and in the process raised over $6,000 for the NSPCC (National Society for the Prevention of Cruelty to Children). I'd had some back and leg pain during the first 20 miles that developed into excruciating pain in the final six. For that last stretch along London's Embankment to the finish line I was stopping every half-mile to stretch and get physiotherapy. Fired by the energy of the crowd I pushed myself way further than I should have. In the weeks that followed I needed lots of physiotherapy and was being careful to manage the pain, taking a lot of Ibuprofen. It was uncomfortable, but manageable.

We left Southampton on *Aretha*, stopping for our first night a little way down the coast in Weymouth. Walking around town, I could feel my right leg tightening in a way that it hadn't before. Five days later, heading back, we stopped at Brixham where I was walking on the quay with Jani when I was suddenly immobilized and doubled over in pain.

"Jani, I can't walk." It was as though I had hot coals in my legs and back. I'd never felt pain like that before—it brought tears to my eyes. So many things flashed into my mind—how could we carry on our plans if I couldn't walk? I'd be a liability; it would be impossible.

Jani and the crew helped me back aboard *Aretha*—one on either side of me to support my weight. Moving was easier on board since I could support myself around the boat with my arms, taking the weight and strain off my back and legs. It took two days to sail back—I spent as little time as possible walking.

At seven weeks away our departure was about to get significantly more challenging.

Back Surgery

My doctor referred me to a back specialist. I instantly liked Dr. Mendoza. I told him we were setting off to sail around the world for two years and we were leaving in seven weeks. He raised an eyebrow at me, then realized I was serious. He gave me my options. I could grit it out, taking Ibuprofen to reduce the swelling and pain and do physiotherapy, on the basis that 50 percent of these conditions sort themselves out. Or I could have the operation to shave a portion of the disc away at the base of my spine, thus relieving nerve pressure—the cause of my pain.

I went home and discussed the situation with Nichola. We were absolutely set on our plan. Yet if we sailed without the operation I could damage my back, potentially ending my ability to walk and function normally if I pushed too hard. Friends and family said, "Oh, we're really sorry—surely you're going to delay your trip by a year now and let yourself heal?"

It was an agonizing choice and not one either Nichola or anyone else could make. It was my decision alone, and our lives depended on it. Normally when I have a tough decision, I go for a long run to clear my head—by the end the decision usually makes itself clear. Oh, the irony—I couldn't run. So instead, I slept on it for a couple of days, taking advice from as many people as I could. It turned out Nichola's dad had had the same operation many years earlier; it had been a success and he hadn't had any problems since then. I made my decision. I was going for the operation—I wanted our adventure to happen and I wanted to be in the best possible physical condition.

Resourcefulness—A.K.A., If It's Not Working, Try Something Different

It was during these final seven weeks that we had our lowest points. We were by now totally committed, having purchased *Aretha*, but my back had just gone and it was extremely uncertain whether I'd be fit in time for our departure.

I was stepping away from Trovus and cash flow in the business was extremely tight. There were questions around how the business would survive and in the worst-case scenario I'd have to put more money into Trovus to meet the personal guarantees that Ed and I had. As our planned departure date drew near we had to set our expectations that we'd get nothing from Trovus. If a sale came through, then that was a bonus.

We had handed over the day-to-day running of the internet business to Morna but it was still sucking in cash as we invested to grow it. The businesses weren't behaving as we wanted or planned.

We calculated we had enough money to last no more than six months if we left and less than six if we stayed. The costs of owning and prepping a boat for sea are substantial—our cash was flowing out at an alarming rate. There had to be another approach we hadn't tried. We had to look again at all our resources and maximize what we had. Once at sea, our marina bills would drop away dramatically and if we rented out our house, we'd gain rental income. We wanted to get going and get to sea. And so, although we'd said at the beginning that we didn't want to rent out our house, by that point it was a no-brainer. We would rent out the house.

We managed to set things up so that the new internet businesses together with our rental income more than covered our boat and living expenses, enabling us to live, sail, and explore with the financial freedom that we'd planned for all those years earlier.

The Final Stretch—Preparation for the Big Voyage

Renting our house meant we had to pack it up. Mountains of household stuff accumulated over the years had to be dealt with—a chore that felt like it would never end. We still had tons of training to take and repairs on the boat to make—our list was large and growing as we figured out what we needed. And we had the young children to look after as well: Bluebell was nine, Columbus was seven, and Willow was two.

We realized that if I had the back operation, we'd need crew to help us sail across the Bay of Biscay. We had no crew lined up, since we'd originally intended to set off with just the five of us. With so many things going on, despite Nichola completing two sailing training courses, she still hadn't done as much sail training as we had intended and hadn't yet sailed out of sight of land. We also planned to attend my youngest sister's wedding in France so had an involved travel schedule. We intended to sail *Aretha* to Portugal, then fly back to the UK, then on to France, and then fly back to Portugal. I can't imagine how we could possibly have had more things going on—we had lists, lists, and more lists.

These were testing times. When we attended a school parents' evening, the questions kept coming regarding safety in the light of the *Cheeki Rafiki* sinking, how we'd deal with medical emergencies, and the children's schooling. On the outside we were confident and in control.

On the inside we were stretched to the limit, trying to juggle the biggest challenge that either of us had ever taken on. We were at our most uncertain and yet we had to press on.

Nichola and I drew strength from each other. There were times when we were tired and tempers flared but it was only ever temporary. The power of the compelling vision uniting us and pulling us into the future was right at the heart of it. We were stretched, we were under pressure, and yet we were resolved to make our vision turn into a reality.

I had my operation just two weeks before our planned departure date of August 1, 2014. It was the first time I'd ever been in hospital. Nichola was busy making our world move forward so I went into the city on the train by myself, feeling lonely and fearful. The operation took several hours under general anesthesia and was a success, and they kept me in overnight to make certain I'd come through the anesthetic. My good friend Ian collected me the following day and drove me home in the back

Notes from Nichola

It's quite true that Caspar and I have different skills and different approaches to life. I always say, jokingly, that if we were both like me, nothing would get started, and if we were both like Caspar, things might not get completed. Working together we complement each other.

My antidote to the stress of uncertainty was planning in detail. I had barely sailed when our idea came together, so I decided that rather than let it stop me I simply needed training. I crossed my fingers that my seasickness wouldn't be a permanent condition and that we could anticipate most issues that would come up, dealing with them by preparation.

I had a large 3-ring binder that became my administration bible. I carried it everywhere. It had lists, notes, ideas, everything. It contained a boat section, one on schooling, as well as one on parties, trips, and events that I had committed to before setting sail—these were varied, everything from taking the children to Harry Potter World and to a departure party, to arranging for Willow and of his car with the seats down so I could lie flat. The only thing now was that I'd have a period of convalescence that would force us to delay our departure date. But for how long? Six to eight weeks minimum.

Those were perhaps six of the toughest weeks of my life. I've always been active and thrive on leading, living in the heart of the action. Now I was incapacitated, barely able to lift anything, and we had an incredible task list: prepare and complete the refit of *Aretha*; set up our affairs so we could manage our lives while at sea; sell our car; hand over Trovus and Nichola's business. And parent three lively children, as well as attending children's birthday parties, and going away parties, where critics told us that we shouldn't be sailing off with our children. The tools and skills that we as a couple had developed over the years to communicate effectively and understand each other were more important than ever now as we were being tested close to our limits.

Columbus to be baptized (a commitment I had made to my mom!). I found it helped to write a list of all the possible issues that could arise. This helped with everything, from working out what sail training I could take as well as the items we needed aboard.

The lists of tasks were long and we were stressed out. We had supportive family and friends but the negative comments hurt, probably more so when I was already stressed. Yet through it all we had a plan—we were excited to be setting off together as a family and that buoyed us up at the low points.

In the 1980s Billy Ocean released a song called "When the Going Gets Tough, the Tough Get Going." That song epitomizes my wife, Nichola. While I was incapacitated, she tackled these final tasks with ruthless efficiency and organization. She pulled things together, enlisting help from friends and family in packing up our lives, taking only the essentials onto *Aretha*. Friends came over to take bags of rubbish to the local dump and ferry our stuff to different storage locations. Ian, who was to join us sailing across the Bay of Biscay, helped us with boat preparation, packing our house, and storing our gear. Mark, another great friend, also helped us pack, bringing his unique style of humor: "Just why do you need to save so much of this stuff?" he cajoled. He was of course right, but arguments over what to keep were saved for another day. Both my mom and Nichola's parents helped with childcare. A host of neighbors and friends helped us juggle our crazy lives. The help from so many people was humbling.

Packing toys was a huge issue. Every year at Christmas, we'd be overwhelmed by the amount of presents the children received. We'd get from one Christmas to the next and find presents still in their cellophane wrapping from the previous year. So we placed strict limits on what the children could take on the boat: a small box of toys plus books. Of what was left, some went to storage, some went to charity, and some to friends.

One of the nicest things about the whole sailing adventure was that we had so few possessions aboard we realized that we didn't need much stuff. On land we had clogged our life with possessions. We found it liberating to live with less. Nichola's favorite birthday party was for Columbus in the December after we left, at Rodney Bay in St. Lucia. She purchased 20 juice boxes and a cake and we had a party by the pool. One present from the family was all that was needed: the focus was on enjoying time together rather than wading through gifts.

Storage Decisions

When deciding what to store we tried to be as ruthless as possible. We recycled what we could, sold items on eBay, gave stuff to charity, and threw things away. Eventually we still had a fair amount of belongings left—we divided these into items that could be stored in a friend's garage and more delicate items that would go in storage. We saved money by finding the smallest container we could find, paying for a year in advance (to get the best deal), and by picking an upper floor container (they are cheaper than ground-floor ones). Storage was expensive and the key question when deciding what to store or get rid of is will it be cheaper to store or buy again new later on? That test certainly helped us.

We also opted for a storage unit we could self-pack, with good accessibility. We didn't need constant access but we might need things to be collected so we picked a storage company a 45-minute drive from relatives who could go to the unit if needed. We left small and valuable items with parents for safekeeping.

We still stored way too much. Now as we start to go through items since our return, the amount of boxes we look through and then toss confirms we should have been more ruthless.

There is no doubt that without help—which we asked for and received—there was no way we could have departed. Having a bold plan and sticking to it galvanized others to help us succeed. Nichola worked long into the nights, often only coming to bed at 3 or 4 in the morning. Rachael, Willow's nanny, was a godsend. Piece by piece it all came together—an effect only a deadline can create.

We moved our departure date back three weeks—this gave me five weeks to convalesce. We were in a tight spot since we needed to cross the Bay of Biscay before September. The Bay's reputation as one of the most dangerous stretches of sea in the world is well deserved—the sooner we could get south of it, the better. We also had to accommodate the schedules for our crew—my brother Max and my good friend Ian had already scheduled leave from work for the passage.

The days flew by. My diary entry on August 19, 2014, the day before departure, reads:

"Insane. Best word I have to describe what's going on.

"The house is upside down. Things to be taken to the boat. Things for storage. Stuff to be sold. Stuff to be chucked. Thank goodness we can laugh. Seriously, this could drive you nuts.

"Minimal sleep last night and back down to *Aretha* today—food shopping, life raft on board, spare lifejackets, electronic charts, spare water, compass fitted. Why does it always end up last minute? Part of life I guess. Nothing ever happens without a deadline.

"Finally feel close to getting going. Sailing will be a doddle.

"It's funny. You can find a million reasons not to do something. Really though. You just need one good Reason Why you should do something. Conquers all the other crap that goes through your head. That thought of creating inspiring life-changing experiences is the reason we are doing this. Good job we've been hanging on to that."

We held a family goodbye party on board *Aretha* so everyone could meet the boat and gain an appreciation of our seagoing home for the next two years. We have marvelous memories of that day in the sun on the Hamble, spending time with the people we cared most about. At another time, a month before we left, we scattered Dad's ashes at sea. It was perhaps the greatest sadness of our travels not being able to share this trip with him—he'd have loved every moment of what we were doing and I was certain we'd have seen him in many far-flung lands. I knew he'd be looking over us, smiling at what we were doing.

Another goodbye party, this one nautically themed for our friends, was held upstairs in a bar by the river. It was a great evening, the DJ one of our friends. The party rocked until the early hours of the morning.

The final couple of days were a blur. An incredibly exciting blur, but a blur all the same. When I cast off with the BT Global Challenge, I was one of 18 people getting everything ready, with full onshore support. This time round, it was just Nichola and me—with family and friends. I went to the wholesale box store (cash and carry) to fill the boat with long-term supplies of pasta, rice, flour, and other basic essentials. Nichola's mom, Sheila, ferried the piles of food to *Aretha* and we carried it aboard and wondered where it would all get stowed.

We picked up lifejackets and got them fitted with AIS (Automatic Identification System) units so that each person and their lifejacket would give off an identifiable digital signal if they went over the side, got the sat-coms sorted, obtained paper charts, electronic charts, and pilot books. There was much help and many hands to help pack—much appreciated as I was still under advice not to lift or pull on lines while my back recovered. Thankfully, my back was feeling better by the day. Nevertheless, since I was still in a delicate state, we enlisted the help of my brother Max.

We left Willow with Nichola's parents for this first passage on *Aretha*, settling into a boat routine without a lively two-year-old.

Bluebell wrote (in several colors) on the blog about her thoughts on the upcoming first passage:

"I feel excited about going sailing around the world but I do feel a bit scared as well. The reason I am scared about this is because I have never been across one country to another country that's why I am a bit scared. But apart from that every thing is fine so I am really excited. The things that I am mostly excited about going around the world is that I will get to see lots of new places and lots of animals like dolphins, turtles, sharks and whales but most of all meeting new friends. And this is why I am excited and scared."

On the night before our departure we worked late into the evening, stowing away the last bits. By midnight the boat looked less like a yard sale. *Aretha* felt as though she had much hidden space—everything or almost everything found a home.

Alarms were set for 5am and we slipped lines just before 6 to catch the tide heading west. Damn, this is really happening, I thought as we glided out of Universal Marina on the Hamble River near Southampton. It was August 20, 2014. There was a slight mist over the water and the sun was rising in a blue sky with wispy white clouds.

Our vision statement for the previous five years had started with the line: "On August 1, 2014, we are setting off to sail around the world." It was five years since we first inked those words with the world before us. We were 19 days after our planned departure date but we were underway.

It was an incredible feeling as we switched off the engine in the Solent and felt the wind filling the sails, powering us along; standing at the helm and steering our sailboat, knowing that we were leaving these waters for two years, off to experience the world. All those 5am starts on freezing cold mornings off to London when I'd visualized standing there at the helm of our boat sailing around the world. And now here we were. Our dream had become our reality. We were off. It was the biggest buzz you can imagine. We had done it.

Bluebell and Columbus were still asleep as we departed, but everyone was awake and on deck by the time we reached mid-Solent with a marginal breeze. As we passed the Isle of Wight, heading out into the English Channel, the stacks of chalk known as The Needles looked fabulous, stark white against a deep blue sea and sky. Columbus took photos. We aimed for Weymouth for the first night, arriving under full sails, with Columbus having caught his first mackerel.

Make the Magic Happen: Actually Going Ahead (Or Not?)— Your Actions

1. Be mentally prepared that things will go wrong in the final stages of preparation. It will happen. It's guaranteed. Much as when sailing around the world, you know that at some point you will have to deal with adversity. This is where working your mindset muscle will pay off. Get resourceful, get creative, and either find a way or make a way (make sure it's legal and moral!).

2. Don't be afraid to ask for help.

3. Work to your team's strengths while making sure to consider everyone's needs. The final buildup to any project can be stressful—this is where teamwork and values will really pay off. Values and focusing on the right behaviors aren't just for the good times. They are for the tough times when nothing seems certain and you don't know how to achieve your goals.

4. Capture and document what you are doing. You might not feel like doing it at the time, but these photos, logs, and journals will contain many of your most valuable memories later on.

5. Stop to appreciate the moment. Notice what you've achieved and allow yourself to feel proud, as a team. Remember where you started and look at where you are now. Make yourself notice the small things—it's far too easy, and habitual, to keep charging on without appreciating the details.

PART TWO

Sailing Around the World

What were you excited about before the experience?

BLUEBELL: I was excited because I was going to see new places I had never been to. Like the Galapagos and Panama and lots of other places. I was also excited that I would be able to go swimming with dolphins, which most people don't get to do. I was also excited that I was going to get to spend more time with my family and in England I only got to spend a few hours with them a day but now we spend 24/7 with them. I mean I was excited about everything. I mean wouldn't you be?

COLUMBUS: OK. Let me think. That we were going to see lots of places and swimming at nice tropical islands with turtles. That we'd see lots of dolphins and catch lots of fish. We'd see sharks.

What were you worried about before you started?

BLUEBELL: Now I was worried I was going to miss my friends and wouldn't meet lots of new friends.

COLUMBUS: That we'd come into big storms and there would be really big waves. Also, the boat might get a leak in the bottom. That we would be seasick.

Chapter 8

Settling in to Life at Sea
The Hamble, Southampton, UK,

to Figueira da Foz, Portugal

(August 2014 to October 2014)

Part of me was expecting that once we left we'd slow down, maybe have time to read a book, and settle into a relaxing rhythm. As we were to discover, life would be full of experiences—reading time wasn't going to happen anytime soon. We completed a little under 1,000 ocean miles in 12 days. Nichola, Bluebell, and Columbus had their first offshore sails (Willow stayed at home with Nichola's parents for the first few weeks), and we had a hatful of rich experiences—exactly what we signed up for.

During the first week we worked our way along the south coast of England. Weymouth, our first stop, was heaving with people and boats when we arrived—it was carnival season. Dinghies filled the harbor entrance and there were a handful of yachts waiting to berth. We tied up in a narrow gap just in time to see the Red Arrow aerobatic display planes flying overhead in perfect formation—it was a party atmosphere complete with fireworks. A great first day to kick things off. The next day we slipped lines at 7am heading for Dartmouth near to where I had grown up. The sea turned a little rougher. We continued to fix things on the boat—now it was a blocked head (toilet) and our satellite communications. What we quickly realized is that there is a permanent to-do list aboard a boat. From time to time I needed to pause and take in the fact that we were really underway on our trip around the world.

The following day we had an emotional departure from Dartmouth, passing the key landmark of Start Point lighthouse near Hallsands where I'd spent my childhood navigating the inshore waters. We continued around the coast past Hope Cove where my dad had lived and where we'd scattered his ashes. Memories of magical times spent with him came flooding back to me—I felt his presence more than ever, wanting him to have been there waving us off, knowing we'd be seeing him at the next port to share a beer and stories.

We had our final family farewells in Plymouth. My mom and her husband, Paul, joined us, as did Nichola's parents, Sheila and Laurie. There was a good deal of trepidation, excitement, and apprehension since this next leg would be our first test as a family—crossing the English Channel to Camaret in France—Nichola's first time sailing out of sight of land.

We were joined aboard by Ian, godfather to all our three children. Ian is as tough as they come, a brilliant sailor and highly resourceful when it comes to fixing things. I'd sailed with him on the BT Global Challenge and was delighted he was able to create the time at short notice to join us as we sailed south across the Bay of Biscay. My brother Max was also aboard.

We slipped lines from Plymouth in perfect conditions, headed out past Drake's Island and the breakwater. The sea was teeming with mackerel. Feathers over the side and within a few minutes we had ten on board to keep a super-excited Columbus happy. Bluebell took a little longer to settle in to all the changes and was missing her sister, Willow, and her school friends. She spent a lot of time below in her cabin.

I was frustrated to still be under doctor's orders with restricted lifting and pulling—I really wanted to get on and do things.

The weather gods blessed us with perfect sailing conditions as we set out across the Channel. By night we were in the middle of the shipping lanes, dodging cargo ships and fishing vessels. We had to be alert. The breeze died, forcing us to start the engine—then the engine decided to cut out. It started again but only ran at low revs. We sailed around Ushant ("Ouessant" in French, an island off the southwest end of the English Channel marking the northwest end of France, notorious for its strong tides) and contacted our Oyster Yacht engineers in the UK for advice. We worked through our diagnostics: raw-water inlet, water separator unit, engine coolant, engine oil, and fuel filters. No use, the diesel still cut out at high revs. We were confident we could reach our first landfall just south of Brest under sail with the engine at low revs. Once we checked that the tides were favorable for our approach we headed east into Camaret.

First Overseas Landfall

It was a huge accomplishment to arrive in Camaret—we were all exhilarated to have made our first overseas landfall in *Aretha*. I was delighted with how well *Aretha* had sailed and how Nichola, Bluebell, and Columbus had taken to life at sea. After clearing in with local customs and immigration at the port captain's office, we headed straight out for supper—fresh seafood and ice cream to celebrate.

We stayed for a few days, checking the online weather forecasts twice a day waiting for a decent weather window to get across the Bay of Biscay. Biscay has a fearsome reputation for high winds and dangerous seas and demands absolute respect. It is one of the three most dangerous sea passages that we would experience in our whole circumnavigation. (The other two were off the northern coast of Colombia and along the east coast of South Africa.) We were anxious to get across safely in relatively calm conditions. We had pushed ourselves to leave the UK in August to avoid Biscay's worst. We were under other time pressures as well since Ian had to get back home. Finally the weather charts showed a small window and we knew that it was the right time to take sail across Biscay.

Those first few days in the Bay of Biscay were wet, cold, and windy. We had 25–30 knots of wind from the southwest giving us headwinds and big seas breaking over *Aretha*. The thoughts were unspoken: what on earth have we signed up for? House rented out, car sold, no time for second thoughts. Columbus was sick for a day but showed amazing resilience, bouncing back straight away. Bluebell is made of stern stuff and got her sea legs pretty quickly.

As the gray weather of North Biscay softened and turned to calmer seas, sunny skies, and gentle breezes, our spirits rose. The wind veered and was now from the north, giving us easy downwind sailing and flat decks with the mainsail on one side and the genoa poled out on the other.

Dolphins swam playfully in *Aretha's* bow wake—a first for the children and a great distraction. In South Biscay we fished for the first time since Plymouth. It was only 30 minutes before the reel started screaming and the rod bent over. We slowed down by furling the genoa and within ten minutes we had landed a 10-pound bluefin tuna. In next to no time Max had the catch filleted and fresh tuna steaks prepped.

Our crossing took four days. We stopped briefly in La Coruña on the northern coast of Spain to allow Ian to catch a flight home. We then continued our journey south to the beautiful and historic town of Baiona, close to the border of Spain and Portugal on the Atlantic coast. There we found an engineer who quickly diagnosed our engine problem as dirty diesel. The quick fix was blowing down the fuel pipe with a compressor to clear the blockage. The complete fix would be to drain and clean the diesel tank, filtering the fuel, and then refilling with clean fuel. Not the nicest of jobs, but it would have to be done.

The children loved the beach at Baiona, but my sister's upcoming wedding meant we were pressed for time and had to get to Povoa de Varzim, Portugal, still a few days' sail away. We left Baiona under pink skies.

In spite of minor leaks and things to be fixed, *Aretha* sailed beautifully both upwind and downwind; she felt solid as a rock. One of the things I loved offshore was night sailing. It was stunning to look at the sky with the stars and moon, glancing astern to see the water alive with phosphorescence streaming in the torpedo-like wakes that the dolphins left behind. The shoals of fish darting like flocks of birds in the bow wave were also aglow. As we sailed down the Portuguese coast Columbus and I spent half an hour just spotting fish from the bow and gazing at the lights of the cargo ships and fishing boats.

We left *Aretha* moored in a marina in Povoa de Varzim and caught flights back to the UK to wrap up our life there, pick up Willow, and then fly to France for my sister Jess's wedding.

I reflected on what Columbus and Bluebell had absorbed so far. They'd been reading the weather, studying the barometer, identifying birds and fish, exploring new towns and learning the history of the places we visited: Baiona, where Christopher Columbus returned from the New World in 1493; and La Coruña, home of the Hercules lighthouse, the oldest in the world. They'd been speaking with the locals, figuring how much things cost, observing engine checks, and learning about changing water filters for the watermaker (our device for turning sea water into fresh water). They both seemed happy and engaged by life at sea.

I was grateful to have Ian and Max on board for our Bay of Biscay crossing. Ian's engineering skills were tested early, working on the engine—he also pulled the short straw when he dismantled the forward head to clear a blockage. Max was a wizard in the galley, whipping up roast meals, fresh bread, and delicately cooked tuna. Max sailed with us only as far as Povoa de Varzim, but would join us later on in our voyage.

Airborne Back to the UK

During our two weeks back in the UK we received our final rabies and hepatitis injections, were reunited with Willow, and finished packing. I was still relatively restricted in movement. What I could do was spend time with the children. We'd come to appreciate the need for each of them to have one-on-one time with us. A great start—and an outing for just Columbus and me—was a trip to the National Maritime Museum in Greenwich, London.

There we discovered the seafarers of the past, the spice routes, and other stories of the Atlantic. We found a huge map of the world on the floor and walked the route we would take around the world. We learned of Christopher Columbus's voyages across the Atlantic starting in 1492 and the lands he discovered. We learned of John Harrison and the discovery of longitude. Columbus showed me how he loved to arrange and collect things—the Maritime Museum had a passport that you got stamped in different exhibitions. I began learning what engaged him. Someone once asked why we persist in teaching children how we want to teach instead of how they want to learn. Our children each had their own ways of learning—Nichola and I knew that for them to learn the most, our teaching had to suit them.

We wrapped up our UK life, said our goodbyes to friends and family, and headed to the airport. After a delayed flight, we arrived in France with three tired children, navigating across the countryside with Google Maps. We were just in time to witness Jess marrying Jules in a picture-perfect vineyard on a balmy hot sunny day with a cloudless sky, celebrating with oysters, pâté, and local wine—all of which helped us forget the headache we had getting there.

Getting back to *Aretha* in Portugal was an epic journey of rental cars, planes, and taxis. We were booked on a flight from Bordeaux to Lisbon: roadworks outside Bordeaux meant that we were delayed, still trying to find a filling station to refuel the rental car 35 minutes before the gate for our flight closed. The gods (and the airline check-in staff) smiled on us. Phew. We made that flight. At Lisbon, who'd have thought that every mid-size rental car would be booked? What doesn't kill you makes you stronger. Flights up the coast were prohibitively expensive; trains and coaches impossible to navigate with no trolleys and 12 bags. We found a taxi, negotiated a half reasonable rate and Paulo, our new best friend, set off fueled by strong coffee on the 185-mile road trip from Lisbon to Povoa de Varzim.

We arrived past midnight and were relieved to find *Aretha* in good shape. We loaded bags and children aboard and crashed. My mantra— life is a swashbuckling audacious daring adventure—felt truer than ever. Our team was awesome, the children flexible, resilient, and as adaptable as ever to changing circumstances. Nichola was heroic with her calmness and organization.

All Aboard, Finally

Autumnal storms were tearing down the Portuguese coast. *Aretha* was docked close to the harbor mouth, close enough to watch the wind whip up huge seas outside the breakwater. Yachts strained at their docking lines. We stayed on *Aretha* to monitor the situation while the wind howled, waves buffeting us through driving rain.

We remained stormbound in Povoa de Varzim for two weeks. The five of us were on *Aretha* for the first time with plenty of work to do to get her in shape. Holding anchor watch with the engine on tick over while tied to a dock that was threatening to break up during the worst of the storm, I discovered a leak. The engine compartment had over 5 gallons of water inside. It was a relief to finally figure out what the problem was—a leaking pipe on the coolant system. An internet search in the middle of the night led us to the solution and the fixes we needed to make to the cooling pipes.

For the growing list of boat jobs we discovered Isak from Nautical Vaga, a local engineer who could carry out many of the fixes we needed: cleaning our diesel tanks, fixing the head, and spray cleaning the hull— all at a reasonable price compared to the UK. Cleaning the dirty diesel tanks was the worst job. The fuel tank had to be drained and the empty tank then cleaned thoroughly by hand. The diesel was hand filtered and then poured back into the diesel tanks. We would later discover that this was not a good idea, as even though the diesel was filtered it would still contain the microbes that cause dirty diesel. The head hoses were blocked solid and needed to be removed and replaced. The bow had been damaged where the dock had moved while we were away, damaging the gelcoat, and had to be repaired.

For a week while *Aretha* was out of the water we were basically living in a car park: our home was 12 feet up in the air, accessed by a ladder. But we met the friendliest people in the local restaurants, supermarkets, ice cream stores, and fishing tackle shops. Columbus obsessed about the gray mullet in the harbor and within 24 hours caught six. Eating marina mullet isn't recommended, so five of them got to live another day, with the sixth becoming bait for the crab net.

While there we also reconnected with Andy who we'd met on the Ship's Doctor's course. I remembered when I walked into the small classroom on the first day of the training course and scanned the room. Most people looked fairly regular, apart from one. Sitting in the far back corner was a guy who stood out with his massive dreadlocks, boat shackles for earrings, and heavily tattooed arms. Over the coming months we'd get to know Andy and his fiancé, Emma, extremely well. Their yacht *Pentagram* was a beautiful Oyster that they had lovingly restored over the previous five years. They would sail the same trade-wind routes as us halfway around the world, becoming lifelong friends. We'd share countless experiences—both highs and lows in far-flung countries. Andy also happened to be a first-rate engineer and we learned much from him with his calm and thoughtful approach. Seeing him in Povoa de Varzim, I simply remembered him as the guy with the dreadlocks who tested out the staple gun on his face...

Allowing ourselves a day off boat duties, we enjoyed a day trip into Porto, a beautiful, vibrant city, joining in a local festival with street artists and theater. The children's schoolwork for the day was finding statues of historic figures; their homework was to find out who each one was and write it up. The children were the happiest we'd seen for months, beginning to settle into their new lives. All was well with the world. The wind at the dock settled down to a steady 20 knots, and warmer waters lay ahead. Life was throwing all manner of things at us but I wouldn't have changed it for the world.

Departure from Povoa, Portugal

Diesel tanks emptied and cleaned by hand. Check.
Head hoses replaced and in pristine condition. Check.
Satellite telephone working. Check.
Bow repaired. Check.
Hull antifouled. Check.
Anchor windlass fixed. Check.
Engine compartment water drained and fixed. Check.
Two adults and three children fractious and landlocked, ready to get going. Check.

Hooray. Three days of stopover that turned into two weeks had passed—we were finally on the move again. I was sitting on deck listening to the best of 80s music. The sea was flat calm with the very occasional puff of wind to ruffle the glassy surface. The sun was warming the decks and spirits were high. Columbus was hand steering *Aretha* to a compass course of 185 degrees at 7 knots with all the confidence of an experienced sailor, easily maneuvering around the fishing buoys that lined that part of the coast. We had 30 miles south to go to reach Figueira da Foz.

Willow had been crawling around the cockpit getting used to her lifejacket. We had a few tears to keep her from climbing outside the cockpit but it was no more than we'd get on land with a two-year-old. She seemed to settle easily and was happy playing down below.

Columbus called out to tell me we had 29 miles to go now. He deftly flicked through the settings to read out the AIS information, letting me know what the boats around us were doing. Electronic navigation was child's play to my seven-year-old. Several hours earlier we'd had a pod of 50 or 60 dolphins surrounding us. Bluebell was beside herself with excitement, holding on to the bow as they played all around her.

Yes, life was definitely an audacious swashbuckling daring adventure.

Ports of Interest—Figueira da Foz, Portugal

Figueira da Foz is a vibrant city of 50,000 inhabitants on the Portuguese coast. With broad sandy beaches and Atlantic surf rolling on to the shore, it's a popular tourist destination. According to legend the city's name is due to a fig tree that stood at the quay of Salmanha, where the fishermen tied their boats. It's a welcoming place and contains a fabulous market stacked with fresh fish like red gurnard, sardines, and tuna, and newly harvested fruit and vegetables like peppers, ripe red tomatoes, and glistening apples and oranges.

Chapter 9

To the Canary Islands
Figueira da Foz, Portugal, to Las Palmas,
Canary Islands
(October 2014 to November 2014)

The best thing about our sailing adventure was spending time with Nichola and the children 24 hours a day, 7 days a week. The hardest thing was exactly the same.

In our previous life in London, Nichola and I would see each other for half an hour a day. I might see the children for half an hour, too, if I was lucky, just in time for bedtime stories. By the weekend I'd generally be pretty spent from a demanding week, yet would ferry the children to tennis or rugby, perhaps play with them a bit, as well as catch up with Nichola and friends; often a good amount of work crept in as well.

We were now at the other end of the spectrum. We all needed to get used to living in the same tiny space. It's hard enough sailing shorthanded (just Nichola and me to handle the boat)—now add in three lively children and we had our hands full. Meanwhile I was also acutely aware that the lives of all five aboard were in my hands. The constant proximity was my hardest adjustment: the noise, both the excited happy sounds as well as the squabbling, and in between, our urging them to do their schoolwork while simultaneously keeping the boat safe. It was also the best thing about the whole adventure—being able to play with them, teaching them what we believed was important in life, getting to know who they were as people, and allowing them to get to know us. Still, in those early weeks I struggled with the lack of peace and quiet. It was why I relished night sailing—all was quiet and I had my own time to write, read, and ponder my thoughts.

In these early days we were all adjusting. Bluebell was understandably missing her friends and was taking a while to acclimatize—her way of dealing with this was to throw a tantrum, a frequent occurrence. In contrast, Columbus charged to his cabin in a sulk, refusing to engage or cooperate when asked to do anything. Clearly we had work to do to ensure the children were on the journey with us emotionally.

School on Board

Homeschooling was a totally new experience for Nichola and me. With no formal teacher training, we were figuring out how to maintain and accelerate the education of a nine-year-old, a seven-year-old, and a two-year-old. We had a lot to learn. We had almost universal acknowledgment that we were doing a great thing for our children by spending so much time with them, exposing them to the wide world— detailing and quantifying what they were learning was much harder.

The pre-prepared homeschooling courses we'd investigated didn't hit the mark with us. Some were by email—hard for us at sea and in far-flung lands. The structures didn't appeal to us either, nor did they offer the flexibility we needed. There were only so many hours in the day and we had to find time for managing and running *Aretha*, for daily living (cooking, cleaning, etc.), for each other, for friends, and exploring. We quickly discovered that one thing took precedence over all other things: *Aretha*. When something needed fixing, it usually needed fixing there and then. Schooling was just one element of life that had to fit in.

So at this point our schooling challenge was motivating the children to do their schoolwork and making time for schooling. Our approach was the same we'd used with other things we'd taken on—do our research and be practical and flexible as we went along. The context for learning was challenging: the children were missing playing with other children and there was a lack of routine and structure aboard. We'd had little time for schooling in a traditional sense in the first few months, so homework started fitfully, and yet the children were absorbing all that we were doing. We took care to expose them to as much learning as we could, explaining and encouraging while in the moment.

One of the things I'd had in mind from the start was that we'd be visiting markets. We'd give the children a bit of local currency and explain the concept of exchange rates, letting them figure out the math. What did they want to buy, how much money did they have, how much change would they get? Simple and practical mathematics—just living in the real world. We encouraged the children to do this at every opportunity as well as mentally converting the prices back into the sterling equivalent so they could appreciate by UK standards how cheap or expensive things were in different countries.

We had also recently launched our blog, www.familysailing.co.uk, and encouraged the children to contribute. Columbus did not want to write. Neither threats nor bribes had any effect. When researching the trip we had spent many hours talking about the best way to educate all three children and the working theory was to follow their passions. We'd find what they were most interested in and let that lead as far as it could, propelled by their own natural enthusiasms and energies. Columbus's passion was fishing. I'd fished all my life in South Devon—netting, potting, line fishing, spear fishing, just about any way you can imagine. My dad had been a keen fisherman, too. Now Columbus had the bug. At every opportunity he was reading fishing books, reciting facts about fish, baits, lures, and what he could catch in different oceans. He would sit down with a fishing book and consume its contents, not coming up for air at all while in the middle of something he found fascinating. Not only that, he was keen to share the knowledge. Fishing became Columbus's educational context.

As a leaving gift, my mom had given Columbus a tape measure plus a pair of weighing scales. He measured each catch, then weighed it, and in this way was practicing his weights, measures, and numeracy. With some encouragement he also started to write in his journal about the fish he was catching: mackerel as we left Plymouth, tuna in the Bay of Biscay, garfish off the Spanish coast, mullet caught from the docks in Povoa de Varzim. We also frequented fish markets when ashore, often finding new species. As soon as we returned aboard Columbus would consult his books to find out what species they were.

Bluebell had always been an avid fiction reader, needing little encouragement to sit down and read. This passion led us to get her engaged in mini research projects. In Sines on the Portuguese Atlantic coast, after visiting the castle where Portuguese explorer Vasco da Gama was born, we encouraged Bluebell to write a mini project about it, including her own illustrations for posting on our blog (see plate section, image 7). Lots of people commented on her projects—including her previous teachers and family. My mom further encouraged all the kids by sending daily email quizzes, as well as asking them to make up silly stories using a range of new and different words.

Making Friends at Sea—Nazares, Portugal

When we talked about the idea of sailing around the world when we were still in our London home, we'd promised the children that they'd meet lots of other boat kids and they'd have loads of other friends to play with. During the seven weeks since we left Southampton—two weeks sailing, two weeks in the UK, two weeks in port, and a week sailing the Portuguese coast, we'd met no other children and I'm certain ours were beginning to doubt us. As we worked our way down the Portuguese coast we put into the charming coastal town of Nazares, tying up on the end of the dock. The

A Life Lesson

In addition to schooling, we contended with *Aretha*'s maintenance, as well as rough seas, seasickness, and a sailing schedule. This was the first of what we considered to be the really important life lessons for each of us: life will throw all manner of things at you—the only thing that you can control is what meaning you attach to those things and how you respond or react to them. Later on, after our adventure, it was remarkable to see how our children responded to challenging situations—calmly, in control, then figuring things out. I didn't realize it at the start, but this would become a vital part of the children's education. We would have many more chances to learn this while sailing *Aretha* around the world.

marina manager came down to tell us that a boat was coming to raft alongside us for the night. Half an hour later a sailboat arrived, crewed by a couple and their two kids with brilliant shocks of blond hair and virtually identical in age to Bluebell and Columbus.

Within minutes Bluebell and Columbus were on board the Dutch yacht, *Pacific*, playing with Hein and Cato, climbing the boat's rigging. They soon announced a sleepover had been arranged and for the next ten days the four were as thick as thieves as both boats worked down the Portuguese coast to Cascais. The children were inseparable and were starting to get the idea of what "boat kids" were all about. It was lovely to see and it took pressure off us to entertain the children; we also got to know their Dutch parents, Eelco and Willemijn.

The friendships we formed at sea were intense. We shared multiple experiences while spending a huge amount of time together—exploring ashore, sharing meals, swapping stories late into the evening. The common bond of the sea—with your life so often in your hands—united us in a way we just didn't experience on land. I remember describing the friendships I'd formed while sailing the BT Global Challenge to an army captain who had just returned from Iraq. He likened shipboard friendships to the military bonds formed amid high degrees of risk where the help you get from those around makes a critical difference.

These intense friendships included joy and connection, as well as the sadness of saying goodbye when departing for the next port. Our children experienced this as keenly as anyone—there were several days of quiet aboard *Aretha* after we waved goodbye to *Pacific* in Cascais—all of us missing our friends.

Blogging Home—South from Cascais

One of the things I intended to do while sailing around the world was communicate as much as possible through our blog, sharing our exploits and location. This was also the best way to relieve concerns of family and friends—they'd get an insight into our lives, what we were coping with, what we were experiencing, and proof we hadn't dropped off the edge of the world. It was always lovely to hear back from people while at sea. Getting a message—reading and savoring a loved one's words—in the peace and quiet of the ocean was extremely meaningful. Every morning over breakfast, I'd read aloud the latest messages—it was one of the few times in the day when the children would actually listen.

We received lots of feedback and comments on Facebook and our blogs—it was encouraging to hear how we were affecting other people's lives.

Bluebell wrote on our blog:

"Hi it's me Bluebell, and we are in Sines in the South of Portugal now. We have had an amazing time. We have met 2 other children called Cato and Hein. They are Dutch, but we can still understand them. We loved playing with them but we could only play with them in the afternoon because we were doing schoolwork in the morning."

The sailing on the south coast of Portugal was good, with full main and full genoa, winds gusting 30 knots. We even started some gentle racing with our friends on *Pentagram*, who had sailed down with us, as we surfed down the Atlantic rollers at 10.5 knots. Wonderful stuff.

From Nazares to Peniche, Willow had a touch of seasickness. The mistake we made was Nichola going down to clean up. I peered down the companionway to see both mother and daughter vomiting into the blue basin.

Across to the Canaries—Seasickness Takes Hold

The 450 miles or so from Lagos on the southern cape of Portugal to Porto Santo by Madeira was a fast, wet, bouncy sail. Nichola's queasiness didn't abate and for the next two days she continued to feel its effects. This woman is tough but three days of seasickness is hard going. I consider myself extremely fortunate to have never experienced *mal de mer*. Nichola tells me that if I imagine my worst ever illness and multiply it by 10 then I'm still not close.

She tried just about every remedy available: patches, pills, sprays. Eventually we learned that the best thing for Nichola was to be up on deck until she started to feel queasy. At that point, she'd pop down the strongest tablets available (three times normal strength) to knock her out, sleep for 12 hours and fingers crossed she'd be up and running after that. It was best to just sleep, stay hydrated, and have a handful of dry crackers to nibble on. Once we made landfall, with the restorative effects of a good meal and walking around, she bounced back quickly.

With Nichola out of action I singlehanded the boat for three days. I was short on sleep and the boat was a mess. Luckily, by now I was able to fully function on board again. Nichola was still able to take a watch and keep a lookout with me resting in the saloon, close by and kitted up should sails need adjusting and so on. It was wearing to be switched on 24 hours a day, though I figured it was no different from what singlehanders like Ellen McArthur experienced.

Our sailing was fast with 15–20 knots of breeze shifting from the beam to aft of the boat and then forward so the sails needed trimming. The sea was building and we were surging along on waves at a good 9–10 knots. If we were racing it would be ideal to have the boat fully powered up with full canvas. But I had to keep reminding myself we weren't racing. We needed to get there safe and happy.

Aretha was soon doing a good impression of a submarine, punching through every sixth wave or so. At least it was cleaning the deck of all the vomit! We discovered a few leaks and some of the cupboards decided to unlock themselves, sending schoolbooks and bowls crashing. This now was life as normal apart from the fact that we were 300 sea miles from our destination and our home was bouncing around. Nichola was keen to make land so we kept up the pace. The children were mixing it up between happy and grizzly. That's something Ellen McArthur didn't have to deal with.

The biggest help with the children were the animal visitors: a flying fish on the deck early one morning, a squid on the deck the following morning, and our feathered friends. Three different small birds joined us on deck and we gave them bread and water. One decided to join us below deck, flying through the boat from the saloon to the forepeak to the aft cabin before I opened the hatch to let him fly back and sit on deck. Birds were welcome visitors—we were happy to let them hitch a lift with us.

 Captain's Log, 35°44'N 010°02'W, October 19, 2014

It's 11.30pm. The only sounds are the sea against the hull as *Aretha* carves through the waves and glides along effortlessly. I'm in shorts and a light jacket and it's pleasantly warm. I'm lying across the cockpit on deck cushions. The sky above me is blanketed with stars. It's just beautiful. I roll over and look at the sea. Phosphorescence lights up our wake.

We're some 80 miles now off the Portuguese coast heading out into the Atlantic. The wind is perfectly positioned on our beam—a steady 12–13 knots which, with a full main and full genoa, we're converting into 7 knots speed over the ground as we point directly toward Porto Santo on the Madeira archipelago, some 360 miles away. At this speed, that's less than 2 days.

Nichola and the children are fast asleep and I think this is the first opportunity I've had for a while to be by myself with my own thoughts.

We've spent the last week in Lagos in southern Portugal, waiting to get a good weather window for fast sailing. It's a proper ex-pat type community complete with Irish bar and English accents. It confirms we enjoy the small local fishing villages as stopovers and getting off the beaten track. That said, they have good facilities—excellent supermarkets, a great museum full of history of the Portuguese explorers, and some lovely beaches.

It's been a week of getting a routine going—the children doing schoolwork in the morning while Nichola and I juggle catching up on our respective businesses, dialing in for management meetings. Nichola found out she has been shortlisted for an award for her business. Outside that, it's normal life stuff—laundry, keeping the home clean and tidy, and boat maintenance. Moving seacocks, adjusting blocks plus sanding back the cockpit table. Our days seem to fill up just as fast as ever and it's nice to be back to sea again, and away from internet and phone calls. The constant information flow is definitely an addiction and the forced abstinence at sea is good.

This is the longest passage we have done with the five of us on board. In fact, it's the first time overnight with just us so we are sailing close to our friends on *Pentagram*—safety in numbers. Nichola and I divide the night into four watches of three hours or so. Nichola does the first from 8pm to 11pm. I set my alarm for 10.45 and with tea in hand take over at 10.55. Nichola tells me she's been sick on the side deck and has been washing it away with bottles of water.

Columbus spent much of yesterday on deck. He feels queasy for the first day out but knows that fresh air is the best thing for him. Our new fishing lure out of the stern is always the perfect distraction and I'm called on regularly to set the drag and check the lure. He spotted a pod of dolphins as we were leaving Portugal, and not long after we saw our first shark. The fin cutting through the water some 10–15 feet away was impressive and it's great to see different wildlife.

Bluebell prefers the sanctum of the saloon (I think she prefers not to wear a lifejacket and shoes—which under our boat rules means you're not allowed on deck). She is great at keeping Willow entertained and is the self-appointed administrator of snacks from the snack cupboard.

Willow feels at home straight away and is happy drawing and playing with Lego. She is sick once and smiles seconds later. The big thing she keeps asking for is dolphins. Now she's seen some, she wants more.

Yes. It's good to be sailing offshore, living a simpler boat life to spend time together.

I'm back to watching to make sure we dodge the shipping—a container ship bound for Houston passed us a little while back and now that we are farther offshore the intensity of shipping leaving and arriving in the Med is reducing.

Time for more stargazing too.

Team *Aretha*, Out.

Late in the evening of the third and final night of the passage we ran out of propane cooking gas for our galley stove. Although we carried three spare propane bottles, I didn't fancy changing tanks on a rolling deck at night so supper was boil-in-the-bag food heated by warm tap water. Columbus was particularly happy—he loved the lamb stew, saying "the gravy tastes just like Nanny's." The rest of the crew were a little less enthusiastic.

First Offshore Landfall

By the morning of the third day since leaving Lagos, Portugal, we made our first offshore landfall. Porto Santo, the northernmost volcanic island of the Madeira archipelago, rose up in jagged, dark peaks. After a long time at sea, the sight of land rising up out of the ocean is incredible. I never got bored of this.

Willow and I checked in with the local police/customs (the GNR, or Guarda Nacional Republicana), and then met

Staying Connected

Having decided to sail in convoy, we were with *Pentagram* at the first sunset but by morning we'd lost them and we sailed alone. We tried calling them on the VHF (Very High Frequency) radio, but were out of range. (The range of our VHF was roughly 10–15 miles.) We decided later on we needed to invest in an SSB (single sideband) radio, which would eventually be installed when we were in Panama. Regular SSB radio chats are a great way of staying connected and sharing weather and stories.

Entertaining the Troops

When we bought *Aretha* we added a large TV with a DVD player plus a hard drive loaded with films and TV programs. It was ideal when Nichola and I needed time to think things through—while coming in and out of port, or if we needed time to talk to figure stuff out—we'd start a film and let it work its magic. Initially we used the DVD player a lot, perhaps more than

Nelson at the marina office, who gave us our local map with directions to shops and the beach. We spent the next six hours washing, cleaning, and airing the boat. It's amazing how just three days at sea turns a boat into a damp environment. Nichola bounced back quickly from her seasickness and the effect of a sparkly boat was a tonic.

We scanned the horizon all day for *Pentagram*. After eight hours she berthed alongside us. They'd been slowed by a thunder and lightning storm that packed 38 knots of breeze.

Madeira is a popular holiday destination and after we moored in a marina on the east of the main island, we spent three days exploring by

we'd have done at home. Bluebell watched the film *Pitch Perfect* over and over again. Columbus was happier watching David Attenborough documentaries.

On one passage I downloaded an eclectic collection of Desert Island discs. Both older children listened to some of these with me. Bluebell was taken with the books of English comedian David Walliams (author of *Gangsta Granny* and *Billionaire Boy* among many others), while Columbus loved the interviews with the adventurer Bear Grylls, singlehanded yachtswoman Dame Ellen McArthur, and naturalist David Attenborough.

rental car and taking in the stunning scenery. We discovered some adrenaline-fueled excitement as we careered down the famous hills in wooden sledges steered by expert locals, slowing down the sledges with shoes soled with the rubber from car tires. Leaving Madeira, a touristy port popular with cruise liners, we had a slow sail south to La Palma—the westernmost Canary Island (not to be confused with the city of Las Palmas on the island of Gran Canaria). With very light winds from astern and after a few hours of only making a couple of knots of boat speed, we motorsailed the last stretch. There was great excitement as always at making landfall, the kids shouting "Land Ho" as we approached, finding the new courtesy flag to fly from the mast for the new country we were entering (the Canary Islands are part of Spain).

Ports of Interest—The Portuguese Island of Porto Santo

Porto Santo was amazing. I'd never heard of it before and would never have come if we had not been sailing around the world. We'd intended to stay for a day or two, and ended up staying four. Christopher Columbus had once lived there—we visited his house, now a museum. It was strange to stand where he would have stood, all of us getting ready to follow his route across the Atlantic. The town—really more of a village—was relaxed and low key, clean and safe. A roadside kiosk sold beer. Our kids played on the Caribbean-style beaches, swimming and surfing. Wi-Fi was pretty much everywhere and password-free—a true sailor's port. The harbor wall, 20 minutes' walk from the town, was adorned with paintings made by different yachts, with the date, the boat name, the crew, and a picture. We didn't add one on this visit and made a mental note to come prepared for this next time. The welcoming marina had a maximum of 10 boats at a time, boats coming and going each day, everyone with a smile and a story to share.

One day we hired a quad bike (a four-wheeler motorized bike) and raced up to the mountain peaks and along the long sandy beaches. Porto Santo is only 4½ by 2½ miles yet the mountains were high rising, 1,640 feet above sea level—breathtaking as we rose above the clouds. Bluebell and I took turns shouting our names and listening for the echoes from the surrounding mountains. This was our favorite port so far: relaxed, understated, beautiful, friendly, and calm. Our last evening was magical. Andy and Emma from *Pentagram* looked after the children on *Aretha* while Nichola and I found a restaurant on the beach. We were the only diners but the place had brilliant ambiance and top-class food. The waves crashed next to us as we sat in the warm night air in shorts and shirts. The following day we'd sail to Madeira, then 250 miles south to the Canaries. Life truly is an adventure and we felt we were living every moment. So far our trip was everything we expected and more.

 Captain's Log, 30°27'N 017°46'W, October 28, 2014

Aretha is shuddering and isn't liking the sailing. It's a grating time. The wind is light at 7 knots and we are motorsailing dead downwind. Clank clank clank from the mainsail every 15 seconds. To my port side are the lights from three other yachts. All this ocean and it's amazing we have converged and sail within a mile of each other. We're 30 hours out from Madeira and 80 miles from Santa Cruz on the island of La Palma.

When I was younger, I always used to wonder how rough the sea would be several hundred miles from the coast. I can tell you today it's pretty flat calm—a gentle, almost imperceptible roll is all. Calm enough I can sit in the cockpit and type undisturbed by the movement.

From La Palma we will day sail to La Gomera, Tenerife, and Gran Canaria where we'll be joined by friends Paul and Jani for the ARC to St. Lucia. For the past six weeks it's just been the five of us, and being at sea now feels natural and home. The children are calm and happy. But we're ready for some fresh company.

We're already planning ahead to the Pacific, having booked our transit through the Panama Canal for February 3, 2015, with a week's sail after that to the Galapagos and then probably three weeks at sea to the Marquesas Islands.

For now, it's all about the buildup to the Atlantic crossing. Some 210 boats are converging in Gran Canaria to sail the Atlantic at the same time.

Checking the weather files—a light 5 to 10 knots NNE for the next 12 hours—is a stark reminder of how far we've come.

My eyes drift to the African coast: Morocco, Western Sahara, Mauritania, Senegal. Sailing down the Solent to Weymouth feels a lifetime ago.

The wind has settled. The clanking has stopped. I can see the lighthouse flashing up ahead on La Palma.

Chapter 10

Crossing the Atlantic

La Palma, Canary Islands, to St. Lucia, Caribbean
(November 2014 to December 2014)

Adapting to Life on Board

We were now starting to settle into sea life as a team and becoming more fluent with daily boat activities. When we were leaving Southampton just over two months ago, Nichola had been reluctant to go 8 inches above the deck up the mast. Now, less than two months in, she was shimmying up the first two mast steps to flake the mainsail with all the confidence and dexterity of an experienced sailor. The children donned their lifejackets and clipped on without being asked, Bluebell tying perfect bowlines, Columbus rigging mooring lines and fenders, operating the winches. Willow moved around the boat with ease and perfect balance—utterly at home on the boat and, when we were sailing, jumping up and down shouting, "Sail faster, sail faster!"

Island Hopping—La Palma to Las Palmas

As we arrived in the Canary Islands the number of sailboats we met increased, in particular those heading across the Atlantic to the Caribbean. Sailors are a distinct community of extremely friendly and helpful people. Conversations revolved around boats, rigging, downwind sail plans, destinations and routes, power management at sea, fishing, and so on. We all had a vested interest in sharing plans—once you're out there, there are no marine stores or engineers to fix things for you, although on our Atlantic crossing we were usually no more than a few hours away from a ship or another yacht, even though we rarely saw other boats.

La Palma was the first marina we'd been to with a McDonald's; I think Columbus was in disbelief for days that Nichola turned down the fresh dorado that we had caught that morning for a Big Mac!

We stayed in La Palma for a couple of days before heading toward La Gomera and Tenerife. It was here we said goodbye temporarily to *Pentagram*, knowing that we'd meet up with them again around Panama as we prepared to cross the Pacific Ocean.

We were now heading east to join the start of the ARC Rally in Las Palmas, Gran Canaria, and decided to island hop our way through the Canary Islands. We had a super-fast sail to La Gomera, arriving just after dark. Here the breeze often cranks up by 10–15 knots in a matter of seconds as the trade winds funnel down through the islands. We surfed downwind in 25–30 knots—rock'n'roll sailing. When it's been dark and breezy, it's always a relief to make landfall and tie up safe and sound in a harbor. As we nosed our way into San Sebastian, the dock attendant signaled us in with a flashlight. We safely navigated our way into the smallest space possible right next to the slipway with zero margin for error.

Our slip neighbors were a Danish family—Haften, his wife, and their four children. It was Halloween and within minutes our children were on the dock with theirs, trick or treating. We'd decorated the boat with Halloween stickers and were ready with candy. It didn't take long for the crews to meet up—15 children walking the docks, parents in tow, visiting all the boats in the marina. That evening we spent time with Haften, exchanging plans. They were heading through the Pacific after the Caribbean crossing too. It was fascinating to meet so many families from other countries—Danish, Dutch, French, Swedish, Norwegian—doing what we were doing.

We continued island hopping from La Gomera to Tenerife and then to Las Palmas on Gran Canaria for the start of our ARC Atlantic crossing. Boats were now starting to congregate in Las Palmas for the November

12 arrival deadline. We went from being in the company of a handful of boats to being surrounded by hundreds—including our friends Paul and Caroline on *Juno* who we'd been sharing plans with for three years. Between 200 and 250 boats were to sail the Atlantic on the rally, making landfall 2–3 weeks later at St. Lucia in the Caribbean.

We had arrived several weeks in advance to make certain we had time to prepare for our first ocean crossing as a family. We felt ahead of the game. *Aretha* had been cleaned from top to bottom, we'd passed our safety checks, we'd had a professional rigger give the boat a thorough check, and the Oyster Yacht maintenance team also came aboard for a final run through of *Aretha* (there were 11 other Oyster Yachts in that year's ARC).

We were put onto S dock—the family dock—surrounded by other boats with children. This was pure magic for the children—they had friends from all over the world right next door. Opposite *Aretha* was *Cygnus Pena* from Denmark and their girls, Camille and Malou. Farther down was *Matilda* from England with Emily and William; on board *Khujada* 2, a French/English boat, were Daisy, James, and Hugo; and Alex and Innes were on board *Take Off* from Sweden. The children started to appreciate different languages and cultures as they played on each other's boats, went fishing off the docks together, and built sandcastles on nearby beaches.

This proximity allowed us to observe other boats' approach to schooling. On one the children enjoyed the familiarity of wearing school uniforms and they followed a school timetable for lessons. On another they had to submit work for marking and assessment back home in France. Nichola and I were asking ourselves if we were doing the right thing for our children by not having a formal structure. The fact was we simply didn't have the time or energy to do more than we were doing. We put our faith in our approach and we knew that a strict system wouldn't work for us. I don't believe it was easy to maintain on other family boats and in the end we were the only family boat to continue on to the Pacific that year. We eventually eased into the view that life at sea was simply different from life on land and became happy with our more relaxed approach to education.

We were all in good spirits and enjoying the company of the other sailboats, looking forward to family and friends joining us as the regatta atmosphere built. We found out that Willow was the youngest person on the ARC and our children would carry the British flag for the opening ceremony.

Helping Hands

For our first long ocean crossing we had decided that we wanted extra hands aboard. We chose two friends I had sailed with extensively and who we knew would easily fit in with family life on *Aretha*.

Paul Covell sailed with me on the BT Global Challenge in 2000. Back then he was the oldest member of the crew at 61. Since 2001 he and I had sailed virtually every year with

A Learning Opportunity

Chris Tibbs, one of the world's leading offshore meteorologists, ran the ARC weather briefings. I had gotten to know Chris when attending his weather course in the UK. Following our schooling approach of using topics that most interested the children, I invited Columbus to join me for these weather briefings in Las Palmas. We were fortunate to get instruction from Chris on celestial navigation—measuring our position relative to the sun and other celestial bodies with a sextant. We spent a lot of time together as Chris explained how sextants worked and how to measure celestial angles from the deck of a sailboat. Back at sea Columbus was the first to get the sextant out to take sun sights during our passages (see plate section, image 8).

a crew in the Mediterranean and I've sailed more miles with him than anyone else. Paul has a brilliant sense of humor, gets involved, and offers to help with anything—always with a positive word. There is never a bad day in Paul Covell's world. He is the perfect person to have on board for an ocean passage.

Our second crew member was Jani, the tough resourceful Hungarian who had come with me on the trial run of *Aretha*. As well as being brilliant with the children, he was a first-class mechanic and an excellent chef. We couldn't have chosen two better crew to join us for *Aretha*'s first Atlantic crossing. With the extra help we'd be able to devote more time to the children's schooling and appreciate more of what was going on around us.

 Captain's Log, 27°01'N 15°47'W, November 24, 2014, 3,000 Miles to Go

> It's 6.34am. The light is just starting to come up. The sea lollops us around, waves bubbling along the hull. The sounds of sleep are all around me. The dawning light signaled the start of Day 2 of our Atlantic Adventure.

Scheduled departure day was November 23, but high winds and squalls delayed the 2014 ARC Rally start. The breeze in the marina touched 43 knots. We found and completed new jobs on the boat: repair work on the Avon tender that hangs from davits on *Aretha*'s stern, cleaning the hanks on the staysail, and spending more time with the Oyster support team discussing alternative downwind sail combinations. All good valuable stuff.

You could feel the buzz of start day—we all just wanted to get going: final trip to the mini market to buy bread, new lures for Columbus, topping up the fresh water tanks and downloading the latest weather. Race/rally starts are always an amazing sight: over 200 boats in a small space, crews settling down, preparing sails. We motored north slowly to get away from the pack, finding quiet water. We had 3,000 miles to go and wanted to stay out of trouble with other boats, so hung back. *Aretha* was one of the last boats to cross the line, but we soon hoisted full canvas, making satisfying progress through the fleet, passing by other boats one by one.

Columbus had been itching to get a fishing line out so we set up one of his new lures—a pink marlin shaker. In just an hour we heard the ratchet scream into action. I grabbed the rod as line streamed out of the reel. In my haste I forgot I was fishing for big Atlantic fish, not bass off the South Devon coast. My efforts to slow down the reel with my thumb on the spool were rewarded with a burnt finger. With a snap the line had gone and we were fishless. Lessons learned for sure as I put burn gel on my thumb.

There is an old classic saying to describe the navigation and routing across the Atlantic. You head south until the butter melts, then turn right and head west until you hit land. The heading south is to get into the trade winds and warmer weather. The route across the Atlantic is pretty straightforward and in November to December the probability of good settled conditions is high.

Life aboard settled into a routine: the children waking and going to bed at the agreed times, meals and routine maintenance becoming established. Sleep patterns were adjusting to watches: sleep when your head hits the pillow during your 3 hours off at night and wake rapidly when called for the next watch. We humans readily adapt to different patterns—it just takes a little time.

There were still boats all around us the first night. On Day 2 it thinned out. Then there was a clear feeling of being in the middle of the Atlantic.

Bluebell: Are we nearly there yet?

Me: No.

Bluebell: How far is it to go?

Me: 3,000 miles.

Bluebell: Oh.

Developing Routines at Sea

By Day 4, Nichola and Jani were back to full strength after bouts of seasickness. Sea legs had been acquired, helped by calmer seas and beautiful sunshine. Seasickness comes to even the most experienced sailors. Jani would go quiet after taking the seasickness medication he was using. Nichola would try to sleep it off.

Columbus learned from Paul how to whip line and Bluebell worked on her knots. Jani wasted no time in creating culinary genius—freshly baked bread with homemade leek and potato soup for lunch, a chicken and rice dish for supper. It was great to sit down and eat together, a practice so often forgotten in the bustle of seagoing life. The clocks shifted by one hour and we had happy hour on deck, basking in the sunshine, celebrating with music and a treasure hunt for the children. Each time we changed the clocks as we passed through different time zones we celebrated with a happy hour party. The sea temperature was 28.2°C and it would only get warmer. This was what we'd been looking forward to.

For the first time on this trip Nichola joined me on my night watches. It was lovely to have the company and to see her in top form.

We caught and lost our second fish. Mental note two: slow the boat down properly before bringing the fish in. Schoolboy error. Again.

How We Spent Our Atlantic Ocean Days—2,000 Miles to Go

1. Watching a pod of dolphins play alongside.
2. Discovering a flying fish on deck—after someone stood on it!
3. Catching a dorado at first light—filleted and sliced for sashimi followed by curry.
4. Bluebell playing guitar to the crew during our evening meal—a piece she'd written herself.
5. Columbus baking his first loaf of bread—the young man justifiably proud of his efforts.
6. Running the watermaker—it's immensely satisfying to make fresh drinking water from sea water.
7. Enjoying hot showers—managing water and power means hot showers only every five days.
8. Checking rigging, sails, and generator.
9. Learning tales from maritime history courtesy of Paul Covell.
10. Exotic meals courtesy of Jani.

Aretha was warming up down below—at night we wore only shorts and t-shirts. We were firmly in the trade winds now, gliding along effortlessly at 8 knots. Over the next 2,000 miles life settled into a pleasant routine. We enjoyed light winds, occasional squalls, and moderate winds up to 20 knots or so. We saw few other boats and became a happy crew content in our own world. By now we were getting to know *Aretha*, testing different sail combinations and becoming much more familiar with the generator, watermaker, engine, and sat-coms. We were happy as a team and the children settled. Children love routines and we could easily have carried on for much longer. This was the sort of thing we had envisaged during our five years of planning.

When the wind becomes light and variable with sailing progress slow, what do you do? Obvious of course—turn the cockpit into a swimming pool by closing off the cockpit drain seacocks and filling it with buckets of sea water. Water temperature was 31.6°C. Result—three happy children splashing and playing in the cockpit, throwing buckets of water over each other—the simple things in life.

On another day we created International Adopt a Star Day—a school project. Find a constellation or star, learn about it, draw a picture, and tell the rest of the crew about it. Here are the stars or constellations we chose:

Bluebell—Draco the Dragon
Columbus—Dorado
Nichola—Perseus
Jani—Pole Star
Paul—Sirius
Willow—Cassiopeia (because it looks like a W)
Caspar—The Northern Cross (also called Cygnus the Swan)

I'm sure a psychologist could have a field day working out what those choices mean.

Update from Nichola

Day 12, December 6, 2014
Just finished morning school with the children—they don't seem to mind that it's Saturday—sticking to the conventional Monday to Friday doesn't work. Today it was geography, oceans and sea, which is a fourth grade topic for geography and fits perfectly with where we are at the moment. As part of the ARC we are participating in a

conservation project studying microplastics in the Atlantic. By asking 100 boats to each collect 6 bottles of water as we crossed the Atlantic, the goal is to collect 600 bottles of water mid-ocean, discerning the level of microplastics present. The findings will be published in *National Geographic*. Combining the research project with schooling brought the topic more to life.

After the success of the cockpit paddling pool yesterday, the plan today is to repeat the fun, though Caspar has suggested we put fairy liquid in the water and hand out sponges so the children can clean the decks at the same time—I don't believe he's joking!

We are going to make fruit juice ice-lollies today as our freezer is now working perfectly. Bluebell is cooking lunch—pizza. She made one the other day and it was quite tasty. She could do with learning about cleaning while cooking—I kept finding brownie mix everywhere for at least another day after she made brownies.

Today is Improvisation Day—we have all given each other a regular object—for example a pencil—by the end of the day we each have to work out a new use for that object. Columbus gave me my object—duct tape!

Willow is sleeping at the moment—hence having the time to sit and write an email. She really is like a Duracell bunny. As soon as she awakes she is at 100 percent. The children have been opening their advent calendars each day, but Willow has already ploughed through 15 of her days. Initially I was stopping her but then decided it will be easier once the chocolate is gone so I am leaving her to it. She is picking up how Caspar gives out the skipper values awards each day. Today she got her books and started handing them out as prizes, sweet although she needs to spend some time on her delivery, as she handed them out to everyone she said, "Do you want one?"

We have roast beef today to mark crossing the 1000 nautical mile mark—we have 904.3 nautical miles left to go. It's getting hot now, I am sitting here writing this email in a bikini and shorts. The children certainly have the advantage that they can walk around in their underwear. I am not too unhappy with that as it saves on laundry.

Microplastics in the Oceans

Microplastics are tiny particles of plastic (less than 5mm in length) that come from a variety of sources, including cosmetics, clothing, and industrial processes. They are found in health and beauty products such as face cleansers and toothpaste. They are also created by the degradation of larger pieces of plastic. They are small enough to pass through the water filtration process and find their way into our oceans. The plastics do not break down for hundreds of years. The tiny particles are ingested by marine life and infuse the marine environment. These plastics contain chemicals harmful to the marine ecosystem. In addition, when these same fish and crustaceans are eaten by humans the plastic poisoning enters the human food chain.

The microplastics survey run by Ocean Conservation specified that the collection bottles had to be filled on a range of evenly spaced dates, noting the exact latitude and longitude where the water was collected. Once we arrived in St. Lucia the bottles were handed in for scientific analysis.

Steps are being taken to reduce the production of products containing microplastics and to clean the environment of plastics— however, the problem is immense. The aim of the Ocean Conservation survey was to collect data to show the extent of the problem in our oceans. Subsequent presentations by Ocean Conservation have shown microplastics are widespread across the oceans. The key conclusion is that we all need to reduce the amount of microplastics that we use.

Autopilot Failure

15°10′N 53°05′W, December 9, 2014, Day 14 of the Atlantic Crossing.

The 14th day of our passage was dramatic. Sailing downwind in 15–18 knots of true wind, Alan our autopilot (the device that automatically steers *Aretha*) sent out an error message: MOT Error. We'd not had this before and it wasn't a welcome sight. Within seconds the sails were flogging as *Aretha* rounded up into the wind. The autopilot had stopped working, forcing us to hand steer.

It's important to convey just how key the autopilot is. When I raced in the BT Global Challenge we had a crew of 18 sailors eager to steer, so we had no need for an autopilot. When you are shorthanded as we were, automated steering is critical. Alan the autopilot was steering *Aretha* 90 percent of the time. If we had to hand steer for an entire ocean passage there wouldn't be much time for us to do anything else.

Nichola and I were on watch together when the autopilot quit. Jani and Paul were sleeping, the children studying in the saloon. We needed to slow the boat down to investigate.

As so often happens on a sailboat, when one thing happens, it compounds itself with other problems.

While I was hand steering, Nichola was reefing the mainsail. She dropped the main halyard but the reefing lines fouled, making it impossible to reef the sail. We had to fully re-hoist to untangle

Skipper's Values Awards

One of the most successful leadership tools I learned from Trovus was the power of regularly and consistently praising people for very specific behaviors. On *Aretha* we did this every day through values prizes. I'd hold these discussions during breakfast, singling out each and every person for a specific behavior or action that they had taken that was in accordance with our values of LAUGH: Love + Learn Something, Action, Understanding, Go Prepared and Happy. Each child had a wall chart and they'd get a sticker to place in the column for the value they had demonstrated that day—for example, Understanding. By consistently talking about the positive behaviors and what we appreciated, we were ingraining an attitude of focusing on what was right rather than what was wrong.

Over time, I'd ask the children to run the values awards discussion so that they became versed in looking for good behaviors and praising other people for specific things they had done, no matter how big or small.

128

the lines. This was hard work but we remained calm and took it all in our stride. Normally, we'd switch on the autopilot and reef together. Now Nichola had to work the reefing controls in the cockpit and at the mast.

We re-hoisted the mainsail and we still couldn't reef. We needed to drop the mainsail completely, bringing *Aretha* up into the wind. To do that, we had to furl (roll in) the headsail. Thankfully this is easier and we slowed the boat down quickly.

Paul was on deck by now, hand steering while we dropped the main, untangled it, and put in the reef. Jani appeared shortly and started to clear out the lazarette (the large locker at the stern that held the spare sails, gangplank [passarelle], and underneath all of this the autopilot linkages) so we could diagnose the problem.

Visual inspection immediately confirmed the issue. There were two rams (port and starboard) controlling the autopilot. The port ram was hanging loose—the bolt fixing it to the steering had sheared off. These are big bolts and it would have taken 4–5 tonnes of load—a powerful force—to shear it off. We examined the autopilot and debated our options. The mechanical system on the port ram still worked. The ram extended. This was encouraging.

The bolt on the starboard side was still good. We detached the starboard ram and took the bolt from starboard and transferred it to port.

One broken ram, one good ram. One good bolt, one sheared bolt.

We made an operational system by connecting the good ram to the good bolt. With over 550 miles to go it was a big relief when we pressed the auto button and the machinery made reassuring whirring sounds and the helm responded.

We put the boat back together and debriefed in the cockpit.

The good news was that the children sensed we had important stuff to fix and stayed below, calm and quiet. We worked extremely well as a team—there was quiet, collaborative focus as we worked through the situation.

It was a great reminder to be pragmatic, solving each problem by looking at what we had and creating practical solutions with the resources at hand. We later discovered that the failure had been caused by a wiring problem with the rams and that the port and starboard rams weren't communicating with each other properly—they were working against each other rather than being synchronized.

Landfall in the Caribbean

We first sighted land at around 7am on December 12, 2014. The shout of "Land Ho" was fantastic, realizing we'd navigated 3,000 miles across the Atlantic to the Caribbean.

We spent the final six hours match racing three other boats. A squall propelled us forward by an extra half mile, placing us comfortably ahead. We gradually extended that lead so that by the time we rounded Pigeon Island at the northern end of St. Lucia we were 4 miles ahead of two other sailboats, *Skiathos* and *Irenka*.

We hailed the committee boat on VHF Channel 72 and spotted the finish line as we sailed into Rodney Bay. The breeze was fresh—we were sailing to windward for the first time in three weeks, *Aretha* heeled over beautifully under full main and genoa—cantering along at 8 knots in flat calm water. The professional photographer zoomed alongside, snapping shots.

Jani counted us down across the line... 5, 4, 3, 2, 1. We'd done it. Atlantic Rally 2014 completed at 13.32 St. Lucia time.

Friends met us in their tender with a bottle of bubbles and lemonade for the children—all of our crew on deck and celebrating—and the children were thrilled to see their friends again.

Sails down and furled, lines stowed, docking lines and fenders retrieved and rigged. We motored through the cut into Rodney Bay Marina, past the brightly colored fishing skiffs, fog horns blasting, other sailors clapping and cheering—a truly amazing feeling. We rounded the docks and reversed into our berth to the sound of steel drums. Our good friends Paul from *Juno* and Meryvn from *El Mundo* took our lines, helping secure *Aretha*. We were grateful to berth safely, especially with a good breeze and a crowd watching.

Once the docking lines were adjusted we were met with more cold drinks and a fruit bowl—a fantastic welcome to a stunningly beautiful St. Lucia.

Over the coming days we shared tales of the crossing, cleaned *Aretha*, and tackled maintenance jobs. Jani and Paul departed. They had been awesome crew and they would be missed greatly.

We made many friends as part of the rally—it was impossible to walk the length of the dock without catching up and swapping tales. We had plenty to fix during our ten days in Rodney Bay: damaged autopilot, chafed halyards and sheets, broken head pump and replacing the seals on the generator's raw-water intake.

Dealing with gear failure on a boat at sea is a skill: you need to quickly figure out what is broken, what you need to fix it (or to jury rig a replacement until you get ashore), and how to do it. Once ashore, the broken items need thorough fixes and all the other systems need thorough checkups.

We were just beginning our apprenticeship.

Chapter 11

The Caribbean Sea to Panama

Rodney Bay, St. Lucia, to Panama City

(December 2014 to February 2015)

We had six weeks in the Caribbean before we needed to head west toward the Panama Canal and out into the Pacific. The driving force behind all of our timing was to cross each ocean in the right weather window, meaning it was the safest time of year for each of our ocean passages. This dictated how much time we could spend in each location before we needed to move on again to take advantage of the most favorable winds and ocean currents. (The primary resource we used for charting routes around the world was *World Cruising Routes* by Jimmy Cornell—see the Bibliography on page 293.)

We wanted to make the most of our time in the Caribbean, spending it with family and friends, plus enjoy the experience alone as a family. Our Caribbean route would take us south from St. Lucia, working our way through the stunning islands of the Grenadines, ending up in Grenada. Then we planned to head west again across the Caribbean Sea to Panama.

A Different Christmas

We planned to rendezvous on Christmas Eve with friends on family boats at Chatham Bay on Union Island, in the Grenadines. Having friends for the children to play with was a large part of our adventure so we often made plans accordingly. Meeting like-minded people was wonderful for all of us.

We headed south from Rodney Bay to spend one night at Marigot Bay, where *Dr. Doolittle* was filmed. Early evening saw us spinning by the mangrove swamps, aiming to catch snapper and small barracuda in this picturesque spot.

From there we sailed through the St. Vincent Passage to the island of Bequia (pronounced "Bek-Way"), anchoring in crowded and blustery Admiralty Bay. We went ashore by dinghy, shopped in the local street markets, found the local cafés with internet access, and spent time exploring. Bequia is one of the few places in the world where they continue to hunt whales—the local market teemed with carvings on whale bones and teeth.

We were relishing the Caribbean: picture-postcard beaches, swimming in beautiful turquoise seas surrounded by fish in glorious sunshine. We weighed anchor early on Christmas Eve, heading south to Chatham Bay on the west coast of Union Island, arriving around lunch and settling quickly into life in this isolated place, our home for the next fortnight.

There are no roads to Chatham Bay. It has four tin shack bar/restaurants dotted along a palm-lined beach. Nothing else. The guys running the bars come 4 miles by boat from the main town of Clifton. We snorkeled every day, seeing lobsters, moray eels, turtles, trumpet fish, and countless other species, all within 100 feet of the beach. We fished from our boats and round the headland, catching jacks weighing up to 2lb (excellent grilled with fresh limes).

In the morning we swam off the boat, ate a lazy breakfast, then took the dinghy ashore so the children could play on the beach, reveling in the sea. Columbus, a tentative swimmer before we left, was now a true water child—always with a mask and snorkel on, diving and playing, rarely out of the water. Willow built sandcastles, running happily in and out of the water. Bluebell surrounded herself with friends.

We sat on the beach and watched magical sunsets every day. This was the most relaxing part of our adventure so far and we loved every moment. We deepened our boat friendships while enjoying our private paradise. It was nice to take the focus off boat maintenance and the mindset of being alert and always "on" while crossing the Atlantic. For these two weeks it was tools down and chill.

Christmas was different, delightfully minimal: one or two gifts each, a small Christmas tree, and to maintain British tradition, one small box of Quality Street chocolates (see plate section, image 11). It was perfect, calm, and happy, incredibly memorable. We got to know Tim, who ran one of the bars and provided us with a Christmas dinner of barbecue grilled lobsters eaten at tables on the beach. At sunset we were swimming in the bay.

We spent time with friends from other boats—*Matilda, Take Off,* and *Khujada 2.* One day we hiked up the rocky path through the hills and met a prearranged taxi for the trip to Clifton—the vibrant one-street capital of Union Island that included a tiny airport and a handful of shops and restaurants. On two days a few of us ran the 4 miles to Clifton—a 2-hour round-trip in the heat. This was the farthest I'd run since my back operation and I was delighted to discover all seemed in good working order. It was good to run again—especially when the cool down included diving into the sea to swim back to our tender anchored just off the beach.

After a fortnight in this relaxed paradise we weighed anchor, heading south toward Grenada. We had another week with friends before they headed north and we headed west toward Panama. Time now to start prepping for our next leg, and I couldn't wait to be back at sea again sailing the 1,000-mile stretch to Panama and what lay beyond—the mighty Pacific Ocean.

More Helping Hands

We were feeling that the children's schooling hadn't taken a particularly high priority after getting from one place to the next safely, so when Paul and Caroline from *Juno* mentioned that a good friend of theirs, Caroline, might be interested in joining us on the long passage to the Pacific we decided to give it serious consideration.

Caroline was a middle school teacher originally from Germany who spoke fluent English, French, and Spanish, with significant sailing experience—her previous Atlantic crossing had been in a boat that had lost all power. From the description she was clearly resourceful and could be just what we needed. Having a third pair of adult hands as well as someone to give the children proper lessons every morning would make life aboard a lot easier. She would also provide Nichola and me with some breathing space. We arranged a Skype call and by the end of it we knew Caroline was a good fit, so that same day we made a plan. Caroline would fly to Grenada where she would join us to sail initially to Panama on a probation period to make sure we were all happy. After that, she'd sail with us to the Galapagos, the Marquesas, the Tuamotos, and then on to Tahiti, where she would leave us. One recommendation and one short Skype call and we had decided on our sailing companion for the next few months. I wonder how long we might have debated that decision back in our land-based world. On the water you make a decision and get on with it. Our judgment with Caroline was spot on—she was a superb addition to the crew of *Aretha*.

From Union Island we had a fast sail to Grenada, dodging an underwater volcano that needed a 1-mile clearance and the occasional rain squall. We headed for Prickly Bay Marina on the south coast. Slightly ramshackle docks meant we couldn't leave our gangplank down—so our tender became the preferred means of getting ashore. The children were as happy as ever playing with their friends from our small flotilla—we rarely saw them.

Nichola's parents, Sheila and Laurie, had flown to Grenada, staying in a hotel just a two-minute dinghy ride away. The children rippled with anticipation as we sped over to meet them—large bags of chocolate and goodies from the UK further increased their excitement!

We spent a week exploring Grenada and prepping the boat. A day on Hog Island with a band and a barbecue was a fabulous, if a rather rude, wet awakening to island life for Sheila and Laurie as our water taxi half filled with water on the way over. We were delighted to be joined by Caroline. We swam in waterfalls in the rainforest, visited the chocolate and rum factories, and got to know friendly and welcoming locals.

Unexpected Time Out

In preparation for our next sailing passage, I needed to take *Aretha* to the fuel dock to fill the diesel tanks. I cranked the engine and nothing happened. We now had an additional boat repair. The engine was soon in many parts and after ruling out different possibilities, attention focused on the gearbox. Several engineers later the problem was identified as a broken clutch. As happens with boats, we also discovered a further problem—our water separator unit on the generator also needed rewelding.

Our planned departure date was out of the window—new parts would take a week to arrive. The plan had been to set off from Grenada on January 10 to meet with friends in Colombia and then cross to the Panama Canal in early February. We'd now be a week behind, playing catch-up to our friends as we sailed the 1,000 or so miles to Panama without other boats to accompany us.

While we awaited parts, some of our other friends sailing back up through the Grenadines toward St. Lucia suggested we join them aboard for a few days, returning to Grenada via inter-island ferry. So Nichola, Caroline, and the children headed off to Tobago Cays on their boats, *Matilda*, *Take Off*, and *Khujada 2*, while I stayed aboard *Aretha* to oversee repairs. It provided a perfect opportunity for Nichola and Caroline to get to know one another and for the children to get used to Caroline. I wonder if Caroline had any idea what she was getting into with our lively bunch! Her easygoing yet firm nature was an instant hit with Bluebell and Willow. Columbus took a little more warming up but she soon won him over, too.

I was left on *Aretha* in the pouring rain. The silver lining was a couple of days of peace and quiet to catch up on work, watch a film, and enjoy some solitude. I realized that for four months the five of us had been together 24 hours a day. When it was good, it was truly fabulous. When it was bad, it was testing. There was nowhere to go. The skills you really need aren't sailing ones (though clearly they help), but emotional mastery and how to deal with relationships on board. This adventure was our opportunity to redefine our relationships, what they meant, and what we all wanted from them. Time on your own is excellent reflection time. Going forward I would be encouraging all the crew to have more "me time."

In among all this, we'd had *Aretha* polished and cleaned, winches serviced, rig checked, sheets washed, and routes planned—prep for the next long voyage at sea. I couldn't wait to get back out there.

Joining the World ARC in Panama

When we departed England our plan was to circumnavigate on our own. We wanted our own experience, the chance to choose our own routes and timeline. However, after months of sailing on our own after our Atlantic ARC experience, we made the decision to join the World ARC in Panama so we could sail in company across the Pacific to Australia.

Why the change? The first reason was for peace of mind—for relatives and friends at home, and for us—that we would be in the company of other boats. Although we'd be spread out over hundreds of miles of ocean, we were part of a community of people we knew well and who were able to help each other out. Secondly, having a liaison to arrange customs and immigration clearances in far-flung countries is a huge time and hassle saving—extremely valuable when you have three small children. Finally, although there is a hefty cost, the benefits of marinas being organized and events planned goes a long way to offset the cost.

An added and unexpected bonus of joining the World ARC meant that we would forge deep friendships with people who understood our stories because they were there at the same time, experiencing the same things, the highs and the lows. The magic of life experiences is sharing them with other people and creating shared memories that last.

Is There Safety in Numbers?

There are always two sides to everything. The upside of a rally is that there is potentially safety in numbers and there are people who are relatively near by who can help you if needed. The other side is that just because there are boats around doesn't mean you can lower your guard when it comes to safety. Each boat and their crew have to maintain the utmost responsibility for their boat and keeping it safe. Lives have been lost in rallies. They are not an insurance of safety. You have to do what is right and safe for your own boat and make your own judgment calls.

Values Off the Coast of Venezuela

Flat seas. Consistent breeze. Good boat speed. Happy, well-fed crew. Nichola walked Caroline through the full briefing for *Aretha* and ran the maneuvers on deck. I think Nichola surprised herself with how much she knew.

After breakfast I usually held the daily skipper's briefing—more so at sea than when we were docked or anchored, but as often as we could. I'd share updates on our position. I'd read aloud email messages we'd received in response to our blogs—the children loved getting feedback from the outside world. Sometimes I'd ask everyone how they were feeling on a scale of 1–10, then I would ask for one or two emotions describing those feelings. It let me gauge how everyone was doing while helping to develop emotional awareness in the children. Sometimes we'd meditate and play calming music. Two-year-old Willow was particularly keen on this and would sit perfectly still, cross-legged. The part the children looked forward to most, though, was the values prize.

In the early days the prize was candy, but over time—as we reduced the amount of sugar we all consumed—we switched to small adhesive paper stickers. Stickers—a vast collection of smiley faces and colored stars—were actually more powerful. The children created their own values charts with columns listing the different values. Each day, they'd add the sticker to the relevant column so they could see which values they were expressing and those they needed to work on.

"My first prize today relates to the value of Action. This person got up early this morning and before they had been asked to, they had already written in their journal for the day. They wrote three pages of

The Time Factor

It would be great to take five or six years to cruise around the world in years to come—to visit more out-of-the-way places, relax in certain islands, meet more locals, experience more diverse cultures. But we had carved out a fixed amount of time for this experience: five years to get the money together, two years for the circumnavigation so we could return in time for Bluebell to start secondary school at the age of 11.

good, well thought-out writing and did so calmly and happily. So, well done Bluebell for demonstrating the value of Action." After the applause Bluebell chose the sticker she wanted to add to her values chart.

Even though Willow didn't always understand the emotions or values we were talking about, I took great care to make sure she was included by asking her feelings. If I asked a question, she'd always be the first to put her hand up, giving her views. We encouraged this and took the time to listen to her, repeating back what she'd said to make sure we'd properly understood her point.

Highlighting and rewarding good behavior had a huge impact. For example, Bluebell went from "I hate fish—throw it overboard" to a helpful and happy crew member—in one day—busy in the galley making tuna fish fingers with egg and breadcrumbs fried in olive oil.

We were by now making rapid progress across the Caribbean Sea with flat seas and moderate wind from the quarter giving us fast boat speed.

Heading for the San Blas Islands

Ten miles off the east coast of Aruba, as we sailed toward Colombia, I was trying to remember the title of a Beach Boys song, "Aruba, Jamaica," etc., etc. Back when I heard the song, Aruba was a far-off place. Now it was a series of lights including a long line of flashing red ones on our port side. Ditto for Curaçao—the drink Blue Curaçao now has a different meaning having sailed past the island it originates from.

We spotted a huge pod of dolphins. Bluebell and Columbus hung over the bow (all clipped on of course), dangling hands over the side as we surfed down the waves at 8 knots surrounded by these joyful creatures, the dolphins rolling over, eyeing the children. Bluebell was convinced she touched one as it leaped out of the water. Willow sat in the cockpit with Caroline, content to watch from there.

We were in the company of many tankers and container ships—our protocol was to call on the VHF to make sure they had seen us. Most were friendly and chatted for a few minutes and if needed one or both of us would alter course to ensure a safe passing distance. We didn't see any other sailboats.

Colombia was one of the three places we'd been told to expect the roughest sailing—it was more demanding than the Bay of Biscay, testing the boat and us. We had 35 knots of breeze with seas from all directions. We topped out our speed one night at 13.6 knots, surfing downwind with three reefs in the main plus a poled-out headsail. Sailing always feels faster in the dark.

The wind softened by day but the confused seas remained. I was sitting in the cockpit with Caroline and Nichola when we were suddenly hit by a massive, cockpit-filling wave that left us completely drenched. Heading across the Colombian Basin, the wind was pushing us north, in the direction of Nicaragua, not toward Panama, our destination. We wanted to gybe but were conscious of gybing back toward the roughest part of the wind acceleration zone; in addition, the idea of gybing the pole and working on the foredeck in bouncy and confused seas wasn't grabbing the crew. We decided to wait for the expected wind shift—eventually we were headed in the right direction.

The children were brilliant. Bluebell now thoroughly loving boat life, cooking meals with us, reading, playing games with Willow and Columbus, utterly charming. Columbus was devouring two Tintin books a day. Willow was pulling things apart faster than we could put them together with a cheeky smile and shrug of her shoulders.

Our fast sailing meant that we made up time so that rather than meeting the World ARC boats in Shelter Bay in Panama, we'd be able to meet them in the San Blas Islands, a collection of 300-plus sparsely populated tropical islands.

 Captain's Log, 09°35'N 078°52'W, 6.30am, January 25, 2015

The boat is quiet apart from the sound of the waves lapping against the hull and the cries of tropical birds on the San Blas Islands.

Nichola woke me some 20 minutes ago to take my turn on anchor watch, to make sure the anchor doesn't drag. Being only yards away from the reef behind us, there is no margin for error. If we do drag anchor we need to respond immediately. Testament to the importance of this was the sight of a yacht on her side on the coral reef as we entered the anchorage last night. She had clearly either missed her navigation marks or had dragged anchor. Either way, she was high and dry with her keel exposed.

Being able to see things by morning, it truly is a tropical paradise here. There are two tiny islands—a small one to windward and a larger one just behind us. The larger one is the size of two football pitches. You can see the waves breaking over the coral reefs. The islands are dense with palm trees and I can see the hand-built shacks where the three families who live on these islands are. By contrast the Caribbean feels very commercial and packed with boats.

There are no shops here—just some coconuts and fish and the embroidery you can buy from the locals who come out in their canoes.

The local people aren't keen on the name the San Blas Islands as it came from the Spanish invaders. They are proud Kuna Indians and are meant to be very friendly and welcoming. They are a short people—the closest tribe in height to pygmies.

There's a whole host of new wildlife here—there are meant to be crocodiles and sharks, which will make the snorkelling interesting. Apparently the crocodiles are friendly (I've not heard of that concept before) and there are no reported attacks. The birds and the monkeys we will learn more about later.

There is a World ARC rendezvous here at midday today so we will catch up with our friends and meet the rest of the fleet.

Over the last eight days, we covered 1,000-plus miles; eight days without any seasickness from any of the crew.

I now have Bluebell and Columbus for company. It's like having two bouncy Tiggers while you are trying to write. They are keen to go swimming and have breakfast and go exploring.

Columbus calls me on deck. He's spotted a parrot.

After eight days at sea, it was good to decompress, spending time in one place. The San Blas archipelago has 370 islands but we didn't stray beyond the first, a tiny island no more than 3 feet high in the center. Columbus, Caroline, and I nosed our way around the coral reefs in the dinghy in unbelievably clear water, exploring beautiful crescent-shaped, sandy beaches surrounded by palm trees.

A dugout canoe arrived with one of the local Kuna Indians selling coconuts and conch. The second one arrived shortly after selling *molas*, the local embroidery. No crocodiles had been sighted so far but on the next island a dog had been eaten by two crocs the previous week so we kept watch. We saw one small shark.

By late morning the rest of the World ARC fleet arrived, filling the bay. We were soon reunited with Paul and Caroline from *Juno*, as well as Andy and Emma from *Pentagram*. We had so much in common from our experiences that the conversations flowed happily and easily. We'd be sharing our journey to Australia with them and another 15 boats: diverse people, ages, backgrounds, nationalities, all united by a desire to sail around the world—that forges a deep connection entailing adventure, exploration, and something of the spiritual side of life, too.

We each brought food for a shared "potluck" beach rendezvous lunch. Drinks were coconuts with a straw: sip the first mouthful of coconut milk, then the coconut is topped up with rum; as simple as it gets for a rum cocktail. A tiny bar served drinks and we were treated to local flute music and dance. As the afternoon wore on, with the children happily playing with Andy and Emma, Nichola and I took an hour to walk around this tiny island. We paddled in the water over white sand, watched colorful fish playing, and savored the moment in this tropical paradise.

The Panama Canal

A few days later we were waiting to pass through the Panama Canal to the Pacific. The level of excitement and anticipation had stepped up a couple of gears since our canal briefing in Shelter Bay on the Caribbean side of the canal. The procedure was that we were to raft up with two other yachts the following afternoon, then around 6pm, provided all went to plan, we'd proceed into the first of the three chambers at Gatun Lock. We'd secure lines to the canal, get moved through the locks, then anchor in Gatun Lake for the night. The next day we'd raft up again to go through the three locks on the other side where we'd be dropped down in height (via the lock) to the Pacific. The landmark moment would be crossing under the Bridge of the Americas as we headed into the Pacific. The sea temperature would be 10°C colder on the Pacific side. We'd also experience huge tidal ranges again—moving from only a few inches rise and fall in the Caribbean Sea to 13 feet rise and fall of tide in the Pacific.

We'd spent the prior few days in a relatively relaxed combination of boat prep, provisioning (getting 3+ months' worth of food on board), and enjoying the sights. We visited another stunningly beautiful San Blas island, El Porvenir, this one with an airstrip. You had to walk across the runway to get to the snack shop—no one monitoring safety—just check in the sky that no planes are landing.

We arrived in Panama with many emotions. We had sailed all the way from England to Central America. We were about to transit through the most famous canal in the world—a daunting prospect to be rafted with other boats while surrounded by the largest commercial ships sailing the globe's oceans. We would soon be heading out into the wilderness of the Pacific, the largest ocean in the world, making the Atlantic and Caribbean seem like paddling pools. It felt like standing at the top of the toughest, steepest, longest ski run in the world with perfect fresh powder that would run for thousands and thousands of miles until we finally reached Australia.

Ports of Interest—Portobello, Shelter Bay, and Panama City

After the San Blas Islands, we made a brief stop at Portobello on the north coast of Panama, learning that Sir Francis Drake was buried there in a lead coffin. Visiting the Church of the Black Christ sent shivers down my spine. Ruins of forts and cannons—to keep off pirates—litter the coastline. The seas are full of commercial shipping—perhaps the busiest sea in the world with vessels heading west and east, avoiding the notoriously rough and dangerous longer route around Cape Horn at the bottom of South America.

On the northern side of the canal entrance was Colon—a busy and rough town serving the shipping industry, not a place for sailboats. Shelter Bay, though, was a well-kept marina full of interesting people with stories of adventure and the seas. It had once been a US Army fort, the ruined buildings now eerily overgrown with creepers. Walk two minutes out of the marina and you are deep in the jungle with howler monkeys swinging from the trees above lines of ants marching through the brush.

Shelter Bay served as a great point from which to explore Panama. After the San Blas Islands with their white sand gently shelving into clear sea, the area around the Chagres River felt dark, flowing out of a tropical Central American jungle, hills carpeted with thick forest. We visited the Emberra tribe, riding in dugout canoes fitted with high-powered outboard engines on a two-hour journey to reach the village, zooming up rapids, across huge lakes filled with wildlife. We were welcomed with pipe music, surrounded by men, women, and children naked from the waist up. Being adorned with a henna tattoo from the women was a rite of passage and most of the guys lined up waiting to be initiated and be part of the tradition (see plate section, image 13). We explored the village, visiting the school, sharing a meal of fish and plantains wrapped in leaves cooked on a fire positioned high in the tree houses where the Emberra Indians live. The warmth of the people left strong memories—in particular seeing Willow playing with an Indian girl, each child fascinated by the color of the other's skin and hair. Laughter and play filled the air.

We also explored Panama City complete with skyscrapers, modern bars, restaurants, and hotels. Less than half a mile away the city plunges into slums where thousands live in abject poverty. The contrasts within Panama could not be starker. It was an intoxicating cocktail of extremes.

My sister Pippa was joining us at Shelter Bay and joked about how much she was looking forward to crocodile-infested Gatun Lake and being woken by howler monkeys and mosquitoes. She wrote on our family sailing blog: "The local practice nurse assures me that the biting mosquitoes in Panama are not restricted to dusk and apparently different varieties carrying different diseases will be attentive throughout the day. Malaria at night, yellow fever in the day, and at least another four gems that I'd rather not think about. I was offered a course of three injections against rabies (I declined and will take my chances against vampire bats by not sleeping on deck)." Her luggage was full of yacht parts—she was understandably nervous about clearing customs with her gear full of large metal objects.

We'd been traveling for so long that it was amusing to see how our adventures looked from Pippa's fresh perspective:

"I joined the boat yesterday morning after a two and a half hour taxi ride from the city. My planned Panamanian railroad trip being scuppered by my foolishly interpreting a daily train service to mean just that. It didn't. Arriving at Gatun Locks a huge queue was forming as a ship was starting to enter the first lock heading south. The taxi driver picked up a couple of locals also heading to Shelter Bay. Communication was tricky, the three Panamanians didn't speak a word of English between them (I had previously negotiated the taxi fare with pen and paper) and the limit of my Spanish is 'two beers please' which wasn't particularly useful. The city taxi driver was clearly out of his territory and not surprisingly had no idea where we were going. There were no road signs, no road markings, lots of potholes and jungle to either side of us out of which leaped three large raccoon-like marsupials. I'm not sure who was more excited to see them, my fellow passengers or me.

"Arriving at Shelter Bay Marina I found Caspar on *Aretha*. He's sporting a primitive tattoo which encircles his upper left arm and combined with the dark tan and long unruly hair, he looks quite wild, but very happy. Mummy, don't worry, it's not a real tattoo.

"*Aretha* is spotless, not at all what I had expected considering the time the family has been on board. I was last on deck in Southampton and then *Aretha* was just a boat. Now she feels like a home and it's a privilege to be here with everyone.

"We head off through the first lock, Gatun, tomorrow evening. It will be dark when we go through so I'm off on a lock visit later with Columbus to see the operation prior to the actual practical. The others have already visited and know the form."

In Gatun Lake we saw iguanas and egrets. Miraflores Lock was full of brown pelicans exploiting the mixing of the Pacific's salt water with the fresh water from the lakes above, pulling the now unwell fish out of the water easily. Pippa said her favorite moment was being at the helm through Gaillard Cut with a crocodile on the right bank and a huge container ship just yards away on her left. When you see the locks filling with water and the boats bouncing around, it makes you realize how small you are compared to the ships that regularly pass through.

Pippa certainly had an amazing albeit brief experience transiting the Panama Canal with us, but it was also a culture shock. As we whizzed around the city to chandleries for boat gear, she was alarmed by large cracks in the taxi windscreens. She also realized that being on *Aretha* was hard work, and physically uncomfortable at times: searing heat on deck in the day, hot and humid below deck, an unceasing workload of meals, washing, cleaning, education, and the boat needing constant attention. While in a normal home repairs can be made when one has the time or inclination, on the boat every part needs to function to keep safe and that's before you can start sailing or throw in squalls and seasickness. Life also included harder bits: three energetic children are always going to argue and test your patience.

It was a reminder that this was our dream, not everyone's.

We were living our adventure, one whose particulars we had planned carefully as a family. There was a party atmosphere as we

trovus
Power up

4th September 2011

Nichola & Caspar Shared Vision

On the 1st August 2014, we are setting sail as a happy contented family, having easily achieved ∧ £5m of net assets enabling us to sail and travel with complete financial freedom and in control of our lives.

a minimum of

In achieving this, we have ensured our shared journey to the start point is as fulfilling, enjoyable and enriching as it can be. We have worked as a team focused on making the most of our combined strengths and the different contribution we all bring. We will measure and celebrate our personal growth on our journey on a regular basis:

We are returning as a happy family invigorated, renewed and full of energy and passion for our next adventure.

1 The vision statement we created that was in full view on our kitchen wall.

2 The Craven Family Winners' Bible: the folder that captured everything and lived on the table in the kitchen.

THE CRAVEN FAMILY WINNERS BIBLE

ABOVE: **3** Bluebell's 8th birthday before we set sail. Note the map of the world on the wall.

MIDDLE: **4** The Craven family values picture that we created together.

BOTTOM: **5** Our family portrait taken a few weeks before we set sail from the UK.

ABOVE: **6** Sailing past Start Point: I spent all my early childhood on this coastline.

RIGHT: **7** Different locations provided ideas for homeschooling: Bluebell created this picture after visiting Sines in Portugal.

BOTTOM: **8** Columbus learning how to use a sextant under the tuition of leading weather expert, Chris Tibbs.

9 Sailing the Atlantic: Nichola, Paul and Jani putting the emergency steering gear into practice.

BELOW: **10** *Aretha* arriving in St. Lucia after completing the first Atlantic crossing © Tim Wright/photoaction.com.

11 Our first Christmas away in Union Island with our small fold-up Christmas tree on board *Aretha*.

12 The children exploring Chichime Cay, one of the many magical San Blas Islands.

13 Getting a henna tattoo in the Emberra village in Panama.

14 Willow enjoying playing and making friends in the Panama jungle © Anna Berg.

ABOVE: **15** Columbus expertly steering *Aretha* on the approach to Panama under my watchful eye.

RIGHT: **16** Sailing the Panama Canal—our route through.

17 The children loved baking and it became a regular routine.

18 Self-sufficiency and humor were key: mending our ripped mainsail sailing the Pacific.

19 Making landfall in the Marquesas Islands after our longest offshore passage: Columbus, Willow, Nichola, Bluebell, me and Caroline.

ABOVE: **20** Willow and me kayaking in the protected lagoon on Fakarava.

BELOW: **21** Bluebell and Columbus swimming with dolphins in French Polynesia—one of the things on Bluebell's wish list.

ABOVE: **22** Columbus being towed by a 10-foot nurse shark in Bora Bora.

BELOW: **23** On the isolated island of Suwarrow deep in the Pacific Ocean.

ABOVE: **24** Bluebell showing huge courage diving into Mariner's Cave in Tonga © Sarah Barthelet.

RIGHT: **25** Nichola doing our regular rig checks.

ABOVE: **26** Bluebell and Columbus studying hard in Australia—snakes and spiders!

BELOW: **27** Sailing in company with *Wayward Wind* inside the Great Barrier Reef.

ABOVE: **28** Enjoying the calm seas of the Arafura Sea as we headed north of Australia.

BELOW: **29** Nichola walking the decks of *Aretha* as we sail fast on our way to Cocos (Keeling).

ABOVE: **30** Max escaping children on deck and setting up his cameras to do some filming.

BELOW: **31** Magical Cocos (Keeling): one of the most captivating islands we visited.

ABOVE: **32** Under a watchful eye, Bluebell expertly running the SSB Radio Net.

RIGHT: **33** Willow was always building dens on board.

BELOW: **34** Teachers all around: Columbus and Willow learning how to build a combustion engine with Sarah from *Makena*.

35 Christmas Day in Cape Town: an international event with all our friends.

ABOVE: **36** *Aretha* surfing down waves after leaving Cape Town.

LEFT: **37** Crossing the equator back into the northern hemisphere.

ABOVE: **38** Celebrating crossing our outbound track and circumnavigating in Grenada.

BELOW LEFT: **39** Bluebell on the bows of *Aretha* in Chatham Bay, Union Island.

BELOW RIGHT: **40** Three circumnavigators—enjoying life back in the Caribbean.

passed under the Bridge of the Americas. This gateway to the Pacific had long been a picture in our minds—well before we ever set out. We played our boat songs at full volume, dancing on deck. It was truly an amazing moment to have sailed the Atlantic, on the cusp of the Pacific, standing at the top of the double black ski run, about to leap off.

Chapter 12

Pacific—The Biggest Ocean in the World

Panama Canal to the Tuamotu Islands

(February 2015 to March 2015)

The Pacific featured as a big step in our trip from the very beginning. It's such a huge ocean and so sparsely populated, it truly is a Mecca for sailors. You could spend a lifetime simply sailing the Pacific, never visiting the same place twice. To sail out from underneath the Bridge of the Americas at the western end of the Panama Canal and head out into its vastness is an indescribable feeling.

We left Panama and motored 50 miles with the sea a glassy calm to the nearby Las Perlas Islands (the "Pearl Islands"). The name is wholly appropriate for this stunning island paradise. We anchored at Mogo Mogo and spent a week savoring the island's tropical atmosphere with our friends.

 Captain's Log, 08°35'N 79°01'W, February 12, 2015, Mogo Mogo, Las Perlas Islands

> We're in the most perfect anchorage. The only sounds are the waves on the beach, the breeze fluttering the flags on *Aretha*, and the noise of the birds. *Aretha* is nestled between two tiny islands —the most beautiful and idyllic we have seen yet. The beach to port is golden sand backed by dense rich green trees and rocks. The water is crystal clear and

from *Aretha* we spotted a ray swimming on the seabed some 26 feet below us.

Yesterday morning, we all dinghied over to Mogo Mogo (the setting for the TV series *Survivor*), and navigated our way around a coral reef. We'd heard there was another stunning beach on the opposite side, so Caroline and I set off through the jungle to explore. The island is totally uninhabited and the vegetation is dense. You're never quite sure what wildlife there is so you carry a stick just in case. We see three large iguanas, the largest of which was bright green and easily blended with the leaves on the trees. After much back and forth weaving around the trees we find the beach, a perfect arc of golden sand and completely deserted. We have found our very own desert island with turquoise blue seas twinkling in the sun. I feel like the guy in Alex Garland's book, *The Beach*. We double back to find Nichola and the children and take them to the beach. They are as spellbound as we are and we spend the morning swimming, playing, and building sandcastles with Willow. I can't imagine how things can get better than this.

It's just us and the islands and the sea here—no bars, no shops, no people other than a handful of other boats. This is the most relaxed I've been since we left and we are all content and happy. Boat maintenance has been suspended and we're enjoying each other and our environment.

In the evenings we had drinks with the crew from other World ARC boats, and last night we lit a fire on the beach with the masses of tinder-dry driftwood. We had plans to barbecue fish, but the Goliath grouper that Columbus and I caught didn't seem big enough to feed us all so we settled for drinks and home-made burgers.

From the Las Perlas Islands we sailed back to Panama so I could fly out to attend a work conference in San Diego. I can't lie: being in a hotel and off the boat for a few days felt pretty good. But after three days of meetings with super-smart people and tuning in to some of the latest ideas, thinking, and opportunity, I was ready to head back to Team *Aretha*.

It was lovely to get an excited welcome from all three children, bursting with energy and stories of what they'd been up to. In Panama, Nichola and Caroline had worked hard to get the boat ready and we now had an SSB radio installed thanks to Mike, a Kiwi rigger with a colorful past, and Dino, a Panamanian electrical expert. Columbus had been working with Mike doing the rigging and probably now knew a lot more about the SSB than I did—he continued to be a sponge for information, learning at every opportunity. Nichola and Caroline had completed the provisioning and stowing of *Aretha* with supplies for the next four months—enough to get us to Australia—an impressive feat, as was their encyclopedic knowledge of where everything was located on board. We had full diesel, water, and gas. We were ready.

I was thrilled to be back at sea, en route to the Galapagos Islands. As we left the Gulf of Panama behind and headed out into the Pacific it was too hot even for a shirt. At 10.30pm it was still roasting on board—even with all the hatches open to get breeze through the boat. It is around 850 miles from Panama to Santa Cruz (Galapagos) and we reckoned on five or six days of sailing. All vessels entering Galapagos are inspected by a diver to make sure they don't bring in unwanted sea life. There are many stories of yachts being sent back to sea to clean their hulls, so we'd spent hours cleaning the hull of barnacles and weed.

It was hard not to be mesmerized on deck at night—the phosphorescence as *Aretha* carves through the water leaves a wake of glittering color and complements the starry night sky. On one watch Caroline saw a whale close by the boat.

A little later the same night we were alerted to the sound of a small child as Willow rolled out of her lower bunk with a clonk. Within 30 seconds she and her toy bunny rabbit were fast asleep again. Lee cloth tied to hold her in, so little chance of a repeat. Getting back into sea routines after time on land always took a little while.

At 5°N, we were only 300 miles from the equator. The only sounds were the steady flow of the engine and the sea as we cut through the calm waters. Only 5 knots of breeze. Headsail furled. Main centered.

The heat was intense below deck at 10pm. We were in the doldrums—more technically known as the ITCZ (Inter Tropical Convergence Zone)—where the northern trade winds meet the southern trade winds, effectively cancelling each other out.

Our first visitor from Galapagos, a red-footed booby about 1 foot 6 inches long, landed on the bow, perching on the pulpit for the afternoon, not even batting an eyelid as we photographed it—content to just sit there, hitching a lift. Galapagos animals have no predators and are therefore fearless.

Caroline was teaching the children South American geography and biology. Bluebell and Columbus watched a Galapagos documentary, making pages of notes, becoming junior experts on the islands. Columbus had gradually become adept at writing at length.

I cooked a roast beef dinner with all the trimmings—a well-fed crew is a happy crew. All were sleeping soundly as I prepared to wake Bluebell to join me for watch. One night she chatted nonstop for two hours while we lay in the cockpit gazing at the stars, looking out for the Southern Cross, steering *Aretha* by our angle to Orion's Belt.

By the next night we were closing in on the equator, on the cusp of leaving the northern hemisphere for some time. There was not a breath of wind, the sea's surface flat and unbroken, the sky utterly cloudless and filled with stars and a half moon lighting up the entire picture.

There was a high level of excitement as we neared the equator, preparing for an age-old mariners' ceremony—presided over by King Neptune—called "crossing the line." I'm cast in the role of King Neptune (having crossed the equator before), dressed in finery with trident in hand. Each of the crew—none of whom had crossed before—will be tried for crimes: Caroline for her hatred of bread (she has a gluten allergy); Columbus for crimes against fish for catching so many; Bluebell for crimes against humanity for stinky feet; Nichola for crimes against chaos for being so organized; and Willow for toy crimes for leaving Lego out all over the boat. The bucket of food slops that had been collecting over the past two days would be dispensed over each crew member found guilty. Naturally all were found guilty—but as we were in the Galapagos National Park, food slops had to give way to buckets of sea water.

Galapagos and Beyond

Our anchorage on Isabela in the Galapagos Islands was surrounded by marine life—swimming and diving sea lions, penguins, pelicans, and blue-footed boobies diving from great heights to catch fish.

We explored the lava tunnels; we snorkeled with white-tipped reef sharks, turtles, and seahorses, seeing huge manta rays and colonies of blue-footed boobies and masked boobies. Over a week in the islands we saw hundreds of marine iguanas and giant tortoises at the Charles Darwin Research Center. We walked to the beach of Tortuga on Santa Cruz and played in the surf on a pristine beach. I still couldn't believe we'd sailed all the way there. Of course I knew about the Galapagos—but I had never really appreciated their significance for species diversity, and now, as our family's major milestone.

From Galapagos we faced the longest single passage in our adventure, a 3,200-mile ocean sail in one of the remotest parts of the world. The Pacific stretching in front of us was exciting and daunting in equal measure. This was the big one.

We were meant to leave the Galapagos with the World ARC fleet but on our final checks we found some minor problems with our rig and the steering that needed fixing. Rather than rush our repairs that night, we sought advice from Oyster, making our repairs in the morning in the calm of our anchorage. The racing me wanted to get going. The prudent me said we'd be crazy to set sail on our longest passage without doing all we could to be ready. Prudence won (as it always does at sea).

As our first day back at sea progressed, we saw whales a mile away—we could see the water spouts every minute or so—and tuna fishing boats, including a main ship and seven or eight smaller vessels like a mother duck and her ducklings. Although we departed a day behind the rest of the fleet, *Aretha* is a fast boat and we gradually started to overtake other sailboats, working our way back into the fleet.

We were still in the doldrums with constant wind shifts: big, confused seas coming from many directions; squalls with strong wind and intense rain; *Aretha*'s sails flogging and clanking violently depending on conditions—a damp boat and we got little sleep.

 Captain's Log, 06°00'S 96°32'W, March 8, 2015, Day 3, Galapagos to Marquesas Islands—Damage to the Mainsail

We are suddenly going slower and there is a flapping sound from on deck. I'm trying to get ready for a 4am call with the UK. *Aretha* won't wait and I have to go investigate immediately.

I look out of the hatch and can see the mainsail is limp and flogging. Instantly I know we have done some damage and can see we have ripped our mainsail. This is not good news. Our mainsail is the primary power force for sailing *Aretha*. Without it, sailing becomes very slow.

The phone rings for my call. I answer and have to break off immediately to go fix the sail. I wake Nichola as I will need help. She wakes instantly and is quickly kitted to go on deck.

It's dark and I put the deck and boom lights on to assess the damage and work out what has happened. I can see the back end of the mainsail near the end of the boom is unattached and flying like a flag in the wind. From a position at the stern I can see the grommet on the clew has ripped out. (The clew grommet is the heavy-duty metal ring that is sewn into the lower aft corner of the mainsail, used to tighten the sail to the end of the boom.)

I figure we can still sail *Aretha* for now—the answer is to reef the sail, reducing the main in size and using the clew reefing line as the outhaul.

Nichola is on deck and operates the sail controls from the cockpit while I clip on and go to the mast to reef the sail. Without any pressure the sail comes down easily and we quickly reef. It's a relief to have a sail we can use and we get underway in time for me to rejoin my call.

Call finished, I go back on deck as the light comes up to figure out what has happened and what we need to do to fix things. I can feel spots of rain and quickly check the radar—we are surrounded by three squalls and change course to dodge the worst of the wind and rain.

We figure it's the flogging sails in the doldrums that have caused the clew to rip out. Every time the mainsail flogs you can feel the loads on the kit and you know it's not doing it any good. We have to take great care of *Aretha* and make sure everything is in good order. We have 2,500 miles to go on this passage alone and every bit of kit is vital. We decide that rather than repair the sail now we will press on until we have lighter winds.

Aretha was now continually lurching, making everything on board harder—cooking, cleaning, schoolwork, sleeping. We all had to adjust. Life below deck remained sweltering hot and the children didn't like sleeping in their cabins; by morning there were usually three small bodies draped around the saloon on the cushions, reminiscent of the sea lions in Galapagos.

Still, we continued to rattle off the miles, moving up through the World ARC fleet. As we reached the midway point of the passage we held a party on *Aretha*. Bluebell and Columbus appeared in fancy dress as rock stars, making sure we had music rocking the boat. Bluebell had carefully planned a series of games including musical statues, tomato ketchup, an animal noises snap-type game, and a dancing competition, as well as performing her own song. The kids had baked chocolate cookies and we celebrated the occasion. These small celebrations were important aboard; everyone loved being involved. Willow added energy, bouncing around dancing throughout.

Seasickness was thankfully a thing of the past now—Nichola and the children all had the demeanor of folks who'd spent lifetimes at sea. The movement of the boat and doing things in our world were second nature. Sometimes it seemed strange to live in such a confined space 24 hours a day, and because of the constant energy of the children, I appreciated the solitude and peacefulness of the night watches. But we all got on exceptionally well and had adjusted to life aboard. Nichola and I got to spend time talking, sharing ideas, and making plans for the future—it was a privilege to have this much time together and was one of the highlights of our adventure. We learned more about ourselves. When I was peeved with something, Nichola would gently ask me if I had a pebble in my shoe. It was a great way to break the pattern—irritations rarely lasted long.

We were getting regular reports of the devastation caused by the cyclone in Vanuatu, one of our planned stops farther across the Pacific. Far-off places become incredibly real when you know you'll be there in a couple of months. Our thoughts turned to how we could help on arrival. One island had no fresh water and had resorted to drinking sea water. We realized that with something as simple as our watermaker we could be a source of aid.

Meanwhile, life on board *Aretha* continued. A pod of short-finned pilot whales swam alongside us one day, surfacing to play for a short while. David, a math professor friend from another boat, sent us math challenges by email that we worked through with the children. We had a day of running the radio net for the fleet, recording the position and weather conditions for each boat and then conducting evening roll call to check that everyone was OK. There were many hundreds of miles between the first and last boats, so we relied on a series of relays on the SSB. We were probably one of the chattier boats on the net, asking other boats how they were doing catching fish, or offering recipes for banana bread muffins.

Our involvement with the internet businesses had reduced to the point where we'd get the weekly update emails and then a once a month call to make sure everything was OK. We'd check if we were needed, too. Invariably, we weren't.

By Day 14 of this passage the breeze had died. We were sailing 3 knots with just the genoa hoisted. It was sweltering below deck and the sails were clanking. Fresh food supplies were running low—1½ onions left. No tomatoes or salad. Meat all gone—just rice, pasta, and tinned food. We certainly wouldn't starve but were fantasizing about fresh food.

Then, again, we were in the Pacific, 630 miles from land in a beautiful blue ocean with millions of stars overhead. We were now closer to New Zealand than Grenada.

Having Caroline with us was a great success. It was wonderful to see Bluebell, Columbus, and Willow looking forward to their lessons each morning. They called her "Miss West" during school time, arrived in the saloon with pencil cases and books ready, and insisted she call the roll, which didn't take long with just three students.

We brought along some great sailing books designed for children (published by the RYA—Royal Yachting Association—see the Resources section), full of quizzes, puzzles, and other interesting approaches that taught the children about sailing techniques and parts of the boat. We also started giving them homework that they could do later in the day, usually in the evening when we had the SSB radio net. We developed new writing prompts: the children now had the responsibility of recording comments about what they were reading, which were collected in and marked at the end of each week. We also gave them notebooks to record interesting words for later use in their writing. As we went along we continually developed new teaching approaches, incorporating the children's interests to best engage them in learning.

Willow loved school time. She insisted on getting her schoolbooks ready and joining in. After starting with a coloring book she progressed to books where she could trace out numbers or recognize shapes to color. She absolutely loved all books, having inherited plenty from both Bluebell and Columbus as well as quite a few new additions. Occasionally if she couldn't find anyone to read to her, she'd pretend to read the story to herself, then make us feel bad by saying, "It's OK, I read the story to myself, there was no one to read to me."

The Value of Routine

With schooling and the radio net, each day crossing the Pacific had a structure. We changed our watch system every five days, allowing the adults to rotate cooking breakfast, lunch, or dinner, all offered at set times. We also took turns cleaning up, which meant that galley duties were shared evenly. During school hours Nichola and I completed boat jobs, such as rig checks. It's not only children that like a routine, adults respond well too. *Aretha* was calm, happy, and relaxed.

The children also enjoyed baking cakes, muffins, and cookies. Usually Bluebell took charge and let Columbus assist. On one occasion they even set up a shop to sell the goodies to the rest of the boat.

We made landfall in the Marquesas at 5.30am on March 24, 2015 after 3,200 miles and 20 days at sea. It was stunning to see mountains rising out of the sea and to smell the rich vegetation and moisture as we approached land. This tiny group of islands with its high mountains and lush vegetation is distinctly French, having been colonized in the late 1800s. The Marquesas Islands form one of the five administrative divisions of French Polynesia. Its history is steeped in cannibalism, referred to as the "land of the long pig." There had been reports of a cannibalism incident within the past four years so we also approached with some trepidation.

Our friends on *Makena*, who had arrived several days earlier, helped us by taking our stern anchor as we anchored in Traitors Bay in Hiva Oa. While anchoring we saw a huge manta ray jump clean out of the water. Garlands, fresh fruit, and lemonade met us ashore, as did the agent who arranged for our entry. The informality of customs and immigration contrasted sharply with the mountain of paperwork and forms required for Galapagos and Panama. Hiva Oa's population is around 2,000 people; a warm and friendly spot—the locals full of advice and help.

The main village was 2 miles from the quay. I had to visit the doctor on our first day, and another patient, Joseph, whom I chatted with in the office, drove me back to the boat. The village was tiny—one bar, one doctor, three shops, two banks—and yet was the largest settlement in the Marquesas. Life was relaxed and laid back; no one was in a hurry. We were deeply touched by the warmth of the people, like nothing we'd experienced before—threats of cannabalism vanished.

On two mornings Nichola and I went running at 6am. It was a true pleasure to watch the sunrise and appreciate the beauty of the islands— mountainsides covered in lush green, the peaks (sharp jagged rocks) tipped with clouds: calm, peaceful, and spiritual. One day we went horseback riding with a local guide, Pakou—just Nichola, me, and a young French couple on their honeymoon (tourists via plane were extremely rare). For four hours, we walked, trotted, and galloped through ancient forests, along mountain ridges. It was extreme riding so we had to be alert; neither of us were experienced on horses so the challenge was exhilarating. The views from the ridges were stunning—over untouched and ancient lands.

On our last evening in Hiva Oa, the locals hosted an evening on the quay for all the sailors, with buffet including *poisson cru* (raw fish marinated in coconut milk with vegetables), breadfruit, and other delicacies. The undisputed highlight of the evening was Marquesan warriors performing their tribal war rituals to the rhythm of fast beating drums. The strength, power, and grace of these islanders is so mesmerizing you can see why their reputation as fearsome warriors extends beyond their shores.

We continued westward the next day in sunny, light sailing conditions to the Bay of Virgins in Fatu Hiva. Again a huge manta ray jumped clean out of the water as we dropped anchor. We were reluctant to swim—some of the yachts reported fins—apparently the waters were full of great white, tiger, hammerhead, and gray sharks.

Ports of Interest—Hiva Oa, Marquesas

On a few afternoons in Hiva Oa we went to Alex's Place. Alex was ex French Foreign Legion and had been involved in the nuclear testing at Mururoa Atoll. His bar/house is high in the mountains and taxi drivers are unable to get their vehicles up the steep road, so the routine is to call Alex who collects you in his specially adapted off-road vehicle. Once at his home, you have open access to the bar and the pool—you just write down what you had and pay for it later. His wife cooks a meal if you're hungry and you pay a fixed price for whatever is offered—our favorite was carrot, mango, avocado salad with lemon—all sourced directly from their garden. Bluebell and Columbus quickly made friends with their daughter. When they brought us back to the boat on the last day the whole family came down to wave us off, plying us with bags of fresh lemons, avocados, and grapefruit.

We awoke early surrounded by mountains, inexpressibly beautiful. We attended the Palm Sunday service at the village church where we were quietly ushered in through a side door to sit up front with the local children. The passion and energy of the singing—accompanied by guitars and drums—sent a shiver down my spine.

We felt well, happy, and rested—without doubt, the Marquesas had cast their spell over us and overtook our previous stops as the number one destination in all our travels so far: visually stunning, low key, tribal, mystical, friendly. And relaxed.

Bluebell's Blog—Hiva Oa in the Marquesas Islands, March 31, 2015

I would like to tell you what we're doing in the Marquesas and what we're experiencing. The mountains are as high as a skyscraper, and as green as limes. I think that the Marquesas are the most jungle like and lush green of all the places we have visited. We are going to the waterfall, and I am very excited about it. The mountains are really steep and hard to get up.

On Palm Sunday we went to a Marquesian church. It was no bigger than a cottage, it was packed with people wearing white clothes. It was a Catholic church but still very different. We didn't understand what they were singing, but the way they were expressing their feelings in their singing was amazing.

One morning we saw dolphins. They were doing summersaults, like on trampolines in the Olympics, and they were teeny. In Hiva Oa we went to a house, and this man called Alex is the only one who can take you up there because it is so steep.

Alex has a daughter called Kohai, I played with her in the swimming pool there. FUN!!!!!!!!

I think that the Marquesas are adventurous, amazing, and the people are cheerful.

I love the Marquesas!!!!!!!!!!!!!!!!!!!!!!!!!!!

Going to School in the Kingdom of Sharks

After visiting Nuku Hiva, one of the northernmost Marquesas Islands, with its village with a French phone box plus a tiny Catholic chapel covered in red flowers, we anchored at nearby Daniel's Bay. Daniel's Bay is a rich paradise. It felt like the garden of Eden, pathways packed with copious quantities of fresh fruit—coconuts, bananas, mangoes, papayas, star fruit, and the huge sweet-tasting pamplemousse (grapefruit). With a boat laden with fresh produce bought from the local farmer, we sailed for the next four days and navigated our way to a lagoon anchorage in the coral atoll of Fakarava.

This spot is known as the Kingdom of Sharks. Stick your head underwater and you see why—sharks everywhere. On a dive outside the lagoon entrance I saw eight or ten sharks, curious and unnervingly swimming straight toward me.

In the protected pristine waters, we spent several days playing in kayaks, enjoying the lagoon's tranquility. The children all took to the small, easily rowed craft, Bluebell and Columbus totally at home paddling out to the bathing platforms supporting tiny huts with seats in the water. Willow was content lying face down on the bow of my kayak, paddling with her hands, pulling the kayak up the beach and then pushing it out to sea again, then jumping in. All of the children were now completely at home in and around the water.

We'd been there for a week, snorkeling and getting work done on *Aretha* by Fakarava Yacht Services (run by a young French couple who'd moved there several years before). We were chatting on the VHF radio with Stephanie, one half of the couple, as she explained that she and her husband would dinghy over to *Aretha* the following morning once they had dropped their children off at school. My ears pricked up straight away, sensing an opportunity. It turned out their children were similar ages to ours and the school was about 300 feet from the dinghy dock.

"Do you think it might be possible for our children to attend school as well for the day?" I asked. She paused for a moment then said she'd call the headmistress.

Several hours later, the VHF crackled.

"*Aretha, Aretha, Aretha*, this is Fakarava Yacht Services, Fakarava Yacht Services, over."

I grabbed the handset. Good news. We were invited the next morning. There were two caveats. One was that Caroline would go along to be with Willow (we'd just celebrated her third birthday and they were concerned she'd be upset at being left on her own). Two, the lessons would all be in French. I figured our kids were pretty resourceful and would work it out.

I broke the good news to the children. Willow couldn't have been more excited at the idea of going to school with the big children. Columbus was a little more muted. Bluebell made clear all the reasons why she didn't want to go to school! We were undeterred.

"We're making you packed lunches and school starts at 9am."

The next morning nothing had diminished Willow's enthusiasm—she was up first getting dressed for school. With the other two, I was reminded of crisp early September mornings in the UK, persuading them to get ready. Memories of my own back-to-school experiences came flooding in, briefly distracting me from the task at hand.

But the school bus was about to go: in this case, climbing down into the dinghy. Nichola, aware of the significance of Willow's first day at school, was a little quieter than usual and waved us off as I pulled the starter cord on the engine. As we neared the dock, we were treated to the sight of a huge manta ray swimming under the boat in 6 feet of water. Not your usual sight on the school run back in England. Lifejackets were left in the dinghy as we headed toward the school gates underneath the coconut trees. I reminded the children not to walk directly under the coconut trees. Falling coconuts kill a significant number of people every year.

We were early—Stephanie was not there yet. A handful of maybe 20 or so children were milling around the school gates. There is only one road in Fakarava—it snakes its way along the coral atoll from one end to the other. Cars are few and far between. Bikes are much more prevalent, although nothing is very far on this tiny outcrop in the middle of the Pacific. Other than the location it was like any morning waiting for school to open, hanging out by the school gates. Some children were playing soccer with a makeshift ball made from cardboard and I joined in, much to their amusement and to my children's embarrassment. Our children stood out with their blond hair—a stark contrast to the dark-haired Pacific islanders. The children were the source of much curiosity.

Stephanie arrived by bike with her two children pedaling behind her. She took us to find the headmistress, a warm, friendly woman who was open to our children joining the school for the day. Willow and Caroline would be in one class with the youngest children. Bluebell and Columbus would be together in another class. We gave the headmistress gifts of books and games—which she wasn't expecting. After her warm appreciation she called for a teacher who took Willow and Caroline off toward their classroom.

"Bye Daddy!" called Willow, trotting off full of excitement.

After leaving Columbus and Bluebell I walked down the street to shop for basics, enjoying the peace, quiet, and beauty of the locale, reflecting on what a great place it was for Willow's first day at school.

Nichola and I had a full day on board servicing, fixing, and checking *Aretha* with help from Andy and Emma of *Pentagram*. It's amazing how productive you can be without three children asking questions or making demands. Come mid-afternoon, I was back waiting at the school gates.

Willow ran out first, bouncing with energy, full of stories. They'd had lessons in how to brush teeth and had all been given toothbrushes. A trove of papers were thrust into my hand—all the drawings she'd done that day. Willow also proudly carried a book she was given—*Mon Ami, Le Raie* (translated as *My Friend, The Ray*).

Bluebell was surrounded by a group of girls, all new friends. Columbus came out twisting his Rubik's Cube, a small group of fascinated boys in tow. The older children had enjoyed the day although they'd struggled with the language a little. All three had felt very welcome. This tiny corner of the world would carry lasting memories for all of us. We closed off the school day by walking to the supermarket for ice cream before the short dinghy ride back to *Aretha* to share all the stories of the day again with Nichola.

We spent the whole next week in Fakarava: the quintessential island paradise. Photos don't come close to conveying the peace and tranquility there. Yet it was actually the busiest of the atolls: two shops, two churches, one school, and one hotel, plus a couple of pearl farms growing the famous black Tahitian pearls. A supply ship came once a month—after that it's back to coconuts, breadfruit, and fish.

During our time there Fakarava saw the launch of two new businesses—Columbus Killer Lures and Bluebell's Bread Delivery. We had great fun planning these ventures with the kids, creating their products, working out pricing and margins, then marketing their offers. Bluebell's service charged $1 per boat for bread delivery on top of the bread costs. Her product extension was rubbish removal for $1 also—potentially $2 a day per boat and with 10 boats per anchorage she was earning dollars that were meaningful for her. Both children made sales, learning to gather testimonials for their marketing collateral. They were loving it as well as learning from it.

We had been at sea or at anchor since Panama—two months—completely self-sufficient: making our own water and creating our own electricity courtesy of our watermaker and generator. This self-sufficiency felt good and yet we looked forward to the security of a marina in Tahiti. Made famous by Captain Cook and the mutiny on the *Bounty*, Tahiti, the largest island in French Polynesia, a bustling metropolis of 130,000 people steeped in history, was our next stop.

Distances seemed to shrink now. We were more than halfway across the Pacific Ocean—it was 4,500 miles back to Panama and only 3,000 miles to Australia. The voyage of 250 miles from Fakarava to Tahiti now seemed a tiny hop. The miles glided by underneath us in this beautiful and empty ocean. Seeing any other vessels at sea was extremely rare.

A Birthday, and the Stolen Dinghy

Bluebell's birthday was on April 21 while we were in Tahiti. She was excited that her Grandad Laurie was coming to visit for a week. The fact that Laurie arrived with bags full of books and chocolate further increased excitement. Her birthday celebrations were a simple affair on board with the birthday flags draped around *Aretha* and all of our friends coming over for birthday cake and drinks while we sang Happy Birthday.

We had a super week with Laurie exploring the Tahiti Museum (more school projects for the children) and visiting the island of Moorea where Captain Cook anchored. A highlight of Bluebell's birthday was swimming with dolphins in Moorea—one of the things that Bluebell had been most excited about for the whole adventure. The dolphins were unbelievably tame, calm, and curious—a truly magical experience that none of us will ever forget (see plate section, image 21).

On another outing Columbus and I took the dinghy out to the pass between two small *motus* (the local name for small island) in front of us. Paul, Andrew, and Jeanette from *Juno* were in their dinghy. We snorkeled on beautiful coral and were sped through the pass quickly by the current as we drift snorkeled, holding on to the dinghy—lots of coral, fish, and a huge Moray eel in the middle of some fire coral. Columbus continued to thrive in this world and was a goldmine of information. He snorkeled with his laminated fish spotter cards. It was all finished off by tea and fruitcake on board *Juno*.

While moored in Marina Taina in Tahiti, Nichola, after a lovely evening out, managed to slip while boarding *Aretha*, gashing her knee against the harbor wall. Stoic throughout, she was hanging on to the davits to stop herself from falling in—we rescued her and despite her insistence it just needed Steri-Strips, on first pass it looked in need of something more substantial. While at sea, I'd be pressed into action with the medical training from our nine-day Ship's Doctor's course we did in Hamble the previous spring. On this occasion I had a better plan—we'd had supper with Luis and Manuela on board *Allegro*—one of the other boats on the World ARC. Luis was previously a surgeon working in the emergency room of a hospital, Manuela was a cardiologist. You couldn't ask for a better combination and within three minutes they were on board and working through our assorted medical kits for iodine, anesthetic, the stitching kit, and so on. With an assembled team of onlookers, it wasn't long before Nichola was down below in our makeshift operating theater and Luis was expertly stitching her up, headlamp on—fanned by Caroline from *Juno* to take the edge off the sweltering heat. Stitches completed and leg bandaged, blood cleaned off the deck, and all was back to normal.

One of the great things about being in Tahiti was the modern facilities there—in particular the huge French Carrefour supermarket stocked with a vast array of Western foods. What always comes with increased civilization though is an increase in crime. We'd not been exposed to this in all the islands we'd visited so far. We were about to get a small reminder.

We were just going through our final preparations to leave and cast our lines off to head west to the island of Raiatea. Just before leaving I went to hoist the dinghy onto the davits. You know those heart-stopping moments when something isn't where it should be? Yes, that. The dinghy that had been tied to the side of the boat was no longer there. The dinghy is such a vital bit of kit—without it we'd struggle since in many places we needed to anchor and move about by dinghy.

I ran over in my mind what could have happened. It was there before and then it wasn't.

Two minutes passed while I figured out what to do. At that point my eyes wandered to the dinghy dock 165 feet away. I saw a familiar engine on a dinghy. I raced along the quay and sure enough there was our tender—the oars in rowlocks, the boat partially full of water with a red t-shirt and black baseball hat on the floor, completely soaked. This was some mystery.

I spoke to the friendly captain of the large motor launch next to us. He told me that another dinghy was stolen off the davits from a catamaran anchored 330 feet away, and an apartment nearby was also broken into overnight. It seemed these events were all connected.

Our engine can be difficult to start without the right technique and I wondered if this is what had saved us. My best guess is they (whoever they were) stole our dinghy and tried to start it. They couldn't start it and so ended up rowing back to the dinghy dock (hence the oars out) and then perhaps swam over and stole the other dinghy. I was grateful for small blessings, and that they left our dinghy tied up is one of them. We reported the events to the marina manager and local *gendarme* (police) and with that we slipped lines and left Tahiti, motoring out through the coral pass with surf breaking literally 165 feet on either side.

Chapter 13

The Mesmerizing Heart of the Pacific Ocean

The Society Islands

(April 2015 to May 2015)

After Tahiti we sailed the 150 miles to Raiatea, one of the Society Islands in this array of gemstones of far-flung French Polynesia, the heart of the Pacific. These are little explored wildernesses of magical islands, with vibrant Polynesian culture and rituals, ukulele music, fast-moving hips dancing to a unique rhythm, home to warm friendly islanders. Utter magic on every level. We were to learn that magic spells, however, can also create a disappearing act, at times.

I'd taken time out to participate in a three-day race known as the Pearl Regatta with Paul and Caroline on *Juno*—the first real competitive short-distance racing I'd done on the trip.

The race was keen tactical sailing, windward beats with shifting winds, navigating lagoons, tacking duels through narrow passes—a stark reminder of the differences between sailing a race boat and sailing with young children: chalk and cheese. We had some truly memorable evening events after the racing, including dancing by magnificently tattooed warriors and lithe hip-shaking women. It was a magical final evening on an island the size of three football fields under a full moon with a sky full of stars. We raced back that day, finishing inside the reef under full sail, screaming along at breakneck speed. Magnificent stuff. I was buoyant and buzzing as I returned to *Aretha*.

The contrast on *Aretha* couldn't have been more stark—it looked like a bomb had exploded: dishes piled high, TV on, listless children and clothes strewn around the boat. I found Nichola in our cabin—looking shattered and feverish. When I'd left *Aretha* three days earlier Bluebell was under the weather but it hadn't been enough to warrant major concern, and Nichola was in good spirits, doing well. Now Bluebell was hot, sweating, and very uncomfortable. Willow and Columbus were running Nichola ragged. They hadn't been off the boat since I left and although we were inside the reef, boats regularly zoomed past, making life uncomfortable as *Aretha* bounced around in their wakes. To compound the issues, getting on and off *Aretha* wasn't easy: climb down her stern into the dinghy, pull the dinghy toward the jetty/quay using the mooring lines, then climb up to the jetty. Not impossible but tricky with small kids who aren't in top form. The excitement and highs of three days of racing quickly evaporated.

A Scare in the South Pacific

I called Victor, our rally liaison, to tell him we needed a doctor. Within the hour he let me know the name and number of a French physician who could see us. It was late on Saturday evening. Nichola and I decided we'd give it one more night then take Bluebell to the doctor in the morning if she hadn't improved. We encouraged her to drink water, cooling her with damp flannels, making her as comfortable as we could.

We all had a broken night's sleep. By 6am Bluebell hadn't improved and was in a lot of pain. Time to get help. Victor arranged for us to go straight to the doctor's office. I encouraged Nichola to stay in bed to recuperate as she was still running a fever. With Bluebell clinging to me, we navigated the tricky route off *Aretha*—over the stern, through the dinghy, and onto the jetty. She was too weak to walk so I carried her—whimpering and hot—in my arms. The roads were empty. We walked for what felt like an age—one village street looking much like another as we tried to find the landmarks near the clinic.

Finally we arrived, climbing the stairs to the reception. There was a small queue awaiting the doctor. The receptionist booked us in, my school French just getting us by. We waited for what felt like an eternity.

Eventually we saw the doctor, who looked in his late 60s—old school. I tried to explain what was wrong with Bluebell. Instead of examining her, he showed me iPhone photos of him skiing in France. I wasn't sure whether to walk out or persist. After several minutes, he made a phone call. He was speaking fast and I couldn't understand what he was saying. He put the phone down and opened his door to call his receptionist into his room. She explained that it would be better to take Bluebell to see a pediatric specialist at the local hospital. She gave me directions and we headed off again in the direction of the hospital.

Two doctors, who thankfully spoke excellent English, met us. They exuded a calm, quiet confidence. We were in good hands. We were ushered into a room where I lowered a weak and tearful Bluebell onto the bed. They needed blood tests. I was asked to hold the gas and air to calm Bluebell while they inserted a cannula. The last time I assisted with gas and air was for Nichola at Bluebell's birth ten years earlier. After providing blood samples Bluebell was hooked up to a saline drip and IV paracetamol to replace fluids and reduce her temperature.

The doctor's suspicion was dengue fever; there had been occurrences of the mosquito-borne disease in French Polynesia. The results of blood tests took an hour and confirmed that there was no bacterial infection and it was viral—they were 70 percent sure it was dengue but we had to wait for the blood to be analyzed in Tahiti to be sure.

There is nothing to treat dengue fever; it takes 5–6 days to work its way through, while fluids and paracetamol are administered. We were on day 5 of Bluebell's illness, so hoped the virus would pass through her soon. Once I had Bluebell settled I fetched Nichola. When she arrived, the doctor suspected that Nichola had the flu and advised she also take fluids and paracetamol.

Bluebell and Nichola started bouncing back several days later with no obvious side effects. The scare reinforced the importance of being vigilant with mosquito repellent and nets. We were heading into areas where malaria—also transmitted by mosquitoes—was more prevalent.

Tropical Illness Prevention

There are no vaccines for dengue fever or malaria. The best course of action is prevention. We were careful, using mosquito repellent, covering up our bodies, burning anti-mosquito coils, and using electric plug-in mosquito repellents. We had anti-malaria tablets for areas of the world with malaria. We avoided visiting areas with stagnant pools of water that encourage mosquitoes. We read up on the latest medications, we researched the best repellents to use and clothing to wear, even what perfumes, shampoos, etc., to avoid. We had mosquito nets in every cabin and we made sure they were used every night. We also had mosquito net inserts for each window/opening in the boat.

Good News from Home—Closing the Chapter on My Business

At Trovus, we had built up a blue chip list of clients, an excellent team of people, as well as a set of processes and intellectual property that we had developed over the years. At the same time, Ed and I had initiated discussions with two global corporations who were interested in buying the business. When we sailed from England, I felt that Trovus had been left in the best possible hands, confident it would thrive with the team Ed and I had created.

Ed and I had spoken regularly once *Aretha* had departed. Contact included dialing in for monthly board meetings as well as one-on-one calls where we shared ideas on the sale. As we sailed the Atlantic we had two offers to buy the business. Discussions deepened and by the time *Aretha* had entered the Pacific we had selected a preferred bidder and were now negotiating the terms of the sale.

It felt surreal sitting below deck negotiating sale and purchase agreements with Ed and our lawyers on the satellite phone while *Aretha* surfed down the backs of large ocean waves at 12 knots on a dark windy night between the Galapagos and the Marquesas. My old world was colliding with my current world. Discussions were usually brief and to the point—dictated by the cost of the satellite calls, lawyers' fees, and my need to turn my attention back to *Aretha*. Our lawyers were always amused by the uniqueness of the situation, requesting location updates at the start of each call.

Before we left, many fellow entrepreneurs said that there was no way they could have left their business as I did. I think the best thing I did for my business was to assemble a team of brilliant people, work with Ed and the team to define the vision and the culture, and then get out of the way to let the team do what they were brilliant at.

Our discussions and negotiations culminated with the sale of Trovus to a large South African group, Datatec, on May 1, 2015. It was an incredible moment. The feeling of achievement and the closing of one chapter of my life meant more than just the money. Ed and I had done what we had set out to do—create, build, and sell a successful business that truly provided value to our customers.

The date of the sale exactly coincided with our 11th wedding anniversary. We had just arrived in Bora Bora and celebrated at the famous Bloody Mary's restaurant. A board outside the restaurant lists celebrities who have dined there—Leonardo DiCaprio, Gwyneth Paltrow, *et al*. I couldn't imagine a better place to celebrate both the end of one chapter of our lives and our ongoing—nine months by then—family adventuring aboard *Aretha*.

Bora Bora

We arranged an outing to swim in the crystal clear waters around Bora Bora with turtles, Moray eels, stingrays, and sharks. The stingrays came right up alongside, flapping their wings while lemon sharks, nurse sharks, and black-tipped reef sharks swam all around. Bluebell took a little coaxing to join me in the water. Columbus was in within minutes with our energetic, friendly guide. A few minutes later the guide called me over—there was Columbus underwater grabbing a tow on the fin of a 10-foot nurse shark—absolutely in his element (see plate section, image 22).

Back to Raiatea

After Bora Bora we returned to Raiatea for the continuation of the World ARC rally.

We continued to connect with exceptional people with fascinating backgrounds and stories. On one hike up a lush green French Polynesian mountain, I spent the day walking with Pete, formerly a high-ranking US Navy officer, in his seventies. Pete had the energy and drive of a man in his twenties—and an encyclopedic knowledge of aircraft carriers, as I was to find out. His curiosity, thirst for learning, and regime of staying physically active was a clear formula for continued good health in old age.

It had been a couple of weeks since we'd said goodbye to Caroline. Tahiti was as far as Caroline had planned to sail with us. In the three months she was aboard she had become part of the family. We loved having her as part of Team *Aretha*. She would be missed on many levels—for her calm authority with the children, her easy-going nature and conversations, and her excellent skills in the galley. The children enjoyed having her around and her patient and engaging schooling would be missed by all of us. It took a few weeks for us to adjust to life again with just the five of us; it would be many months later, midway across the Indian Ocean, that we had other crew join *Aretha*.

We left French Polynesia with many happy memories, with Bluebell fully recovered from dengue fever, with Nichola fever-free and the stitches removed from her knee. It was just the five of us on board for the offshore passage. We had received and declined many kind offers from people offering to crew—but the decision to sail this part of the Pacific on our own felt right. Our vision was to experience life together as a family unit; with considerable experience under our belt working together as a team, we wanted to sail alone.

We played and laughed on deck—it felt much like Sunday afternoon in our London living room. The autopilot alarm beeped, signaling another wind shift and the need to trim sails. The lights on Maupiti were bright against the pitch black. The only sounds were those of

Aretha carving through the water and the gurgle of the waves as we slipped through the warm Pacific. It was dry and a perfect temperature: shorts, t-shirt, and lifejacket only on deck. Trouser-wearing days seemed long ago.

Suwarrow—A Deserted Pacific Island

From Raiatea most of our friends on other sailboats made the decision to sail directly to Niue (an island country east of Tonga). Five boats, including us, decided to sail an extra three days to reach Suwarrow, one of the tiniest islands in the Pacific.

We arrived through squalls—30 knots of wind plus torrential rain. I wasn't fully dressed (to say the least) when they hit yet we needed someone at the helm. I only had time to put on one item—and safety won, so I spent the next hour at the helm in the driving rain wearing only a lifejacket. Liberating is a word that springs to mind.

We picked our way slowly through the coral reefs to enter the lagoon, Nichola and Columbus on the bow signaling whether to turn to port or starboard. Dark blue is deep water, light blue is shallow water—watch out, brown is coral. The bow thrusters were switched on, ready to turn the bow one way or the other to dodge the coral.

"Welcome to Suwarrow"—the radio crackled on Channel 16 as the warden welcomed us. Harry and his wife were the island's only residents, except for the cohorts of black-tipped reef sharks swimming everywhere—Columbus counted just shy of 60 within 15 minutes of arriving. The water was a glorious crystal blue with perfect coral. We'd been to many stunning places but Suwarrow made everything before seem busy and commercial. No lights, no cars, no hustle, no bustle: tranquility and beauty. For the first evening we simply stayed on board *Aretha*, watching the stars, listening to the waves crash against the reef. After days of sailing through squalls, the gentle stillness was lovely.

I woke at 5.30 to watch the sunrise in peace on deck; no movement apart from the frigate birds circling the skies and the reef sharks swimming round the boat.

Harry, an extremely affable, powerful looking Cook Islander in a rugby shirt, arrived early to clear us in. We offered him fresh coffee and toast as we imagined that living there he had limited resources, but he said he'd already had porridge and tea. We spent an hour or so going through our clearance and immigration papers, getting the lowdown on the island. He said swimming was fine: "But watch out for the gray sharks and the tiger sharks—if you see any, swim calmly back to the boat and get out of the water." We'd be staying out of the water.

We motored to the little pier, allowing the dinghy to gently ground on the coral. There was a buzz of adventurer excitement as we landed. Columbus—in his Tilley hat, rucksack holding his fish- and shell-spotting books, a small fishing net, snacks, and water—looked every inch the explorer.

The beach was rough and bright with brilliant white coral, hermit crabs scurrying everywhere, fallen coconuts sprouting new shoots. The vegetation was thick and the trees full of coconuts. Based on what Harry told us, we estimated that no more than 300 people a year visited Suwarrow. We walked to the other side of the island, stopping at Pylades Bay to take it all in—the coral reef, fish and sharks swimming round, frigate birds and terns, coconut crabs scurrying along the beach with their strong bright colors. Willow delighted in finding rock pools to sit and splash in, cooling off. It was warm but breezy. We returned to the dinghy, motoring around the edge of the coral reef, spotting fish and glorious coral heads towering up off the seabed.

On the beach in Suwarrow we stopped to take photos by a sign with arrows: 9,500 miles to London, 5,200 miles to Panama, 1,850 miles to Auckland, 2,800 miles to Sydney (see plate section, image 23). We had journeyed far—we were very remote indeed on that tiny dot in the middle of the Pacific Ocean.

Back on *Aretha*, Nichola and I set the children to watch a film while we sat on deck with cold drinks, pausing to reflect on our journey. It was almost nine months since we left and we'd come so far—not just miles but in so many ways. We were happy, content, and enjoying working in harmony as a family team. There had been ups and downs but we were proud of what we'd managed, experienced, and learned. Instead of limiting our lives with the many reasons not to sail around the world we had found one good Reason Why we wanted to do it—to create magical life-changing experiences for us and our children. We were certainly doing that. And we weren't even halfway around the world.

Back in the UK, in my sister's garden on that day the sailing trip was first conceived, I don't think either of us had any idea what was in store for our relationship: how much it would be tested, how much we would learn, how much we would grow, how deep the lows would feel, how high the highs would soar. Our relationship above all else had been my single biggest source of joy—and pain. That bond took us to the edge and back again.

Reflecting on Our Relationship

As mentioned in Part One, before conceiving our trip Nichola and I were like many other couples navigating the usual stresses and strains of daily life. I was working long hours; Nichola was juggling the childcare, running our home, and managing her own part-time work. The time that we made for each other was minuscule, squeezed out by everything else.

Where was the time and energy for us? We had time enough to argue. Making time and paying attention to each other was not our priority. When I raised the subject with Nichola—let's go find an expert so we can figure out how to communicate better to avoid the arguments—her first reaction was reluctance, but I persisted. So, in late 2007, Nichola and I had spent several months with a relationship coach.

Over the following years, while we planned our family sailing adventure, we reinforced what we'd learned from that coach, attending courses and seminars about getting more out of life and understanding our own behaviors. There was so much to discover about self-awareness, communication, and getting greater enjoyment from life. One of the results of this work was the knowledge that during our sailing trip we wanted to help our children understand self-motivation: explore underlying beliefs and values, why we do things, what drives us, what causes things to happen in our lives.

Of course Nichola and I still have our disagreements, just like any couple. The difference for us now is that they seldom last long. We have the tools and the understanding to see these arguments for what they are, to not get caught up in the emotions, instead recognizing the emotions at play, talking about them, and moving on. We had to develop emotionally. We wouldn't have survived if we hadn't. And one continued take away was the desire to help our own children develop emotionally.

Chapter 14

Power Plays in the Pacific
Suwarrow to Niue

(May 2015)

Developing self-awareness, as well as understanding and learning how we all worked best together as a team, was crucial to the success of our adventure. This was tested 500 miles from land in the Pacific when we suffered a complete power failure aboard *Aretha*.

We cleared out of customs on Suwarrow on the morning of May 18, 2015, motoring out of the narrow passage on our own. Immediately we were confronted by a strong wind blowing against a tidal current, creating rough seas. We had 4 knots of current beneath us and 25 knots of wind on the nose. The seas banked up, *Aretha* crashed off the wavetops and into the troughs—sea water streaming over the bow, pouring down her topsides. Nichola and Columbus, who had been on coral watch on the bow, beat hasty retreats aft, joining me in the cockpit as we powered through the waves. Coral reefs flanked *Aretha* with just 10 feet beneath the keel at one point. The conditions kept us focused—we all heaved a sigh of relief when the swells finally flattened as the depth quickly increased to hundreds of feet.

We motored round north of Turtle Island and hoisted sails as we headed west and south past Suwarrow, setting a course to Niue 550 miles away. We were in good company—our friends on *Hugur* and *Ayama* had left a few hours ahead of us; *Garlix* and *Exody* were leaving a couple of hours after us. We tuned in to the SSB radio net in the early evening to hear the news of the fleet sailing directly to Niue. They reported gales in excess of 50 knots—in one case 60 knots—conditions we needed to prepare for. Aggressive squalls laden with rain and wind were hitting the fleet with some ferocity.

We settled in for the night—at this point we had only 15 knots of wind and were sailing comfortably with full main and full headsail—making good progress. As the first squall came with driving rain, the wind rattled up to 25 knots. We held our sail configuration for 5 minutes to see if the squall would pass, bearing away, sailing downwind. Our speed accelerated—we were quickly surfing along at 10–11 knots—fast, wet sailing. The wind showed no signs of abating so we decided to reduce sail.

Reducing the headsail is easiest: bear away, ease the sheet, pull in the roller furling line. We did this and got a third of the sail in. So far, so good.

Reefing the main is more involved: use the autopilot to steer *Aretha*, while one cockpit crew handles the main halyard (the line that pulls the sail to the top of the mast) and the other crew is at the mast hauling down the main while operating the reefing lines. Nichola and I jumped into action like a well-oiled machine—Nichola on the halyard from the safety of the cockpit, me at the mast. Our communication was good and clear and within two minutes I was safely back in the cockpit. We had two reefs in the mainsail—prepared for winds up to 30–35 knots.

We sailed through the night at fast speeds, enjoying 30-knots winds with driving rain. All was well and comfortable on board *Aretha*.

Not for long.

By mid-morning we were settled into the day's routines. The batteries were down to 65 percent—time to run the generator, recharging for the day. I pressed the generator's glow button, letting it run for 10 seconds before pressing start. The generator fired into action—15 seconds later it coughed, spluttered, strained, and stopped; never a good sign. We tried restarting three or four times—the same thing.

We had two ways to charge *Aretha*'s batteries—via the generator or the engine. OK, we said, we need power so let's run the engine for a while, topping the batteries up while we fix the generator.

I started the engine—it ran for a minute, then strained, coughed, and stopped. Four more attempts yielded the same result.

Things were definitely not looking good—we had over 450 miles to go in gale force winds with no electrical power. We needed a plan, and we needed it fast.

To give you a sense of the importance of electricity aboard *Aretha*, here's the list of gear requiring electrical power:

- autopilot (without autopilot you need to hand steer the boat 24 hours a day)
- chartplotter (including our electronic charts and navigation software)
- electric winches
- lights, in particular navigation lights (mast head, port and starboard, bow and stern)
- radio (VHF and SSB)
- AIS (enables other boats to see *Aretha* on their chartplotters)
- toilets
- taps to draw fresh water or drain water out
- fridge/freezer
- watermaker
- bilge pumps
- stove (our gas/propane stove has a solenoid that switches it on)
- satellite phones and computers.

No power was not good news. However, we did have backup paper charts, a sextant, a spare battery-operated GPS (two of them), handheld battery-operated VHF radio, flashlights, battery-operated navigation lights, and a set of sails—with plenty of wind power—that we could work manually without electric winches; that and a ton of food and water. Theoretically we could be at sea for a month and not worry— we'd bobble around and sooner or later we'd make landfall and come in under sail. Captain Cook would have found this positively luxurious!

Thinking fast, we drew up two plans:

Plan A—restore power and continue to sail comfortably with all systems.

Plan B—sail with no electrical power and make landfall safely.

The first step, though, was to buy time and let the rest of the fleet know our situation so we could get help if needed.

Buying Time

The fridge, the freezer, and all the lights were off. The toilets were shut down. The children were introduced to Billy Bucket—our new toilet. They found this hilarious and in no time were queuing up to test out the "bucket-and-chuck-it" system.

Usually our batteries were never allowed to drop below 60 percent charge for fear of damaging them—we had 5 percent left before we reached a level where the batteries might be compromised. Immediately we reduced our hourly power usage to 4 amps. I calculated that the lowest we could drop was 50 percent charge—that gave us 15 percent or 69 amps. At 4 amps an hour of electrical consumption we had 17 hours before we went completely dark, losing all power. If we hand steered, we could reduce the amps to 2 an hour—buying us 34 hours. We had roughly 400 miles to go. If we sailed 150 miles a day, it would take us 2.5 days. That's 60 hours. Not even close.

We sent out an email to our friends on *Juno* and the other boats nearby to let them know our predicament.

Plan A

With power consumption reduced to 4 amps, we started to troubleshoot. We tried the engine and generator again. It sounded like the engine was fuel-starved. We started with the engine and drained off the Racor water separator filter. This pointed to the same thing—the diesel drained off looked dirty: shades of our old friend dirty diesel experienced in Portugal nine months earlier. Surely this can't have come back again? The engine started after changing the fuel filter. I ran it in neutral at 1500 rpms for 1–2 minutes before it shut down and wouldn't start again.

We then changed the fuel and Racor filters on the generator. There was a good amount of black sludge sitting on top of the filter—the size of half a dozen peas slugged together. We checked the raw-water inlet (we found strands of seaweed). We changed the Racor, filled it with diesel, and pressed the glow button with the bleed switch open until fuel bubbled from the bleed switch. It made a sound as though it was half starting and then cut out.

Both the generator and the engine had been serviced in Fakarava four weeks earlier with new filters.

We took turns hand steering *Aretha* while reading the manuals and applying what we'd learned already from our dirty diesel experience. Meanwhile we had 30 knots of wind, rain, and heavy seas, *Aretha* crashing from one wave to another. We worked through the day and by 5pm we had 425 miles to go. We were tired and flagging. The children had been great, playing and reading, working well together with little complaint, largely enabling us to work. Now we needed to think, regroup, and rest.

Hove-to for the Night

I decided to heave-to—i.e., tack the boat but leave the headsail backed, effectively stalling the boat. This tactic left *Aretha* in a stable, balanced position so we could ride out the storm. My stepfather, Paul, taught me this in his boat *Blue Dragon*, a Contessa 32, years ago off the South Devon coast, where we'd heave-to to eat lunch while the boat stayed as steady as a rock. It's a maneuver you can't get easily from a textbook—you have to experience it before you truly understand it. Once hove-to, a sailboat does not need anyone at the helm—the sails are balanced and the boat slowly makes its way along, usually slightly to leeward.

Aretha, once hove-to, settled down. Oysters are well designed (some modern cruisers don't heave-to well) and finely built—rock-solid, ocean-going sailboats. We powered down everything to preserve amps and ran a night watch between Nichola and me to keep a lookout for shipping. Sitting there with no lights or AIS was a vulnerable situation so we needed to be alert. If we saw a vessel we'd switch on AIS and navigation lights, then call them on the VHF. I wrote an email to Eddie, our customer care manager at Oyster, explaining our situation in detail and asking for advice.

I slept fitfully. By 7am when the sun came up the wind was still howling but we were stable and a little restored by some rest.

Oyster World-Class Support

At first light I checked our emails and Eddie had replied—even though he was actually on annual leave. Eddie's email was practical, specific, and encouraging.

After breakfast we set to work disassembling all the fuel lines—cleaning each section by hand, changing filters, rodding the line through with wire—we even created our own pressure system using a dinghy pump with a Sikaflex nozzle over the end. Necessity, is, after all, the mother of invention.

We worked relentlessly—it was hot and the boat stank so badly of diesel that we kept the children in our cabin with the door shut. It was also the best place for the children to be—in the stern where there was less movement than in the bow. We couldn't open any portholes as waves were still pounding outside with the wind now up to 35 knots.

By 11am we'd cleaned the generator hoses and bled the engine, cracked open the injectors, and started the engine. It ran for a minute, then two minutes, then three. This was the longest we'd had so far. Have we fixed it—did we dare believe we'd solved it? We decided to stay put, just let the diesel run. We made lunch, waited. After an hour, we heard it strain, finally giving up. Our batteries were 50 amps higher than before but that was all. We tried everything we could think of but couldn't get the engine started again.

Plan B

We decided to revert to Plan B, hand steering to Niue. It was early afternoon and it was almost 18 hours since heaving-to. Time had literally flown.

When I switched on the navigation instruments my heart sank. We had been 425 miles from our destination when we'd stopped. While hove-to we'd drifted back 80 miles—half a day's sailing to make up for lost ground. But there was nothing to do but dig in and crack on.

I started to hand steer. We sailed on. It was still rough. Nichola joined me on deck. We debated whether to head for Niue or press on to

Tonga where they have a boatyard that could help us—as recommended by Eddie.

Nichola and I hand steered *Aretha* through heavy seas and driving rain for the next three days. We worked together as a team, finding the humor in our situation and playing to our strengths as we figured things one step at a time. We decided to head for Niue, to meet up with the fleet and get help fixing our engine.

It was hard work. I slept in the cockpit while Nichola steered, and I catnapped where/when I could. I rationalized this was child's play compared to the round-the-world solo sailors who do this for 80 days at a time in far worse conditions. When I steered I encouraged Nichola to go below to get proper rest.

On our final night, with 180 miles to Niue, head winds forced us to beat to windward—waves crashing over *Aretha*, our cockpit filling with water once in a while—certainly one way to wake yourself up. The kids were great—Bluebell in particular had come into her own looking after the other two, making sure they were read to and able to fall asleep.

We sailed hard, topping our speed at 14 knots—we were pushing to get there and arrive comfortably in daylight. By mid-morning we were 30 miles from Niue—as we sighted land and shouted out "Land Ho."

As we sailed into the bay toward the mooring buoys we were met by *Makena*, *Juno*, and *A Plus* from the fleet. They helped us the final half-mile, giving us a tow, passing the mooring line buoy. Luc from *Makena* sourced a generator for us (from *Garlix*) so we could charge our batteries. Sarah kindly offered to take the children. *Juno* offered us hot showers.

We were tired, relieved, and a lot wiser.

Gratitude

Reflecting a few days later, I felt grateful for many things about our loss of power experience:

- We worked as a team. With our strength together I now felt we could crack anything; Nichola is an amazingly resourceful person and I couldn't have wished for a better copilot on this venture.

- We lived our values as a family. The power of values and training one's mind to look for what is right rather than what is wrong became blindingly clear. Focusing and dwelling on the behaviors we wanted to see more of allowed us to work our way through this situation. Imagine what would have happened if we hadn't been grounded in our values. We'd have done the natural thing, focusing on what was wrong using language like "the problem is..." —a fast route to blame and getting people's hackles up. Those behaviors don't save you in a situation like ours.
- We'd been tested and we'd grown. We now knew about diesel systems and how they worked, could strip and clean them— and subsequently we actually got the engine working ourselves with the addition of a couple of extra resources (compressed air to clean the hoses and fresh hose to run the engine directly from a jerry can). Backup solar power and a spare generator were now on our must-have list.
- We were grateful to our fellow sailors—they had been amazing—full of support, advice, and help.

Teamwork

As a tightly knit unit, we had worked as the perfect team through all of this. We approached everything with humor, strong communication, happiness, and a shared focus on the outcome—arriving safely and happily. Never had we worked together so well. We thrived under adversity. In the old days, I'm certain the cracks would have shown with old arguments and blame statements flying about. We realized we had grown into an incredible team.

It was also important that the children saw how we reacted to our mid-ocean loss of power. The children were extremely understanding and let us focus. To their credit they were never fazed by our situation and our challenge was more in getting them to take our instructions and direction seriously. They never showed fear or concern—their trust in us was complete and we had no intention of letting them down.

When asked about the ordeal afterward they certainly remembered the situation, especially having to stay in the aft cabin while we worked things out. Later, when our rig failed in the Indian Ocean, Bluebell was straight onto it: "OK, so we just stay calm and go to the back cabin again—don't worry, I'll look after the other two." She met adversity with a calm approach, just figuring things out, making decisions that needed to be made.

Chapter 15

Completing Our Pacific Crossing
Niue, Tonga, Fiji to Australia
(June 2015 to July 2015)

The six months sailing the Pacific flew by—Panama, Las Perlas, Galapagos, Marquesas, Tuamotus, Tahiti, Raiatea, Bora Bora, Suwarrow, Niue, Tonga, Fiji—all with their unique experiences and rich memories. We had high levels of expectation and reality surpassed them all—the Pacific's reputation as a magical place is rightly deserved.

Niue was named the Savage Islands by Captain Cook, and Tonga the Friendly Islands (it's a strange feeling to be recreating part of Captain Cook's voyages and makes you feel very connected with history, particularly as many of the Islands will look today exactly as they looked then). In our experience both were extremely friendly, the Tongans particularly with their easy-going charm.

In Tonga we visited Mariner's Cave—an underwater cave where you have to swim down 6 feet and along 12 feet before you pop up into the cave. Hats off for courage and determination to Bluebell—nothing was going to stop her doing this and she couldn't have been more excited when she reached the cave (see plate section, image 24).

We had a true Tongan welcome and feast at the Mango Cafe on the dockside in Neiafu—another huge buffet of local food—the suckling pig is a big deal there, and lots of local dancing and speeches from the dignitaries. Another evening saw us visit the Bounty Bar to watch a Faka Ladies show—think Priscilla, Queen of the Desert but with huge Tongan guys dressed up!

As our travels continued we were extremely privileged to be introduced to local culture in many different parts of the world, finding warmth, friendship, and openness beyond our wildest dreams. One experience that left an indelible mark on all of us was our next stop, Vanuatu.

As mentioned earlier, when we were sailing from the Galapagos to the Marquesas we received a flurry of emails asking if we were OK. We had no idea what our friends were talking about. It transpired that farther west in the Pacific a cyclone had devastated the Vanuatu islands. We expected to be there in three months' time, and it became apparent that we could help. We worked with the World ARC organizers who had started a relief fund, stocking our sailboats with needed items.

We arrived in Port Resolution on the island of Tanna, one of the Vanuatu islands, on July 7, 2015 in the early morning hours after a fast and wet crossing from Fiji. Customs and immigration came the $2\frac{1}{2}$ hours by road, arriving after 10am and setting up shop in the yacht club, a wooden shack with a few sofas and a fridge adorned with flags from visiting boats. A handwritten sign above the bar read "Bank"—two tellers from the bank had set up shop to change our US and Fijian dollars into Vanuatu vatus. Sixteen sailboats were cleared in.

Later that afternoon we were given an island tour. In a nearby village we saw the original school left in disarray, yet instructions on how to avoid malaria remained written in white chalk on the blackboard. Other buildings, complete with computers, remained, as did tents newly erected by UNICEF for use as makeshift classrooms. Children—curious, playful, and full of smiles—swarmed us, racing ahead, then running back toward us.

Cyclone devastation was evident: stone home foundations reduced to sinks standing alone, attached only to freestanding pipes; felled coconut trees; spare frames of rebuilt houses; bare dirt plots awaiting new homes. We chatted with locals rebuilding their houses. They told of how the cyclone started at 3am, blowing for two days with a relentless howling noise, uprooting trees, tearing houses out of the ground. Most islanders fled to the brick school building for shelter. The story of the three pigs came to mind—houses built of straw, sticks, and bricks. The cyclone wind clearly huffed and puffed and blew the Vanuatu homes all down, apart from the brick school.

Offering Help

Columbus and I went fishing the next morning with Luc from *Makena*, catching a large tuna that we gave to the fishermen. The day was dedicated to helping the village. The sailors split into two work parties. The first worked on rewiring, including the lighting for the yacht club, which offers rented accommodation to travelers—an important source of income for the village. The second work party, including *Aretha*, cleared the land of fallen coconut trees and cut the grass so another volunteer group could continue the building project. Willow played on the beach with the village children, sharing her bucket and spade, making sandcastles. We spent time talking with Sarah who ran the coffee shop, its gleaming kitchen immaculate. She gave us a fruit-and-vegetable gift basket as a thank you for the help we were bringing to the village. Children—ours and the locals'—sat around in a circle outside, playing ball, laughing together.

The following day we all took ashore donations of cooking pots, tools, rice, and clothes. Paul from *Juno* also announced an initiative to fund the building of two new houses in order to attract qualified teachers. We needed to raise $30,000—they already had $20,000; we pulled together as a fleet and met the goal.

At noon we were welcomed to the village with an official ceremony. The islanders stamped the ground in a welcoming dance, the minister prayed, and we all proceeded to shake hands. We walked under an arch of flowers while locals adorned us with colorful headpieces and necklaces made of leaves and flowers. Children sang to us in the pouring rain, but the children didn't flinch—the rain did nothing to douse their spirits and energy—they sang loudly and with conviction. Their final offering was woven baskets and bags of fruit and vegetables in gratitude for the gifts we had brought.

Our donations were divided out into 12 piles: there were two main families per village, and six villages. It was humbling to see that the excess children's clothing we had on *Aretha* clothed what seemed like an entire village of children. Before long we were spotting Bluebell's trainers and Columbus's t-shirts on the local children. That evening we feasted on roast pig, fish, and vegetables, the finest food imaginable. The villagers who had so little gave so much. Port Resolution and its 200 inhabitants had given us an incredibly warm experience. These villagers, only three months after Cyclone Pam, were resilient and happy. They had also made great progress putting their island back together.

Climbing a Volcano

We had a chance to climb the world's most active accessible volcano, Mount Yasur. Before departing, Simon, one of the guides, asked if I had any shoes I could give him. I asked him what size feet he had. He looked at me blankly—I guessed a size 9 and said I would see what I could do.

At 4pm we clambered into four-wheel-drive trucks, sitting under a tarpaulin in the back, heading off on what I can officially call the world's worst road: potholed, muddy, steeply sloping, and broken. We bounced along in the pouring rain, passing villages under huge banyan trees. At one point, the truck slid sideways off the concrete tracks—stuck. After we all climbed out the truck managed to mount the tracks again—after much sliding and spinning. Steam—burning hot if you ventured your hand too close—spewed from the earth at our feet as we chased the truck up the road.

Next was a booming deep in our eardrums.

Once near, we walked up the mountain. The ground at our feet— black sand with large lumps of basalt rock—resembled a lunar landscape. No vegetation survives there.

The wind howled in a driving rain. As we neared the edge of the crater in the dark we watched a gray sky change to orange and then red. Lava bubbled. Every few minutes the volcano boomed—a huge rumble in our bones. We could feel the power of the Earth speaking to us. The children loved every minute of this incredible experience.

As we walked back down in the dark, drenched, I looked over at Simon, our guide, barefoot in shorts and t-shirt. The reason for his question earlier became blindingly obvious. I returned later with a pair of shoes that I hoped would fit.

Halfway Around the World

We left Vanuatu sailing fast at the front of the fleet in perfect conditions with flat seas and steady winds for two days. That gave way as we rounded the northern end of New Caledonia, the breeze filling in to 25+ knots with 10-foot seas. *Aretha* became a bucking bronco—every 10 minutes or so a wave broke over her, partially filling the cockpit. As we sailed through the roughest seas we'd had for a while, thankfully Nichola was sleeping—the second best cure for seasickness. (The first is sitting under an oak tree.) Thankfully the children also slept.

We now had just under 700 miles until Hydrographers Passage—our entry point through the Great Barrier Reef into Australian waters. It's then another 100 miles inside the reef to reach Mackay. This would be our last Pacific crossing—sailing to Australia. It seemed like only yesterday we felt the buzz of approaching Shelter Bay on the Caribbean side of Panama anticipating our transit under the Bridge of the Americas.

Our chartplotter showed the straight-line distance from where we were back to Panama as 7,200 miles. By my estimates, we'd probably sailed close to 12,000 miles in the Pacific with all the different routes we'd taken.

Australia was the halfway point for the World ARC; some crews would leave the group there, but we were excited to be continuing on a route in company around Australia to Darwin, up to Lombok in Indonesia, to Christmas Island, the Cocos (Keeling) Islands, Mauritius, South Africa, St. Helena, Brazil, and then back to Grenada and St. Lucia in the Caribbean.

As we approached Hydrographers Passage, we'd have to complete some intricate navigation through the treacherous reefs. The charts were filled with evocative names such as Wyatt Earp Reef, Bugatti Reef, and Deliverance Bank.

It was a fast, wet, bumpy passage. We hit 14.5 knots and decided to reduce sail to slow the boat. Half an hour later—reefed—we hit 16.3

knots. That's so fast the whole boat vibrates. You are literally surfing down the back of the waves: waves curl up behind you, some breaking, some not, and the stern lifts up, and whoosh—you are off, cantering down the wave until you stop at the trough where the speed stalls to 5 knots until you are picked up by the next wave. The first time you look at the wave in disbelief, wondering how it's going to break over you. Once you get in the rhythm you flow with the waves, almost carving your way through.

Squalls were everywhere—pounding rain with 30–40 knots of breeze. It was cold too—the southern hemisphere winter. I was sitting in full foul-weather gear. We heard Queensland had the worst snow for 30 years. So much for chasing the sun!

Thankfully the kids were rock stars and I was able to sail the boat while they did schoolwork with minimal guidance. They were also cooking, cleaning, and helping with the sailing—proper boat kids now. After five days at sea they were totally relaxed in the squally conditions.

As we neared Australia we were racing, hoping to secure our first podium finish. Safety was always paramount but it was hard not to get sucked into the competition when boats were all around. We were spurred on by regular position reports, too.

The Whitsunday Islands

 Captain's Log, 20°09'S 149°03'E, August 10, 2015, Whitehaven Beach, Whitsunday Islands, Australia

It still feels surreal.

When we first cooked up the idea of sailing round the world six years ago, it always seemed a long way off, and I suspect to many people, half-baked given that we didn't even have a yacht three months before our departure date.

Here we are anchored off Whitehaven Beach in the Whitsunday Islands inside the Australian Great Barrier Reef. I sit on deck in the perfectly still night air and watch the stars with the occasional shooting star. The air has a slight chill to it. In ten days' time it will be the one-year anniversary of us leaving the UK on our "madcap" adventure and we're over halfway round and now starting the journey back toward the UK.

The year has been everything I expected and more—a truly magical set of experiences—of magnificent highs and challenging lows—we are certainly emerging stronger and wiser from just half of our adventure and we are all relishing the second half.

While exploring the town of Mackay I was immediately struck by a strong feeling. We'd been in the Pacific living on the most primitive islands in the world for the past six months—now we were suddenly back in the modern world and the contrast was unbelievably striking. We were met with super-efficient service, supermarkets, bars, and restaurants selling well-recognized foods and brands. It all felt like being back home. I was thankful for the modern conveniences (especially fast internet), but it felt bland and sterile. The Pacific islands were so rich in their diversity, their culture, their vibrancy—I felt desperately sad, missing island life. In many ways this was a dry run of what it would feel like when we returned to the Western world in a year.

As with all emotions, the feeling passed. The lure and simplicity of modern life sucked me in—I certainly appreciated how much easier it made living.

We toured the area, visiting Eungella National Park to see platypus and turtles in the wild, and Cape Hillsborough at sunrise to see kangaroos and wallabies on the beach. Australia truly has some of the most stunning scenery in the world. The kids played with their boat friends— kids from *Hugur* and Kai from *Makena*—pushing one another up and down the wide docks in boat trollies, as well as discovering the best hot chocolate in town at Casu Jack's coffee shop.

Mackay is a working town built on coal mining and sugarcane. I stocked up on spares at chandleries, working down through the list of boat repairs: engine and generator service, rig checks, fitting our Watt & Sea hydrogenerator (one of our new pieces of gear in the wake of our mid-Pacific power failure—this is a propeller on a small rudder attached to the stern; it turns the prop revolutions [via a regulator] into power, charging *Aretha*'s batteries) and plenty more to boot.

Five days after arriving, we had the race ceremony. I'm delighted to say that we were announced as winners of the leg from Vanuatu. Our first podium place—by a decent margin as well. After allowances for boat handicaps (some boats are quicker than others by virtue of their size/design) and for engine hours (we barely used our engine on this leg), we won by a margin of eight hours. It was a great feeling.

Two days later we were on a plane to Sydney to meet Nichola's parents for a week with them. We left *Aretha* in the capable hands of Pete, who was staying aboard, and Andy and Emma who were doing maintenance work for us. It felt like a holiday to leave the boat behind—we had that usual excitement of going somewhere on a plane.

Time Out in Sydney

It was a pleasure to spend time in Sydney with Sheila and Laurie, Nichola's parents. We packed a lot into the week—going to the aquarium, the zoo, Manly and Shelly Beach, visiting the North Heads, the Opal Museum. Nichola and I went running in the mornings around the Botanical Gardens and the Opera House. The last time I had been there was in 2000-01 on the BT Global Challenge. This was the first time I crossed routes with my previous circumnavigation. It was lovely to relive old memories—happy times spent with my dad at Sydney Fish Market, others with Ian, Dan, and the boat guys at the bars at Pyrmont Bridge Hotel and around Darling Harbour. We met our friends Mindy and Victor from *Wayward Wind* in town as well. Mindy and her friend Heather kindly took Bluebell to see *Les Miserables*—Bluebell even got a new dress for the occasion. Fun times indeed.

It was a great opportunity for us to refresh ourselves too—haircuts, new clothes (and foul-weather gear from the boat show). We started to feel a bit smarter again, less like scruffy yachties. Less exciting was the doctor's visit for the last of our Hepatitis B injections!

The children were fascinated by walking round the replica of *Endeavour*, Captain Cook's ship, at the maritime museum, learning more about him. They were thrilled to hear we had been following much of his route. We took in the Shackleton Exhibition, too—all of it plenty of material for school projects.

The World Cruising Club was organizing a talk for 70–80 people on the World ARC and asked a few of our fleet to share their experiences. I was delighted to speak there, encouraging other young families on their journey. It was warming to realize how far we had come on our own journey—in what we had learned and what we had seen.

Sailing the Coast of Australia

As we voyaged from Mackay north up the east coast of Australia, we worked our way inside the Great Barrier Reef watching humpback whales put on a stunning show, and regularly seeing dolphins. The sailing was spectacular—strong southeast trade winds of 20–25 knots on flat calm seas (the sea was protected by the Great Barrier Reef). We cantered up the coast.

The kids (and us) were fractious and grumpy at first. It took a while to readjust to our boating life after a chunk of time on land, reconnected with home life and comforts. Some days I questioned the wisdom of 24 hours a day with our children. I rationalized they'd have strops and tantrums wherever they were—it just so happened we were sharing the same 53 feet of living space so had to resolve disagreements quickly.

We arrived at Torres Strait, the narrow band of water separating Australia from Papua New Guinea, a passage dotted with islands and reefs. The current runs through at a fearsome 8 knots plus. Time your passage wrong and you're sailing in high speed reverse—time your passage right and you're on a flying carpet covering big distances in no time. When heading west you want to arrive for the flood tide when the current flows westward. We were a little early—by about two hours—so we slowed *Aretha*, waiting for the current to flow with us. We were 1 mile away from Turtle Island—we'd then round Albany Island, passing Cape York, the northern tip of mainland Australia. From there it was west across the Gulf of Carpentaria toward Arnhem Land and then to Darwin. One of the day's school subjects was, unsurprisingly, geography. If the children learned nothing else, at least they would have a pretty darn good view of the world and the locations of different countries.

As we waited to cross, I was on a constant watch for cargo ships that barrel up and down the coast at 20 knots—they appear from nowhere and are on top of you before you know it. The wind was largely behind us, meaning that *Aretha* needed careful handling to avoid gybing (the boom flying from one side to the other). It was perhaps the most demanding passage we had done since leaving the UK, requiring a high level of concentration.

We were in good company—*Wayward Wind* left Cairns with us. We spoke several times a day on the VHF. At one point, 5 miles to our starboard side we passed a charity event called Kite the Reef: seven kite surfers along with three support vessels heading from Cairns to Cape York. Each of the kite surfers had a VHF—they were all in constant contact and we listened in to their chatter on the radio. As the kiters approached one island to

Schoolwork

Schoolwork progressed on *Aretha*—daily journal writing became more routine, with longer pieces. Bluebell in particular was more motivated to study from her books. Columbus had decided he wanted to be a zoologist, taking every opportunity to learn about the animals around him, reporting in great detail a whole host of facts. One afternoon the kids watched a DVD about killer whales that captivated all three of them. Each day we studied the charts, learning new names and places—this northern part of Australia was rich with English heritage: Buckingham Bay, the English Company Islands, Sir Edward Pellew Group of Islands, Prince of Wales Island. All have their own stories inspiring further learning and research. Learning that Cook and Bligh also traversed these waters (Bligh in an open boat in 1789 after being cast adrift from the *Bounty*) made the kids feel connected to their stories, encouraging further questions.

change to larger kites for the falling breeze, we heard their chatter "Oh my—look at the size of those turtles," "Whoah there are sharks here," and "Not that beach—there is a small croc there." The afternoon also included a music quiz over the VHF—we joined in but pitifully won zero points (*Wayward Wind* won 4 points).

It was in these waters that we caught our biggest fish. We were below deck when the reel sang out as line was stripped off at high speed. I donned a lifejacket, racing aft to grab the rod. As I tightened the clutch on the reel, the rod bent double as the fish leaped, out of the water.

We stopped *Aretha*. The fish and I tussled back and forth for the next 30 minutes.

Our reward was a new species for *Aretha*—the fish that Columbus had been desperate to catch—a wahoo measuring over 4 feet—taller than Columbus. We didn't have scales big enough—our guesstimate was 25–30lb of fish, enough to fill all our Tupperware boxes with fillets, leaving the fridge bursting at the seams. We planned to make sushi. Not long afterward, we went on to catch the largest fish that *Aretha* had seen—a stunningly beautiful sailfish, which we estimated as being between 6½ and 8 feet long. We made the decision that this beautiful creature deserved to be swimming free in the sea rather than in our frying pan and we let it go.

 Captain's Log, 11°00'S 137°23'E, August 22, 2015, Sailing the Arafura Sea

Our Watt & Sea hydrogenerator stopped working last night. We're still getting used to it and the noises that it makes so to have it stop was worrying.

By day, the problem was clear—a big clog of seaweed had wrapped itself into the prop. We stopped *Aretha* and with Columbus on crocodile watch, I found myself balancing on the step by the stern clearing the prop using the ship's boathook. Problem resolved and we are back in business creating power. 450 miles to Darwin—we're looking forward to exploring more of Australia and beyond. We can already see on the same charts the Indonesian Islands opening up in front of us—Sumba, Flores, Sumbawa, and Lombok (our next destinations after Darwin).

The sea has changed color. The royal blue color of the sea that we have been so used to all the way across the Pacific has changed to a beautiful jade green. The sky somehow seems softer as well and you can feel we are entering a different ocean. It's good to be progressing.

We spent time reflecting. One year in, what is it that we are giving to our children—what are they getting from this experience? How are we doing with the children's schooling, what are we teaching them?

Conversations of all sorts showed us what the trip was providing. One night in Darwin, Columbus and I were on deck watching the stars, chatting. I'd made hot chocolate for us both—for Columbus in his favorite Taronga Zoo mug with a koala on the front.

We fell silent after a while (unusual for Columbus) and he asked if we could play Desert Island Discs. In particular he wanted to listen again to Sir David Attenborough's choice of the Lyre Bird from South Australia. He listened with silent intent. As the show neared its end Columbus picked up on Sir David's recollection of creating a museum of his fossils and snake skin collection for friends and family when he was eight. Columbus began to understand that adults began as kids, and that his own experiences and interests were a clue to the adult he might become.

Columbus seemed primed to connect the rich living experience he was having with his life's path and meaning. Over the previous week, since watching *Blue Planet* and visiting several more amazing places, Columbus had announced he wanted to become a zoologist. Columbus is a serious boy and doesn't make statements like this lightly. This desire provided great leverage for me re his writing: "Columbus, if you want to become a zoologist, you need to up your game with your writing, documenting what you see."

Up to this point, getting Columbus to write had been like pushing water uphill. Now he was transformed. Every day, 1–2 pages of notes and drawings were added to his journal, with prompting.

After we had arrived in Darwin, Columbus presented each of us with a small ticket with a drawing of a common wombat with writing alongside. It was an invitation to the Columbus Museum. Next Columbus announced on the VHF radio that he had set up his museum and proceeded to distribute ticket invitations to the entire fleet of yachts.

The saloon table overflowed with artifacts Columbus had collected on our travels. A steady stream of people came aboard to view his exhibits. Columbus introduced each and every item with great passion—names and details that had long passed me by: coral and shells from different Pacific Islands; volcanic rock from Porto Santo and Mount Yasur in Vanuatu; sand collected from Kakadu National Park and Whitehaven Beach in Australia; other assorted treasures assembled from all over the world.

The wealth and depth of knowledge he'd acquired left Nichola and me marveling. Our real-world education aboard *Aretha* was having an impact. Seeds were being sown for the future. As Bluebell wrote: "At school we'd only be reading about this in books, but we're actually out here seeing it and doing it."

As we progressed from Darwin to Indonesia—a calm and largely windless stretch of 1,000 miles of sailing and motoring—we had lots of time to write. Columbus and Bluebell penned these words to boat friends who had stopped in Australia, updating them on our voyage:

"Dear John and Jilly

We are going to tell you about what is happening. We will start with Darwin, when we arrived in our anchorage the water was all murky and as calm as a mouse pitched on a rock and the moon high in the sky.

The next day we got up early and set off to our marina, the sun was shining bright so it was very hot, then some people came over to our boat to do our seacocks. Then we set off to do some exploring in town. The town was very nice and Darwin was very nice too, but I preferred Mackay.

And yes we did see lots of crocodiles it was exciting and a little bit scary, they were massive and huge.

And last of all I am going to tell you about the sail fish we caught, on a sunny day we were all relaxing until the reel started screaming, in less than 10 seconds we were all up on deck pulling the fish in, we knew it was monster. We could hardly bring it up to the surface in the end we took the hook out and let it go, we knew it was a sail fish because of its huge dorsal fin and it was even bigger than daddy.

Love from Bluebell and Columbus"

Having Fun with the Children's Quiz

It was at this time that the children decided to put all our followers to the sword and test their knowledge. They designed a quiz that we sent out to our blog and email list:

Bluebell and Columbus World Tour Quiz

To win a unique well-traveled Koala bear complete with its own passport, we're delighted to bring you Bluebell and Columbus World Tour Quiz.

The questions have been compiled by Bluebell and Columbus based on some of what they've learned and experienced from the past year sailing from England to Australia.

There are two prizes—an adult's prize and a children's prize of a Koala bear. Our Koalas will travel from Australia, to Lombok in Indonesia, to Christmas Island to Cocos (Keeling) Island and on to South Africa. They will have their own passports and journals stamped from each place and their own maps of the world with their travels on them.

The winners will be judged solely by Bluebell and Columbus and the Koalas will be sent from South Africa in time to arrive for Christmas, and to then be able to start their future travels with their new owners. Good luck!

1. What is the most venomous snake on earth?
2. What shark can get water through its gills without swimming or using current?
3. How big is Australia? As in Australia is the x largest country in the world by land mass size?
4. What is the biggest ocean on earth?
5. How do kangaroos keep cool?
6. What is the youngest island in Galapagos and how old is it?
7. How can you tell the difference between a seal and a sea lion?
8. How many types of boobies are there in the Galapagos and can you name them?
9. Can you name 3 animals unique to the Galapagos Islands?
10. What did Captain James Cook call the Island of Niue?
11. What is the capital of Fiji?
12. What effect does eating eucalyptus have on koalas?
13. How long is the Panama Canal?
14. Who funded Christopher Columbus' voyage and how many times did he cross the Atlantic?
15. What is another name for Grenada?
16. What African animal went to Grenada?
17. What are the 2 fruits that grow in the Tuamotus?
18. Which is the most active volcano in Vanuatu and what island is it on?
19. How many islands are there in the Canary Islands?
20. What's the capital of Tonga?
21. What was the name of Captain James Cook's ship?
22. Who was the architect behind the Sydney Opera House and how many years did it take to build?
23. What famous explorer lived in Porto Santo?
24. What is the latitude and longitude of Suwarrow?
25. How long can an adult crocodile hold its breath?

26. Can you guess how many miles we have sailed since leaving Southampton in England to reach Darwin in Australia? (Tie Breaker Question)

The children had great fun creating the quiz, telling everyone about it, making videos to promote it, and then marking the fabulous wealth of answers they received. There is great truth in the saying that often the best way to learn something is to teach it. Asking and putting the questions out there certainly anchored their knowledge!

Chapter 16

The Magical Indian Ocean

Darwin (Australia), Lombok (Indonesia),
Christmas Island, Cocos (Keeling) Island,
Mauritius, Réunion, South Africa
(September 2015 to November 2015)

We made the decision that, having enjoyed our time with the World ARC and having made so many close friends, we would continue sailing back to St. Lucia in the Caribbean in the company of the World ARC. Our route took us from Darwin in Northern Australia to Lombok in Indonesia. It was a windless passage, motoring many hours, passing close to the coast of Papua New Guinea and several oil and gas platforms. There are parts of Indonesia that are extremely touristy, such as Bali (just west of Lombok) and many places on Lombok. There are also many places that are incredibly poor where basic sanitation, fresh water, and hygiene are extremely limited. Gili Gede (an island on the west coast of Lombok) where we were headed and the surrounding villages fell into the latter. We were far from the tourist route.

One evening over drinks I chatted with Abu, a nearby landowner, and his friend Abraham, the local teacher. Younger children were educated on the island and the older children, if their parents could afford it, were ferried to a larger school on mainland Lombok. Abraham held classes Monday, Wednesday, and Saturday between 4pm and 5pm under the tamarind tree at Abu's house; the curriculum was English, Good Manners, and Good Conduct.

I asked if I could bring our children the next day—Abraham welcomed us with open arms, so it was agreed that the next afternoon we'd take our three to school along with 14-year-old Oscar from *Chat Eau Bleu*.

School in Indonesia

We headed up the coast of Gili Gede by dinghy for the mile-long journey to Abu's house. It was low tide when we arrived so we anchored among the coral and waded ashore, taking great care not to step on the sharp coral. We headed up the beach in search of the tamarind tree. On this occasion—in contrast to the Fakarava school mutterings—our children were engaged. It helped that Oscar was with us—the children looked up to him and wanted to be on their best behavior. Peer pressure can be a wonderful thing.

Sure enough there was a small grove of tamarinds, large, leafy trees providing protection from the harsh sun. Abraham and his class sat underneath the largest tree.

The class had eagerly anticipated our arrival. Abraham's desk and a chair were placed next to a whiteboard nailed to the tamarind tree. Sixteen children aged between 7 and 18 were seated on an orange tarp before him. The students wore handwritten name badges and big quizzical smiles. Some adults were there too—perhaps also curious to meet us. We were warmly gestured into chairs placed in front of the cross-legged children.

Abraham welcomed us and then asked each of his students to introduce themselves in English and to shake our hands. Much smiling and laughter accompanied this as Willow, not quite sure what to make of it all, hid behind my legs. I asked our crew to introduce themselves by saying their ages and where they were from. Abraham wrote the names of our four down on the whiteboard.

The local students had created gifts for us, newspaper-wrapped packets tied with string and filled with beautiful cowrie shells and coral, fantastic keepsakes. Bluebell presented the students with coloring books and pens. I then suggested to Abraham that our children could tell some stories and share some of the things they'd seen on their travels. It was an idea that came to me in the moment. I was curious to see how our children responded to this request. A test of confidence and composure indeed.

Nervously, the older three got up to speak, Oscar first sharing his journey from Australia to Lombok, Bluebell telling stories of the Galapagos and the islands we visited across the Pacific, and Columbus, the Walking Wikipedia as he'd come to be known, giving a talk on animals, islands, and volcanoes. The children spoke a sentence at a time while Abraham translated for his students. Our young Western ambassadors were worldly, knowledgeable, and articulate, ready and willing to share what they had learned. To say I was proud of all the children would be a vast understatement.

School finished with the students singing local songs, then escorting us to our dinghy, stopping along the way for photos. Visitors seldom came to Gili Gede. We were the first to visit the school—as Abraham remarked, our presence was enough to show their children different ideas, manners, and knowledge. As we headed back, a silence fell over the boat as the children reflected on what they'd experienced. I let the children draw the comparisons with their own schooling back home. The next day I heard from Oscar's aunt that he'd told her it was one of his best experiences of the entire voyage.

Inspired by my Family

We left the peaceful and quiet anchorage of Gili Gede on September 13, 2015 and set off for our next destination, Christmas Island. We were sailing downwind in 15 knots of breeze when we decided to hoist the staysail to see if we could go faster (it's amazing how Nichola and Columbus had become ocean racers wanting to win). We discovered we had wrapped a halyard at the masthead.

We quickly reviewed our options. Drop the sails and re-hoist or use a different halyard (not ideal). Nichola piped up, "It's fine—I'll go up the rig and unwrap it." Really?! We were mid-Indian Ocean with the sea rolling—not so much at deck—but probably rolling some 6–8 feet to either side at *Aretha*'s masthead. "No way," was my answer, "I don't think that's a good idea."

Nichola was not to be dissuaded. "I'm fine—we're racing, let's get on with it." Armed with a Petzl climbing helmet, she shot up the rig on the offending staysail halyard, climbed over the line that was causing the twist, and was back on deck within two minutes. Didn't even break a sweat.

On another day in the Indian Ocean, I realized we'd planted the traveling bug when Bluebell announced that she'd really like to explore China, while Columbus was planning a two-month tour around Australia and New Zealand covering the parts we missed.

Before we left Indonesia, Mindy on *Wayward Wind* shared this quote with us: "I'd rather have a passport full of stamps than a house full of possessions."

It seemed we had a crew wholeheartedly behind this.

Christmas Island and the Kindness of Strangers

Leaving Lombok we had a 700-mile passage to Christmas Island, a tiny jewel in the Indian Ocean. It's fair to say we knew pretty much nothing about Christmas Island when we set off. It has a population of 1,500 people—a mix of Australian, Malay, and others. It's an Australian territory—as strategically important as Cocos (Keeling) farther west, allowing Australia to lay claim to the large oil and gas fields lying off the northwest coast of Australia.

Christmas Island is home to many endemic species and is often called the undiscovered Galapagos of the Indian Ocean. Particularly famous are its crab migrations—16 species of land crab live on the island. We saw the red crab, blue crab, and the most predatory, the robber crab (also known as the coconut crab). These crabs migrate seasonally to the coast—a big deal for the islanders, who close certain roads to accommodate them. On parts of the island, special crab bridges have been built, allowing the crabs to migrate over the roads. In other areas barriers and underpasses have been built. It's amazing to see just how much work goes into protecting these crabs.

Bird-watchers make up a large number of the 1,000 annual visitors to Christmas Island. They can spot the beautiful indigenous golden bosun, as well as the ever-present frigate birds patrolling the skies, warding off other species.

Christmas Island has many similarities to Niue—the first of which is the mooring field. Aside from large commercial moorings (used for the ships that collect phosphate—the only heavy industry on the island), there are only six mooring buoys. Anchoring is not recommended here, to protect the coral as well as the practical difficulties of a very steeply shelving ocean floor diving to hundreds of feet just offshore. We arrived as the fifth boat picking up a mooring and waited for the police to come and clear us in. The authorities were friendly and efficient—when they learned we had kids on board, police bags full of goodies were procured (stickers, coloring pencils, a baby koala)—and were much appreciated. Officer Adam from Perth was on his third post of two years on the island and offered to pick us up the following day to take us to the local school sports day.

We walked into town at Flying Fish Cove and were pleasantly surprised by an extremely well stocked, duty-free supermarket. Next door was the visitor center. After Willow decided to make a mess in the middle of the shop, we got chatting with Julie, the gracious, helpful proprietor, and asked for advice on where to lunch. After a list of options she advised us our best bet was 20 minutes' walk away. She looked at us and said, "Why don't you take my car? The keys are in the ignition and it's never locked." I was speechless.

This friendly island cast its spell on us. We visited the said restaurant and were the only customers on a large veranda looking out to sea, with a large grassy area under the coconut trees where the children ran happily, letting off steam. It was the perfect island introduction—while sipping cold drinks, we watched friends sail across the vista.

Our two days on the island were rich. We managed a half-day tour learning about the flora and fauna, saw red crabs, showered under a waterfall, viewed the blowhole rocks. There was much to appreciate.

The underwater world was stunning as well—including the coral just 20 feet beneath *Aretha*'s keel. The kids and I had many happy times playing in the water.

On our passage from Lombok, we were pleased that there was little repair work needed aboard *Aretha*. That was all about to change. Because of the limited moorings and the number of boats, our boats had to raft up. Our rafting partner was the classic Hans Christian 43-foot *Wayward Wind*—Pete, Mindy, and their crew, Victor. While we were ashore, they came alongside *Aretha* to raft up. Unfortunately the bow of *Aretha* swung round at the last moment and the rather large bowsprit on *Wayward Wind* caught the lifelines and stanchions on the starboard bow. The bowsprit from *Wayward* snapped off, bending our bow pulpit (the stainless steel fitting all around the bow) by 12–18 inches, leaving the starboard lifelines hanging loose. Not good. When we returned from our trip to town we found *Aretha* in a sorry state and a rather ashen Pete.

In sailing (as in life), nothing is ever as bad as it first seems. We began by getting our head around the situation, working out what could and couldn't be done. After some thought and deliberation we found a stainless steel guy on the island, who advised that a proper repair might be possible by removing the whole pulpit then heat-treating it to bend it back into shape (although this could be difficult, given the bends were at the stanchion bases).

The short-term fix was getting four big guys on board to bend the pulpit back into place. Given our time constraint we opted for this, moving the pulpit back 10 inches or so, although it still looked misshapen. Equally troublesome were the slack lifelines, which posed the biggest safety threat—lean on a lifeline where it's slack and you'll quickly find yourself over the side in the wet stuff. Stefan from *Ayama* came aboard with stainless steel wire and bulldog clips to create tension using a second line, which seemed to work. We emailed ahead to Oyster, planning a more permanent solution in either Mauritius or, more likely, Cape Town.

We had to learn to smile and move on—fixing stuff is all part of boat life. Taking it in your stride without drama is the way to get through it.

The final evening on Christmas Island included a barbecue ashore hosted by our tour guides, Lisa and James. Our tiny glimpse into life here had been truly fascinating—a place absolutely worth revisiting. Another fabulous if brief stopover—reconnaissance for future travels.

The next morning saw an early start, stowing the boat with the latest provisions, nipping ashore for the strongest Wi-Fi to upload pictures to Facebook, rigging checks that sent Nichola up the mast. A last chance for the kids to swim in the pristine waters. Not so great were the jellyfish stings that Bluebell picked up—she still had red sores two days later.

We had cleared immigration by 10am, and headed to the start line of the 530-mile passage to Cocos (Keeling) Islands—by all accounts another gem of the Indian Ocean. We were straight away into the breeze—a great start for a stretch of sailing at 200 plus miles a day.

We suggested before leaving that the kids run a children's daily midday SSB net on 6 Bravo (one of the radio channels). It's hard to appreciate just what a radio net does for you thousands of miles from anywhere. There was a lot of variation in boat speeds across our fellow sailors and after just a week at sea, there could easily be some 300 miles between the lead boats and back markers. Each day a different boat is appointed Radio Net Controller. At 9am and 6pm there is a roll call going through each of the boats, checking in. The morning roll call is where everyone's position and wind/sea state is collected. The evening call is simply a courtesy check to make sure each boat is OK. It's then followed by chat—often about weather, fishing boat sightings, fishing, details about the next destination provided by the first boats to arrive, and so on. The radio call—sharing daily, intimate experiences at sea—forges unique bonds among sailors.

On the first day of the kids running their own net, Bluebell was the Radio Net Controller. I listened from the aft cabin as Nichola, providing minimal guidance, handed the airwaves to Bluebell. With astonishing confidence and clarity she ran the net, chatting to other boats and setting a mathematics puzzle given to her by Sarah from *Makena*. She closed the net for the day by announcing she'd be running a music quiz the following day.

The Magical Cocos (Keeling) Islands

After a fast three-day sail, we approached magical Cocos, a tiny group of islands in the Indian Ocean, at first light. We picked our way through the coral to the anchorage in the lee of uninhabited Direction Island. We had a few anxious moments as we got as shallow as 1 foot beneath our keel.

Safely through the pass, we were greeted by stunning colors—the deep turquoise blue of the anchorage, the brilliant white sand, and the rich green of the coconut trees on Direction Island.

In a voyage of many superlatives and stunning paradises where each one seemed to better the last, we decided that Cocos won hands down—in fact the best tropical island that we had visited. These islands have a fascinating history, having been owned by the Scottish Clunies-Ross family since the 1700s with a thriving Copra (coconut) business on the islands. Charles Darwin visited in the *Beagle*, forming his theory of atoll development there.

It was also an important communications center in World War II as well as the scene of a historical battle where the German warship *Emden* was sunk by HMAS *Sydney*. The island was bought from the Clunies-Ross family by the Australian government in the late 20th century and now falls under Australian rule. The territory consists of two atolls and 27 coral islands, of which two, West Island and Home Island, are inhabited with a total population of approximately 600 people. The total land area is just 3,500 acres. The name Cocos (Keeling) derives from Cocos—a reference to the abundant coconut trees on the islands, while Keeling is a reference to William Keeling, reputedly the first European to sight the islands in 1609.

With the dinghy at anchor a few yards off the beach on Direction Island, we found an unexpected bonus. Sitting under the roof of the shelter—despite this being an uninhabited island—there was super-good Wi-Fi set up for visiting sailors and before long there was a small cluster of people catching up on emails and Facebook updates.

Ports of Interest—Clearing Customs at Cocos (Keeling)

Clearing customs at Cocos (Keeling) under the auspices of the AFP (Australian Federal Police) was a relaxed affair. The police officers dinghied over to Direction Island and, sitting under one of the three covered shelters, cleared us in on the beach—checking immigration forms and stamping passports. Shorts, sand, and coral attest to the informality of the process and Andrew, the police sergeant, advised us on the best place to snorkel once we had cleared in. I think his job is one of the better jobs in the world—there is no crime here and it's a relaxed, charming way of life on this tiny dot of an island in the vast Indian Ocean.

That afternoon we snorkeled the famous rip. Running around one end of the island there is a continuous flow of 2–3 knots through a channel with a wide gully. Dinghy to one end, jump over the side, and the current sweeps you along for some 1,000 feet or so past white-tipped reef sharks, and copious quantities of fish. As we were swept down current we spotted eye-catching unicorn fish, napoleon fish, parrot fish, and Moray eels, some bigger than Willow. We glided over acres of coral. In the pristine turquoise unpolluted waters the colors were stunning and unblemished. Without doubt it was the best snorkeling I'd ever experienced.

This island paradise was our home for the next week and the children reveled in it, swimming, playing on the beach, hopping between boats, and exploring the island. We made several trips to Home Island, 1 mile away by dinghy but which could only be undertaken by day—the coral is everywhere and you pick your route very carefully. On the final day we managed to ding our propeller, losing most of our power (new prop promptly on order to Mauritius with the help of Oyster). Home Island had three shops—including the well-stocked Shamrock supermarket where we picked up our pre-ordered, excellent quality fresh fruit and vegetables—as well as a Post Office.

One of the keepsakes we purchased from each country was first-day covers of the local postage stamps. They took up little space on the boat—providing inexpensive and distinctive memories from each of our round-the-world destinations. In many ways I was channeling my youth—when I was Columbus's age I had a stamp collection. The children enjoyed the collecting aspect and we stuck stamps from each country in the logbook as well.

My favorite place in Cocos (Keeling) was Prison Island—a tiny island with four coconut trees and four deck chairs (from Ikea!) that someone kindly left there. We sat comfortably surrounded by sea the color of a bottle of Bombay Sapphire Gin, on our own private island. Back in the day there used to be a two-story house here. The owner had a harem of 30 wives, locked in each night—hence Prison Island. It was a terrific spot for Nichola and I to escape the children and share a cold drink and swim.

The shelters on Direction Island were adorned with woodcarvings of boat names left by previous visiting yachts. I discovered one left by Pete, one of my stepbrothers, who had sailed there in the 90s on a square-rigger. I sent him a photo.

A number of evenings were spent on the beach sitting around a fire, enjoying a barbecue, and sharing stories with our fellow sailors. Memories that will last a lifetime.

The Return of Max

The return of my younger brother, Max, was long awaited. Max rejoined us on Cocos (Keeling) to sail on our 4,000-mile passage to South Africa. His epic journey to arrive took over six days including a two-day stop in Dubai, to Perth, then to the Cocos (Keeling) Islands. It's not a standard route so he had to piece together different flights to join us. He was due to land on West Island and then ferry across to Home Island.

On the night he arrived it was too late in the evening for us to collect him so he stayed at Oceania House, the former Clunies-Ross residence. Willow and I took the dinghy over to Home Island at first light to collect him. He was tired after his long journey but had energy for catch-ups, meeting the other crews, as well as snorkeling the rip. This was our last full day on Cocos so it was also spent on boat preparation and provisioning for the long ocean passage to Mauritius.

Max had sailed with us on Day 1 as we left Southampton heading to Portugal. He was the first crew to join us since Caroline flew back from Tahiti many thousands of miles ago. Max penned these words about the changes aboard *Aretha* several days after he joined us in the Indian Ocean:

"I meet up with some overexcited kids who try and tell me eight stories all at once for three hours. Nichola and Caspar look healthy and relaxed, and Willow has found her voice and talks more than the other two combined. The children's confidence has grown immeasurably since I last saw them; they talk to just about everyone now and there aren't many kids you go swimming with who, when you point out a five-foot shark several meters away, casually say 'Yeah, it's just a white tip nurse shark'... Are these the same kids who I struggled to get out the shallow end of the swimming pool just over a year ago? Now they jump off diving platforms, snorkel in deep water and are willing to try most new ideas people put to them. Time at sea has changed them...

"The kids are far more mature than when I left them. They're a dab hand at dealing with the boat, I feel a novice around them. Bluebell is a different character altogether, largely helpful, wanting to be involved and does what she is told. She seems to relish being given added responsibility and even takes night watch sometimes. Columbus is a stickler for the rules and knows the boat inside out, and if you don't do things right he soon lets you know about it.

"Nichola and Caspar to me seem to have also changed. The conversation is now about the kids, each other, and what there is to look forward to. There is more of a noticeable spark in their eyes when they look at each other. I for one, when I live in the city lose the blueness to my eyes and they turn grey. I think all the time in the blue sea enjoying life away from work and the city has definitely made this couple's eyes shine a little more.

"I feel the kids' changes in maturity level has something to do with getting quality time from both parents—something often unattainable in the daily modern grind of life. The travels and life on board have been like a vitamin boost: everyone seems younger, healthier, and doing something that very few families actually get to do, spending quality time with the kids while they grow up."

Cocos (Keeling) Islands to Mauritius

(September 28, 2015 to October 11, 2015)
After leaving Cocos, we sailed fast, magical miles. We were properly in the trade winds with consistent breezes of 20–25 knots, averaging 200 miles a day. It was one of our fastest passages taking us just 14 days, surfing downwind at 10–12 knots and rapidly covering the 2,700 miles. This part of the Indian Ocean can be rough—the weather gods were kind and sent us happily on our way.

It was brilliant having Max back on board and with some guidance from the children he easily settled back into life at sea. We all loved having him back on *Aretha*.

Schooling continued. Geography was a key topic. We'd regularly take a geographical fix to see what was north, south, east, and west of us. For example, on October 5, we noted: due north of us—we've passed Bangladesh, Calcutta, Sri Lanka, and are currently due south from Mount Dilli in India. The chart to the west shows Madagascar and Mozambique. Due east of us, we're on the same latitude as Cairns.

Mauritius to South Africa

Mauritius, a large island off the east coast of Madagascar, was yet another magical destination where we spent a relaxing couple of weeks catching up with family who flew out to join us. Our marina berth was right in the center of the capital, Port Louis. The yachts with their full dress flags made a spectacular sight. We had a regular stream of visitors—locals and tourists alike gazing at the boats, having photos taken with the crews. Mauritius, formerly a British colony and famous for its sugarcane plantations, gained independence from Great Britain in 1968. It has a population of 1.3 million and has recently developed into a popular tourist destination. Mauritius was the only known habitat of the now extinct flightless bird, the dodo.

We then sailed west the short hop—200 miles—berthing at Le Port on the French Island of Réunion, where we spent another couple of weeks exploring the stunning beauty of this mountainous island (complete with volcanoes). We also won first place racing from Mauritius to Réunion—we once again unleashed the competitive side of all of our crew and got Max fully into the continuous trimming and racing.

We now faced one of the most dangerous sections of the whole voyage: the 1,600 miles from Réunion south of Madagascar across the Agulhas Current to Richards Bay on the southeastern coast of South Africa. This passage is fearsome because the Agulhas Current can run up to 6 knots, especially where the ocean depth changes from several miles to several hundred feet. Huge mountainous seas can arise quickly when the current meets strong winds from the opposite direction. Many large ships have gone to their graves on this section of water. It demands respect, preparation, and timing. Anything less can be fatal.

As we passed south of Madagascar, we experienced the single scariest moment of our entire voyage.

Our Logbook

When we set off, our logbook was a place for sailing information only, recording position, course, boat speed, wind, and weather data.

As we progressed, we adapted our ship's log. Rather than a lined notebook, we used a blank journal. All the necessary sailing information was included, but we expanded it to include notes on what we'd been doing, drew pictures, and wrote in-depth descriptions of locales, etc. We'd also stick in stamps from the different countries, getting the log pages stamped by passport control officers when we smiled enough (and they were obliging!).

We encouraged all crew to contribute, including the children, who had begun writing log entries. We'd sometimes record the humor we found with our children—such as the time Bluebell had been reading David Walliams and asked, "Mummy, what is a torrid affair?" These logbooks remain brilliant and engaging records of our voyage.

Chapter 17

Every Parent's Worst Nightmare
Réunion to Richards Bay, South Africa
26°37'S 46°50'E
(November 3, 2015)

It was early evening and we were making great speed, heading on a direct course toward Richards Bay in South Africa. We had 20 knots of wind from the north-northeast averaging between 7 and 8 knots of boat speed. From our weather charts, we expected the wind to shift and increase as a weather front approached. We were watching the barometer closely for pressure changes and watching the radar for squalls. We prepared by reefing the sails early with one reef in the main and a reduced genoa in anticipation. I sent the kids to the forward cabin to settle down while we finished the boat preparations.

The calm was pierced by a child's screams.

Any parent knows when their child is playing or when they are hurt. This one was the latter. I ran forward and found three-year-old Willow screaming. I picked her up and as I held her in my arms with her face covered in blood, my heart was pounding as I tried to work out what had happened and what I needed to do.

My practical side kicked into gear straight away. Deal with it Caspar. Own the situation. I focused on what we needed to do. We were 900 miles from the nearest medical facilities in South Africa—at least six days of sailing. It was going to be down to us to figure out what to do.

I carried Willow to our cabin at the back of *Aretha*, where Nichola had been resting and was now quickly waking up. By the time I got there my white t-shirt was soaked with Willow's blood. Amid her screams we examined her to find a cut on her forehead—half above and half below the hairline—where she'd hit her head. Bluebell and Columbus were there and explained that they had been playing and she had fallen off the bunk and had hit her head on the cupboard beside the bunk. It's the sort of thing that can and does happen to any child at home.

No amount of medical training prepares you for this. It's one thing to know the theory. It's another thing to put it into practice with a stranger. And it's another thing again to put it into practice when it's your three-year-old child.

At exactly the same time, the front that we had been expecting went through and the wind shifted through 180 degrees, rapidly increasing by 10–15 knots to over 30 knots. Thunder and lightning added to the drama of the situation as *Aretha* heeled over to starboard with the increased wind.

There is an unwritten rule that when things go wrong, they all go wrong at the same time.

My first priority suddenly shifted: get *Aretha* under control so we were safe, then attend to Willow. I left Nichola in charge of Willow to assess the situation and raced on deck to settle *Aretha*. I changed the autopilot control to steer *Aretha* downwind and eased the mainsail. *Aretha* responded quickly, her decks flattening to give us a stable platform to deal with Willow.

By now Max was on deck too: "Max—you need to be on the mainsheet—we don't have time to reef right now so when the breeze gusts hard, ease the sheet to depower the sail, when the wind softens, power the sail back up."

I furled in the genoa while Max eased the sheet.

With Max on deck nursing *Aretha* through the gales, I could now focus on treating Willow. I needed to get a clear head and some advice.

I also needed to make sure the other children were OK. I sat Bluebell and Columbus down in the saloon, crouching down to be at their eye level. I spoke firmly and calmly.

"Remember when we sailed to Niue and we lost all power? We figured things out then and we'll figure them out again now. Keep yourselves safe and let us work this out. Remember our values? That's how we are going to deal with this. We're going to be calm and follow our values like Understanding and Get into Action." They nodded and let me get on with dealing with the situation.

When things go wrong, the world seems to go into slow motion. I remember the time distinctly. It was 17.55. Our 18.00 SSB radio call was about to start. Preceding the call, there was always a silent listening watch for ten minutes when anyone with an emergency called in first.

I took the radio handset and broke the silence.

"*Allegro, Allegro, Allegro,* this is *Aretha, Aretha, Aretha.* I need some medical advice."

You could feel the collective intake of breath across the fleet. When you are at sea, medical situations are your worst nightmare. Luis on *Allegro* was formerly an emergency room surgeon in Portugal. Although his yacht was over 100 miles away from us, he was the best person I could think of to ask for advice.

I repeated my call.

"*Allegro, Allegro, Allegro,* this is *Aretha, Aretha, Aretha.* I need some medical advice." The radio crackled and I strained to hear the reply. He had responded but he was too far away to hear clearly. I asked another boat to relay the messages.

Peter from *Exody* stepped in straight away. I explained to Peter as slowly and clearly as I was able what had happened and our situation. He repeated what he heard. I confirmed he had understood it correctly.

He relayed the message to Luis. We had to wait for Luis to receive and understand the message and then relay his advice back via Peter.

After what felt like an age, Peter asked for more details on where the cut was and how deep it was. Standby Peter. I have to go back to check. Nichola had Willow cradled in her arms and was holding the wound together. I asked her to let me examine it. It was about an inch long, in her hairline. It was hard to tell how deep it was.

I rushed back to the radio. I relayed the information to Peter who relayed to Luis.

I waited for the answer Peter relayed: It will be too hard to get a needle in there to stitch it together. Use loops of her own hair as the stitches—tie her hair together in a knot and let it mat together to bind the wound. Via Peter, Luis talked us through what we needed to do.

Willow was settling now as Nichola and I placed her between us. Nichola held Willow while I tried to tie knots with her hair. Hair is slippery at the best of times and even more so when it's wet with blood. After 10 minutes on our makeshift operating table in our cabin, Nichola, with smaller fingers than me, finally managed to tie three knots that effectively pulled the wound together. Our medical kit included large bandages so we covered the whole wound with one of the largest we could find.

Things seemed to be calming down.

The radio crackled into life with Peter asking for an update. I let the fleet know we had the situation under control. I got advice from Svanfridur, a former pediatric nurse on board the Icelandic boat *Hugur*, which was within radio range. She advised us to make sure Willow stayed alert. We agreed to a plan of action that took Nichola out of the watch system to stay with Willow, waking her every hour to make sure she was OK.

I went on deck where Max had been sailing *Aretha*, keeping us level. We needed to reduce sail to slow us down and make *Aretha* more stable. We reduced the mainsail down to the two reefs and furled more of the genoa.

For the next three hours as the front passed, lightning, accompanied by torrential rain and strong winds, surrounded *Aretha*. Lightning on a boat is a scary thing. A direct hit knocks out all power systems: navigation, autopilot, battery starter motor on the engine—you name it and it's gone. There isn't much you can do about it. The best thing is to preserve your spares, which we did by putting our handheld devices (GPS, handheld VHF, iPhone, and navigation iPad) in a Faraday cage (metal box)—in our case, a cookie tin inside the microwave.

Max and I took the watch in turns overnight. I checked regularly on Willow, who was resting. Much to her disdain we woke her every hour. Her grumpiness at being awoken let us know she was conscious and OK.

As first light came, we seemed to have the situation under control— Willow was alert and awake. Apart from the large bandage on her head she seemed utterly normal and unaffected.

Yet again we had been tested. I was grateful for the way we responded as a team. Everyone played their part—no shouting, no dramatics, no blame. Just deal with the situation and move on. If I would want to teach my children any lesson in life, it is this kind of emotional resilience. How do you respond when things don't work out the way you want? How do you react? What do you do? Anyone can deal with things when they are easy. It takes character to deal with things when the chips are down and life throws whatever it has at you. My children now had several powerful anchors of how to react when things go wrong.

Just when we thought we had things settled, another drama was about to unfold.

Rigging Failure

It was 6.50, the next morning. I was just coming on watch to relieve Max. The seas were still big with *Aretha* slamming off waves.

Max was providing the watch handover: here's what has happened with the wind, sail combinations, boat speed, shipping traffic, etc. Nearing the end he mentioned, "Oh, there was one other thing. There was a really large twanging noise in the night—it was almost like a gun going off."

There is absolutely nothing good about unexpected sounds on a boat. We had to find the source of the noise and fast. I knew this could be serious. Max had already explored and discovered the source. For the third time in a small number of hours, I was fired by adrenaline as he pointed from the comfort of the saloon to where on the rig the metal had broken.

Lifejacket and harness on, I was forward in a flash. "Max, come and keep an eye on me while I investigate."

The culprit was the port side D1 (lower) shroud. A D1 is a thick wire going at a diagonal (hence the "D") angle from the deck to the first set of spreaders (see diagram on page 273). Every single piece of standing rigging is critical—it holds the mast securely in place. If any piece of the standing rigging breaks or fails, a full rig failure—the mast toppling over—is imminent. That's extremely dangerous in its own right but another danger comes from the mast falling by the side of the sailboat, punching a hole in the hull. Then not only do you have a boat with no means of sailing, but you have a sinking boat as well. It really couldn't get much worse. Except, of course, the mast falling and hitting someone.

Safety Routines at Sea

Safety on board was my number one priority. As well as our personal safety routines of wearing lifejackets and shoes on deck (and clipping into lifelines), we also checked rigging, sails, and all lines for signs of chafe and wear—every single day. Checking things daily—at deck level and by using binoculars to check the upper rig—made us extremely familiar with all parts of *Aretha* so it was much easier to spot anything wrong. Sails and rigging are critical to sailing the boat—if we found something wrong we fixed it immediately.

There is a D1 on each side of the mast—port and starboard. Our D1s consist of one x 19 wire rope—a core of six inner wires laid up around one straight center wire (making seven wires); 12 more wires are laid up around this core. We discovered that one of the wires had snapped—we were now holding our mast up on the lower port side with 18 wires.

The adrenaline started to flow again with this new challenge, complicated by *Aretha* slamming into seas that remained short and steep. When we lurched forward into another wave the boat slammed, our momentum throwing everything forward. With each drop onto a wave, the load on the rig increased dramatically. This pumping on the rig was almost certainly the reason our D1 failed.

Thinking on my feet, I decided we needed to stop the pumping right away. "Max—we need to reef the main right now," I called back to the cockpit. "Prep for the reef, we are going from two reefs to three reefs to depower the boat." We had the reef secured within a few minutes, effectively reducing pressure on the D1. I maneuvered back to the cockpit where we roller-furled the headsail to a hankie, further slowing *Aretha*.

We were now sailing slowly at around 3 knots. With 800 miles ahead and still wanting to be certain that Willow was OK, this speed was less than optimal. We had to figure out another solution.

I woke Nichola. It was just after 7am. I wanted all three brains working on solving this. While she got up, I made coffee, working the problem in my head.

We needed to secure the rig. Eighteen wires might hold but it was clearly not ideal. We needed to find a way to make sure that the mast was secure. That could mean adding extra lines to the mast on the port side to provide support for the rig if the D1 failed completely. I started thinking through different options of fitting additional lines. Where on the mast would we fit them? Where on the deck would we fit them? What lines could we use? What material would be strong enough to secure the mast? There were more questions than answers.

Coffee in hand, we debated our options. We emailed Eddie at Oyster as well as asking for advice on the 9am SSB call.

After much debate, the favored option was to strengthen the D1 by securing a length of Dyneema (an extremely strong fiber rigging material), attached with a series of eight hose clamps—four on either side of the break on the existing D1. Nichola and I took to the deck and within an hour we had made a jury rig of sorts. We emailed Eddie to let him know what we had done.

Within the hour Eddie had emailed back to say that the hose clamps we had used probably wouldn't hold it and that we were right to reduce sail and nurse *Aretha* through at slow speed. Ideally we'd need rigging wire and bulldog (cable) clamps. We had rigging wire, but we didn't have spare bulldog clamps. Eddie signed off his email with this stark reminder: "Make a plan if the worst should happen. Have your rig cutters ready. Tell the net controller of your situation. Above all, stay calm. Eddie."

We spent more time debating what to do. We didn't have enough fuel to motor the whole way—we needed to sail some part of the passage. It didn't help that we had several knots of current flowing against us and that the predicted southerly breeze doggedly remained from the east, forcing us to sail into the wind, getting bounced around on 13-foot waves.

As the day progressed, the choices became apparent. Our friends on *Ayama* appeared on AIS (our vessel tracking system) 11 miles behind us. We called Stefan—who is a brilliant engineer—and talked through our options. Stefan had bulldog clamps and offered to let us borrow them so we could make a more robust repair. We planned to slow down to let him catch us by the following daybreak when we would make a ship-to-ship transfer.

As we reduced sail, one of the mainsail cars (which attach the sail to the mast) broke and the reefing lines jammed. Ho hum. Just more stuff to fix. We unjammed the reefing lines—the car would have to wait.

An eventful time indeed.

By nightfall we were nursing *Aretha* along in 30 knots of wind, sailing 5 knots, planning at-sea repairs. The children seemed fine, sleeping in our aft cabin.

Just after midnight, we got hit by squalls with 35-knot gusts, surfing at over 12 knots. That was nowhere near the definition of nursing the boat. We decided to drop all sails. Naturally, the headsail furling unit jammed with 20 percent of the genoa still out (I was pretty confident I could fix that in daylight). The main came down more easily, aided by Max at the mast securing the halyard and the sail with sail ties. We switched the engine on to maintain speed and were making slow but steady progress through big and confused seas. The motion was extremely uncomfortable—everything that wasn't stowed was finding its own new home. Every few minutes or so a wave broke over the boat, flooding the cockpit.

Ayama was now 1 mile to starboard ready for our mid-ocean repair kit transfer the next day. I was hoping the swells would abate by then.

As if we needed more to deal with, the pin securing the Watt & Sea hydrogenerator had come out, which needed securing from the stern of *Aretha*. The final twist was we had lost all our eggs as they flew out of the microwave, smashing everywhere—the end of pancakes for this leg!

I sat, thinking that normal life problems wouldn't seem quite the same after this.

Someone had once told me that life isn't about what happens to you, it's about what you do when it happens to you. Right then, Team *Aretha* was working extraordinarily well under testing circumstances, finding resourceful solutions. As with Willow's accident, we were giving the children a good grounding in what to do when life chucks a whole bunch of stuff at you: stay calm and work through each issue one at a time with a smile. Not stuff you can teach in a classroom: real life lessons. It was interesting to hear Bluebell and Columbus that day refer to our previous "situation" sailing to Niue aboard a dark boat with no power for three days. They had a frame of reference already for dealing with challenging stuff and it was starting to seem normal to them to approach challenges without any fuss.

Morning Brings Fresh Challenges

By 4am the wind had abated and we re-hoisted the triple-reefed main so the boat movement was more steady with a small amount of genoa, allowing us to shut down the engine and progress under sail again, albeit at reduced speed.

I came back on deck at first light to discover a fresh challenge. My check of our jury rig showed that one broken wire on the D1 had become three broken wires. We were down to 16 out of 19 strands.

This was seriously dangerous—we needed to take immediate action to stop the mast coming down. I called below to Max that we were tacking. By turning the boat around—heading away from South Africa back toward Réunion—we would take all the load off the port D1, transferring it to the still-intact starboard D1. Within a minute we were tacking the boat.

I felt immediate relief as now the mast was held up on the strong side. The obvious downside was we were heading in the wrong direction, away from our destination.

I called *Ayama* on the VHF and explained our situation. They had been sailing faster than us and were 20 miles ahead and agreed to turn around to come back toward us with the repair equipment.

We slowed the boat as much as we could. At the same time we decided to give the mast extra support on the port side. We took a spare Dyneema halyard and tied it around the mast at the first spreaders and then brought it down through a block near the base of the D1 and then onto a winch, putting tension on the halyard so that it could start to share the load of the mast with the port D1.

Nichola readied herself to be winched up the mast to secure the line around the spreaders. After a detailed safety brief and making sure she was absolutely secure with helmet on, she climbed the mast. The seas were rough, bouncing her around; it was taking what seemed like an age to tie the halyard around the spreader—after 10 minutes she said she was happy with it. We lowered her to the deck. I could feel her shaking as I held on to her, lowering her the last few feet. Being 30 feet above the deck in 13-foot seas is no small feat when you're being thrown violently from side to side.

We put the other end of the halyard (now a makeshift shroud) through the block, tensioning it on the winch. We looked up and saw the line around the spreader slipping. It needed to be resecured. Max worked the winch to hoist me up the mast. It was bouncy stuff. I was holding on with one arm to stop myself being thrown around against the mast like a rag doll while tying the knots with the other hand. I made the adjustments and was lowered back on deck.

We tensioned the new D1 again and she held. We cranked it some more and I was happy to see the load now being shared between the D1 and the new halyard.

Given that we had three broken wires on the original D1, I wanted to have two backup solutions in place—the new line we'd just attached, plus the rigging wire and bulldog clamps that *Ayama* was bringing.

While we waited for *Ayama*, we discovered another problem. The engine was overheating. That could wait. We had to deal with one problem at a time.

Our pressing challenge was how to work out a boat-to-boat transfer in 13-foot seas. It's not as easy as you might think. It was way too dangerous to bring the boats alongside—two boats weighing 25–30 tonnes each crashing into each other as they tried to come side by side just isn't worth thinking about. It was too rough to launch a dinghy to go from one boat to the other.

We debated asking *Ayama* to drop a buoy over the side with the equipment securely attached to it so we could pick it up with a boathook. It was a possibility, but not without the danger of getting ropes wrapped around the propeller. Or of missing the buoy.

Another option was to get a water bottle and half fill it with water with a very long thin line tied to it. We'd bring the boats as close as we dared to throw over the bottle with the line to *Ayama*. They'd catch the line, tie it to the container with the equipment safely inside it, throw it over the side and we'd pull the line in with the equipment. It sounded like a workable plan.

Two hours later *Ayama* appeared on the horizon and we communicated the plan over the VHF radio. They were ready to go. I took the helm to steer *Aretha*. Max put on his foul-weather gear, lifejacket, and harness and moved to the stern to throw the bottle and line to *Ayama*.

First attempt went flying. It fell short.

Ayama looked huge as she came close, rising and falling with a crash. We needed to be extremely careful. With some expert seamanship by Captain Stefan, he nudged her as close as possible.

Max threw again: again, just short.

Third time lucky. The water bottle landed on deck and I called to Max to have line ready to pay out and at the same time make sure there was no slack line in the water that could tangle our propeller. *Ayama* dropped back a little to keep a safer distance between us while Pelle, one of their crew, secured the container to the line and threw it over the side.

Max hauled the line in and within minutes we had a large yellow waterproof container on deck. We thanked Stefan and the crew of *Ayama* as they wheeled around and headed toward Africa. We now had work to do.

I opened the box to find the bulldog clamps. Within an hour we had secured the super-strong bulldog clamps on either side of the broken rigging using spare rigging wire. We linked it back through a block and loaded it on to our biggest and most powerful winch. We tensioned it up, inch by inch, to make sure the clamps were holding. We needed to be totally confident this would hold. When it became bar tight, I was happy that the repaired shroud was fully loaded. Max had the idea to mark the levels on the rigging wire with permanent pen so we could monitor the jury rig in case there was any movement.

Once we were done, we gently tacked the boat and loaded up the repaired D1. It looked fine so we shook out a reef, increasing our sail area. I needed to repair the furling system on the headsail next. That was a relatively quick fix. Ten minutes later we had both sails set, *Aretha* pointing toward Richards Bay in South Africa. Just 716 miles to go!

We celebrated with a packet of chicken-flavored two-minute noodles. The children had been exceptionally calm throughout, earning praise and special sweet treats from us.

Could we have been better prepared? Of course. We could have taken every spare ever needed. If we had done that, there probably wouldn't have been enough space on the boat for us. The key lesson for us was to be creative, resourceful, and not afraid to ask for help. It was humbling to have had so much help both on the radio and in emails. Fellow sailors contributed ideas on how to fix the rigging and engine, on weather routing, as well as shipping traffic in case we urgently needed help. It's one of the first rules of the sea. Always be prepared to help others. It's a pretty useful rule on land as well. It also goes without saying that I'd now recommend that bulldog clamps should be an essential part of anyone's spares kit for sailing.

Max's Blog On Risk

I am sure after reading Caspar's blog about the incident with Willow, many people may have been filled with the thought of this trip as proof of the terror and potential recklessness of being aboard a boat—so many things can go wrong. I have to say terror is too strong a word, though it is a little unnerving being on a boat where we have reinforced the rigging ourselves and have to sail more miles in the next three days than the average yacht will sail in a year, with our repair in place.

Both Nichola and Caspar are fastidious when it comes to safety on board and rightly so. Not many people in the sailing world check the rigging daily, check the engine daily, never go on deck without a lifejacket... It's funny that some people gasp at the thought of the family going sailing when in my opinion, it's far more dangerous to get a lift in a person's car—I can guarantee they haven't checked the tires before they set out, they didn't check the brake fluid, check the lights, oil or water... Yet you will happily drive down a road at 60 mph with someone else coming the other way at 60 mph who also hasn't checked any of the above. It's a perspective thing.

 Captain's Log (343 Miles to South Africa) 27°22'S 38°24'E, November 7, 2015

3.33am. All is calm on board tonight.

The wind has finally backed to the northeast meaning we can sail directly to Richards Bay. For the past six hours we had been pushed north so it's good to be going direct at 8 knots and closing the miles. Children, Nichola, and Max are all sleeping soundly. It's been a calmer day and we've diagnosed the engine overheating to a leak on the heat exchanger. We can run the engine for several hours before we have to stop it, let it cool down, and then top up with coolant. Hopefully the wind will let us sail all the way without needing too much motoring and we can repair the leak once ashore.

Nature highlight of the day was a large squid that got washed on deck overnight—one for Columbus's (who is currently getting inspiration from reading Gerald Durrell—classic stuff— thank you Sharon) wildlife journal.

Weather highlight was spending time with Bluebell reading the weather with me and her interpreting the GRIB (General Regularly-distributed Information in Binary) files and comparing what we have and predicting our weather for the next 12 hours—getting lots of practice on angles and degrees.

Willow's head seems to be healing nicely. Her hair has helped knit the wound together, which will be fine until we arrive in Richards Bay and can get it examined more thoroughly. She seems full of beans—which is worrying as she's more likely to injure herself again! Read children bedtime stories—first for a few nights. Dinner was pretty basic—baked beans for the children, two-minute noodles for adults. Boat looks like a bomb has exploded inside. Thankfully it only ever seems to take a short while to tidy again.

Checked the rigging, new line seems nice and tight. Deck is completely covered in salt. Every time you come back from being outside it looks like you have been rolling in icing [confectioners'] sugar.

Clearly going crazy—that is the second pen I have put down and when I come back the pen is missing. Final drama, after shrouds breaking, Willow's head, engine running too hot... I broke the sodding coffee pot. Yes another has had a watery grave. Very depressing.

Today's Memories in the Logbook by Nichola

1. Clinging on for dear life up the mast mid-ocean.
2. Willow's face of glee when Max dressed her in clothes this morning.

3. Columbus and I having a cuddle while reading *Oliver and the Seawigs.*
4. Bluebell playing mom, feeding "the children" while adults spent the full day on deck.
5. Max throwing the line to *Ayama* as they charged up to us.
6. Tucking Willow in tonight she said, "Mummy will you sit and talk with me a little? Is it Christmas tomorrow, or maybe your birthday, or maybe my birthday? Maybe my birthday and I will be 6?" I suggested maybe 4, she said, "Will there be flags?" "It's not tomorrow but soon will be Christmas." Her response, "I'm so excited—I can't wait." She then snuggled down to sleep.
7. Directly north of us is Mozambique, Tanzania, Kenya, Ethiopia, Eritrea (and the border of Sudan), and Jeddah in Saudi Arabia. Directly south of us are the very isolated Prince Edward Islands, the Enderby Abyssal Plain, and Padda in Antarctica. Due east of us is Brisbane. Due west of us is Swaziland and Namibia.

Team *Aretha* in the Mozambique Basin, out.

Chapter 18

South Africa to Brazil—Our Second Atlantic Crossing
(Mid-November 2015 to February 2016)

We faced our final Indian Ocean test during the last six hours with *Aretha* pushing through the waves into headwinds and heavy seas as we crossed the Agulhas Current. We were making 3 knots while doing our best to protect our jury rig and keep things safe. When we finally made safe harbor inside Richards Bay—South Africa's largest commercial port, with many ships in and out every day—we were met by my mom aboard the World ARC welcome boat, with Victor guiding us the final mile through shallow waters. Safely tied up to the dock, it was lovely to see Mom and Paul for the first time in a year. We were also greeted by the Richards Bay Yacht Club Commodore with a bottle of bubbles, congratulating us on crossing the Indian Ocean.

We had passed a huge test as a crew. We had lived our values, working together as a team, dealing with everything that had been thrown at us.

We spent two weeks around Richards Bay, exploring the bushland of KwaZulu-Natal—a truly amazing part of Africa. We planned a variety of safaris to see the finest wildlife Africa has to offer—elephants, giraffes, rhinos, hippos, lions, crocs, antelopes of many varieties—just about everything you can imagine. The highlight was staying at Thula Thula, camping wild in the bush, waking up in the morning to vervet monkeys, nyalas, and vultures just outside the tent. We went on game treks through the bush, seeing the animals at close quarters. At night we enjoyed watching game from jeeps.

There was a wealth of new experiences for the children. It was magical to see them spellbound by the game parks, talking to rangers, devouring animal books, and writing journals with an energy we'd not seen for a while. Coming to Africa—sleeping under African skies and walking through the bush—was one of the experiences I was most looking forward to when we envisaged our adventure seven years earlier. It didn't disappoint. I was also under the spell and began reading *The Elephant Whisperer* by Lawrence Anthony (creator of the Thula Thula reserve and lodge that we stayed at), a beautifully written insight into his part of Africa and his relationship with his herd of elephants.

We pressed on with *Aretha* work, led by Warren, an extremely experienced rigger recommended by Oyster. Warren brought the new D1s, surveyed our rig completely, and declared us safe to press on to Cape Town where we would replace more of the rigging, strengthening certain parts. *Aretha* would be practically a new boat by the time we circumnavigated! The leaking engine water-cooling pipe was repaired, broken navigation lights were replaced, and broken mainsail cars repaired.

The Richards Bay Yacht Club fêted us with a Zulu welcome dance and a feast—one of the World ARC highlights. The club had superb child-friendly grounds and during our time there the children played with a host of other boat kids. Playing on the wide-open spaces, the pool, and the play area was perfect for them after a long passage. Kids bond quickly—they were running around playing games and carving wooden sticks in next to no time. For us, the yacht club bar and restaurant was the perfect welcoming place to share tales of past passages and make plans for our next legs.

The strong British pound combined with a weak South African rand meant everything was cheap—it was less expensive to eat out than cook aboard. It was also interesting to learn more of South African politics and the ongoing challenging political situation, and to witness the effect this was having on the country. The different struggles this magnificent country faced bubbled up in most conversations with people we met.

The passage south to Cape Town was a favored topic of conversation among the skippers—the Agulhas Current was the factor that demanded careful weather assessment. The current flows south at up to 6 knots and because of the dangers of rapidly changing weather conditions, we had to become weather experts with the assistance of the local briefing as well as the wisdom of local delivery skippers. We waited a week longer than planned in Richards Bay to get a better weather window. The plus side was more time with my mom, catching up.

Every single boat has repair work to do. It's just normal after a passage at sea. Some were more serious than others. *Hugur* had been out of the water fixing structural hull leaks; *Chat Eau Bleu* was replacing a cracked bulkhead, and *Garlix* needed to replace all their electronics after a direct lightning strike had torched anything electrical on board. Sailing offshore is a demanding adventure. No safety element can be overlooked—the consequences of neglect don't bear thinking about.

After riding out a 50-knot storm in Richards Bay (our dock was scarily breaking up), we refueled and headed southbound for East London with five other boats. We had planned to put into Durban (forever etched in my mind as the place my super-talented business partner Ed started his career, working on the ships), but the window for heading south lengthened so we used the current to make the 340-mile hop south to East London in one go. East London is South Africa's only natural river harbor, a welcome port offering safe haven on this exposed coastline. We put in there, anchoring near the 15 or so other yachts taking shelter.

We'd already discovered via VHF that there were other boat kids at the dock and within hours Bluebell and Columbus were charging around the grounds of the Buffalo River Yacht Club with new friends, making dens, using the wheelbarrow and supermarket carts to push each other around at high speed. All totally non-PC back at home—out here it's all fair game. The first night we had a *braai* (barbecue) at the yacht club with plentiful steaks and cold drinks—we were getting used to this South African way of living!

Many years ago I read a book called *A Fish Caught in Time* about a coelacanth caught off East London in 1938. Scientists had thought the species—which dated back 65 million years, a time before the dinosaurs—was extinct. I sought out the East London museum where the taxidermied specimen was on display with the full history of the species, as well as a treasure trove of other information on local animals, culture, and shipping. I returned with Nichola and the children the next day—we found school projects there to last a month. Truly fascinating—great to connect the dots from previous learning.

We stayed for three days and planned for the next part of our passage to take just under a week to get to Cape Town. As we left East London, the South African base for Mercedes and BMW, we had to wait for a huge car transporter vessel docked 100 yards ahead of us to load up with freshly baked C-Class Mercedes. When we finally departed the safe harbor we were met by huge waves and a pod of dolphins leaping all around.

Cape Town in December

Cape Town is without doubt my favorite landfall, tucked underneath stunning Table Mountain with a rugged coastline stretching down to the Cape of Good Hope. After a relatively uneventful passage, we rounded the Cape of Good Hope on December 2, 2015 at sunrise with calm seas. It brought back happy memories of sailing there in 2000 during the BT Global Challenge. On this passage the "Cape of Storms" had been kind to us, providing benign conditions. We sailed up the Cape in the company of dozens of whales, dolphins, and seals.

Our planned home for the upcoming month (our longest time in any one place since leaving the UK) was the Victoria & Alfred Waterfront—a truly stunning first-rate development of shops and restaurants next to the marina. We felt as if we had our own private marina at the base of Table Mountain, with direct access to the waterfront wildlife all around—especially the South African fur seals that regularly hopped onto the docks to laze in the sun.

Of course, the month flew by. Our personal and dedicated tour guides were friends from back home who now lived in Cape Town—their daughter was the same age as Bluebell. They showed us their city, introduced us to their friends, and we spent marvelous times eating out, touring vineyards, attending parties, watching car races, and partaking in all kinds of kids' activities.

The children and I stayed at a guesthouse while Nichola attended a course in the States for ten days. The kids and I had a great deal of fun.

It was here that Willow learned to swim. With her usual determination for everything in life, she simply made the decision that it was time for her to swim and just went for it. Columbus and I took a bus tour around the city one day—the highlight was finding rock dassies on Table Mountain. (Dassies are also known as rock badgers—they resemble guinea pigs, and their closest relative is the modern-day elephant.) Bluebell and I took a tour of the townships (government designated areas where some of the indigenous populations still live) around Langa and Khayelitsha. We saw the local witch doctor—Bluebell made a miraculous recovery from her "not feeling very well" when asked to tell the witch doctor what was wrong.

We spent Christmas Day with the crews of six World ARC yachts—a potluck feast with dishes provided by each boat, followed by an afternoon playing games, along with a visit from Father Christmas. For Nichola's birthday we enjoyed a picnic in the sun at nearby Constantia with her parents, Sheila and Laurie, who'd just arrived the previous day. The children took surfing lessons at Muizenberg and we all stroked cheetahs at a wildlife sanctuary. We watched penguins on Boulders Beach. We met many old friends. On New Year's Eve we had a *braai* (barbecue) with the World ARC yachts followed by a party on *Makena*.

Aretha received much attention, too: new rigging, all sails refreshed, new seat cushion covers, new mainsail cover, hull antifouled, and engine fully serviced—bringing her back to A1 condition.

We were sad to wave goodbye to Max after a great three months. He had been brilliant with the children, calmly dealing with Willow's accident and our rigging failure, and had meshed superbly with our family. It's hard stepping into a boat, sailing offshore for weeks at a time—tensions can surface easily. I cannot remember a single cross word from Max through all of it. He was steady as a rock and a most able shipmate—very much a part of Team *Aretha*.

In short, the Cape Town layover was incredible and it was hard to leave. Africa had got under our skin—it's a place to which we intend to return.

So, onward. We planned to sail first to the tiny island of St. Helena (population 4,000) in the middle of the Atlantic. The first ever airport was due to open in 2016, but for now the only way to get there was via the ocean. After St. Helena we intended to sail 2,000 miles to Salvador de Bahia in Brazil.

Off the Namibian Coast

We had been rejoined in Cape Town by Paul and Jani, who had both sailed from the Canaries to St. Lucia with us the first time we crossed the Atlantic, 14 months earlier. It was terrific to have them back aboard for the crossing to Brazil. We looked forward to sharing the next stage of our adventure with them.

We recorded *Aretha*'s highest speed ever in the following seas off the coast of Namibia. Nichola was on watch when we clocked an unbelievable 19.6 knots. We were surfing on a 30-tonne surfboard in 16-foot waves. Rock'n'roll.

It always took a few days to get settled into an ocean passage. After three and a half days of strong winds up to 40 knots, the breeze finally settled down to a more manageable 20–25 knots with the seas reducing from 16-foot to 10-foot swells. The movement of *Aretha* became more fluid, in tune with the seas, and we were now sailing downwind with the genoa poled out to one side and the mainsail on the other side, providing a stable boat.

Now that we had a very experienced crew on board, I made the decision to change the watch system. I created three watches run by Nichola, Paul, and Jani of three hours on, six hours off. Bluebell and Columbus by now were keen to join night watches and usually took at least one night watch with a different adult each time. They enjoyed being part of the system. I would be available when needed and spent more time with the children, reading to them—*The Owl and the Pussy Cat* to Willow, and *The Elephant Whisperer* to Columbus.

Values Lessons—Food for Thought

We always sought to include new crew in our routines. To help with this, the children created values charts for Paul and Jani so they could participate in the morning discussions and have somewhere to mount their stickers.

I had been varying how we ran our values sessions to make sure the children were actively engaged. One day I'd ask each person aboard to nominate someone for a values prize, including a succinct reason for the nomination. This allowed the children to appreciate the values and behaviors demonstrated by others. Another variation as we sat around in the saloon was for each person to pick a value that the person on their left-hand side demonstrated. If for any reason I missed anyone as we worked our way around our circle—which I sometimes did deliberately to make sure everyone was paying attention—it was only seconds before this omission was pointed out to me. On other days I'd ask everyone to say what value they themselves had best demonstrated during the past 24 hours, including an explanation as to why they deserved a values prize. Like any of us, the children were eager to be praised for their positive contributions.

Back in the Indian Ocean when he first rejoined us, Max had been skeptical about our values prizes and discussions. It took him a while to see the positive side. Despite not being a morning person, after a week he made sure he was awake and at the breakfast table ahead of time for our sessions and was as honest as possible about his feelings. He started to enjoy the sessions and looked forward to the values prizes each morning. Why wouldn't you want to hear something nice about yourself and have the chance to tell someone something they'd done well? To see the smile on their face, to see them flourish with positive praise? Everyone thrives from feedback on what they do well.

Paul, like Max, had observed changes in the children. After one year he sensed that they all took much more interest in what was happening on the boat, were more settled in their environment, and proactively thinking about what they could do to help.

The Leading Edge

A concept I took from my business training was the "leading edge," the top skill or area that is the most important for you to develop. Framing one's areas of focus is much more constructive than saying you are weak in this area and need to develop. Rather than providing criticism, the concept works to guide and steer. What you focus on most is usually what happens in your life most. If you say "Don't panic" to someone, the first thing they do is panic because the subconscious mind struggles to process negative commands. The mind responds quicker to clear direction, saying do this or do that. So, if you want to avoid panic, uttering the words "Stay calm" is more likely to lead to your intended outcome. It was this understanding that led us to focus on behaviors we DID want aboard *Aretha* rather than those we didn't want.

Don't get me wrong: I've fallen into the trap many times of raising my voice with my children, telling them off, focusing on exactly what they are doing wrong. This is my issue—I get caught up in the emotion of the moment. It would be virtually impossible to never revert to this behavior. But we've consciously strived to focus on the desired behavior—and that includes our own!

Daily Questions

Another technique we used to engage everyone on board was a set of morning and evening questions. To remind us of these, we had two laminated lists posted on the saloon wall that Bluebell had worked with me to illustrate:

The five morning questions:
· What am I grateful for right now?
· What am I committed to achieving today?
· What am I excited about today?
· What am I happy about?
· What am I proud of?

The three evening questions:
· What have I given today?
· How have I invested in my future today?
· How have I contributed to other people today?

At every breakfast and dinner I asked one of the children to choose one of the questions to ask the group. We then went around the table so each person could answer. In the evening, without fail, Bluebell wanted to hold everyone accountable as to whether they had delivered on their commitments.

Continued Learning

For the first time in a while we had flying fish on deck. We were looking forward to getting the lines out for some fresh dorado and wahoo as the breeze calmed. We settled into life at sea again. St. Helena was 1,000 miles away.

Paul, after a career as a marketing director, had gone back to university to learn maritime history and now lectured on cruise liners on his special interest subjects. As on his earlier passage with us, Paul treated us to several maritime lectures including ones on Captain Cook, Christopher Columbus, and St. Helena. We learned that Napoleon was imprisoned on St. Helena for many years, and that it was now home to the oldest animal in the world, a tortoise of more than 180 years.

Sailing from South Africa to Brazil, Columbus, who was capable of remembering vast numbers of facts, delighted in setting up pre-dinner quizzes for the adults, asking us questions about fish, as well as African and Australian animals. During the day he'd come to all the adults with his animal books and offer them to us so we could learn as much as we could before the quiz.

Poetry Readings

Having Paul and Jani aboard gave me more time than usual so I was working my way through our extensive library. We'd just left St. Helena to sail the 1,900 miles to Brazil when I found a book of poetry by Walt Whitman, a Christmas gift from Sharon. As I read at the chart table I decided that poetry actually should be read out loud rather than silently.

So began our poetry readings—after half a dozen readings of Whitman, the crew were hungry for more.

Nichola suggested we email our blog readers to send us their favorite poems. We were amazed with the response—within an hour our inbox was alive and bubbling with Tennyson, Yeats, Kipling, Lewis Carol, Robert Louis Stevenson, Ogden Nash. Poems flowed in steadily over the following days.

I began reading poetry at the skipper's morning briefing, at lunchtime, and in the evening, with as much theatrical impact and intonation as I could muster. Trying to hold the attention of a three-year-old requires you to be more engaging than usual. Bluebell and Columbus were absorbed—unusually quiet and engaged.

We thanked our followers for this wealth of words and inspiration. My mom, ever the teacher, spotted an opportunity, emailing back to ask whether the children could write and email her their own poems. Bluebell and Columbus sat down straight away with pen and paper at the saloon table.

In a short time Bluebell brought her poem to us. She composed herself to read it aloud—a little shaky at first, but she soon got into the flow. It was lovely and we applauded. When our children were engaged and interested they were a thousand times more likely to absorb knowledge than when pushed, or when we imposed our own topics. We became much more aware of what caught their attention in the world around us, seizing the learning opportunities to keep the children's minds open and growing.

Time for What Matters—Nichola's Reflections

17 months at sea ... 630 miles to Salvador in Brazil.

As I am sitting here on watch (06.00-09.00) the children are not yet awake so all is peaceful as we continue to make our way to Brazil.

We only have a few more months at sea. The last 17 months sailing together as a family has flown by—we have become a close family unit. When we left the UK with the five of us together 24 hours it was a challenge—24 hours a day in a small space with three young children takes getting used to—as does spending 24/7 with your husband—especially when you have become distant partners due to long hours of work.

Those gritty first months are behind us. Now we enjoy our extended times together. We still have our disagreements and the children do fall out from time to time, but it never lasts long and underneath all of that there is a close bond formed from our shared sailing experience.

People often ask, "Don't the children get bored?" and "What do you do on those long passages, all stuck together in the boat?"

We keep so busy there simply isn't the time to be bored. We are three weeks into our passage from Cape Town to Brazil; we had a 72-hour stopover in St. Helena but for the most part it has been the five of us joined by our good friends Paul and Jani, sailing and enjoying each other's company.

There are many activities on board. For example we have "games night" which the children absolutely love. On this leg we introduced the children to bingo. Columbus and Bluebell mastered the rules quickly. Willow—just getting used to the numbers from 1 to 10—took longer. As I called out the numbers she'd look at her card for a minute, then turn to Paul on her left and whisper "have I got that one?" Paul let her know whether she was a step closer to winning. She obviously had beginner's luck, romping away with the numbers. When she got one she'd shout "yes," punching the air while trying not to shake all the counters off her card.

We have also discovered Bananagrams. It's like Scrabble but easier and much more fun for children. Columbus and Bluebell love it and it's been great for their literacy (we certainly have fewer dodgy words each time we play). It's great learning a game from your children—they are so much more invested in sticking with it when they realize they are quicker at it than their mom!

We also play Monopoly—we have my old board, which the children tell me is "ancient" but great because the pieces are made of metal rather than plastic. The kids love the property dealing and money handling. And we play cards—Columbus is keen to learn poker from Caspar, especially as Columbus was told by someone he met on our travels that they paid for their first home with poker winnings.

We create lots of quizzes. The children pick teams and compete against one other. Other activities for Bluebell and Columbus are cooking and baking. Bluebell has also reignited a passion for sewing, making the rest of the crew sewn felt gifts, e.g., the lovely heart bookmark residing in my current novel.

Schoolwork takes up the mornings—journal writing, mathematics, geography, with some science, sailing, philosophy, and art thrown in for good measure. Yesterday the children learned the phonetic alphabet, testing it out on each other's names. Columbus built a balsa wood model lion. Willow completed every jigsaw she could find on the boat and then she and Bluebell built a great Lego house. We have DVD films, and games on iPods and Kindles, but these devices could be thrown over the side today and the children would delight in entertaining themselves.

This morning I looked through my computer and found a poem that touched me back on January 23, 2014—we were knee deep in preparation for this trip, busy with work and "life." At the time the poem made me stop and think so much that I copied it out on my phone, carrying it with me so I would remember what mattered.

Slow down mummy, there is no need to rush,
Slow down mummy, what is all the fuss?
Slow down mummy, make yourself a cup tea.
Slow down mummy, come and spend some time with me.
Slow down mummy, let's put our boots on and go out for a walk,
Let's kick at piles of leaves, and smile and laugh and talk.
Slow down mummy, you look ever so tired,
Come sit and snuggle under the duvet and rest with me a while.
Slow down mummy, those dirty dishes can wait,
Slow down mummy, let's have some fun, let's bake a cake!

Slow down mummy I know you work a lot, but sometimes mummy, it's nice when you just stop.

Sit with us a minute, and listen to our day, spend a cherished moment, because our childhood is not here to stay!

By Rebekah Knight

That got me thinking about how we live as a family now—it made me smile :) We have come a long way not just in miles but in terms of how we are as a family and how we all enjoy spending time with one another.

Chapter 19

Circumnavigating the World
Brazil to Grenada
(February 2016 to March 2016)

Landfall in Brazil

We made landfall in Brazil on January 31, 2016. After 25 days at sea since leaving Cape Town, we were safely in Brazil, having completed our second Team *Aretha* Atlantic crossing. Expectations were high as we approached the buzzing city of Salvador, home to three million Brazilians gearing up for Carnival, during which the city shuts down for ten days. We had heard Carnival's reputation as the largest street party in the world and we were excited to be part of it.

The final approaches to Salvador were a little anxious—our engine was cutting out every half an hour or so. We'd dissected most parts of the fuel system but still couldn't resolve the problem. As we approached Salvador close inshore past the Barra Lighthouse and Christ the Redeemer monument, we were close to a large sandbank with the sails and anchor ready in case the engine cut out. We navigated in the dark through the shipping channels and past ferries buzzing around—the lights moving against a background of light and music as the pre-carnival noises filled the warm evening air.

We safely docked in time to celebrate Sarah's birthday, joining *Makena* for celebratory drinks on board. Mooring up was classic Mediterranean style: anchor off the bow, stern to the dock, and the gangplank (passarelle) over to the quay. It was a lively dock to say the least, requiring some deft moves from all of us to get off *Aretha* safely.

The luxury and stability of Cape Town V&A Marina seemed a distant memory.

We explored Salvador, sampling Carnival for ten days. Our first experience was a men's night down the main road leading to the lighthouse. Although it was still two nights before Carnival properly started, the city was roaring. Groups of drummers and dancers were working their way along the road. With ten sailors in a bustling crowd, it wasn't long before we lost each other and were fragmented into four groups. Despite warnings to only take what we wanted to lose, I had brought my iPhone. Within an hour I'd had it pinched from my hand. By the time I'd turned around, the thief was long gone. I was warned. An expensive lesson.

Another evening saw us and the *Makena* crew walking alongside the carnival trucks for several hours. We walked alongside Olodum, probably the most famous group there—they'd recorded with Paul Simon and Michael Jackson. The crowds were huge, as was the police presence. Cohorts of five armed and helmeted officers followed a strict routine, working their way through the crowds. Every two minutes another five walked by. Offenses were dealt with severely and quickly— fast whacks with long truncheons and handcuffs. Thankfully, their revolvers stayed in their holsters. This was not a place for the faint-hearted: blasting music, flowing beers, dancing crowds. If you didn't want to dance, well you didn't have a choice. The movement of the crowd carried everyone along. A street party of epic proportions. It was vibrant and buzzing.

We found afternoon events for the children so they, too, could experience Carnival. We sat in the square in the old town of Pelourinho as different groups paraded the streets. Vibrant colors shimmered while the music blasted. One of the groups of revelers, The Sons of Gandhi, stood out magnificently in their blue and white costumes—several thousand of them.

Paul and Jani stayed with us for the week after our arrival. We explored the old town, the countless churches—some with fantastic amounts of gold and ornamentation, in stark contrast to the poverty in Salvador and the *favelas* (slums). We'd been warned by friends before we arrived about the Zika virus. Amazingly there was barely a mention of it and without notice from our friends we'd have been unaware. Thankfully, there were few mosquitoes around but we didn't take chances—we used bug spray and set up netting at night.

The weather was searingly hot and it was great to escape to a truly first-rate air-conditioned mall to cool down. The mall had every brand and store you could imagine in London and was full of wealthy Brazilians. Another haunt we found was Bahia Marina—a smart marina a mile down the road with great sushi and Wi-Fi. Wi-Fi as always was the essential commodity among sailors—especially so for us as this time we were planning our next adventures.

A year before, we had been heading toward the Galapagos—the whole world was ahead of us. The end of our trip was now in sight, generating a range of emotions. Elation that we'd have circumnavigated by the time we reached Grenada; sadness that the World ARC was coming to an end and we'd be saying goodbye to this incredible group of sailors we'd called our family for the past year; excitement at the adventures that lay ahead; uncertainty at what the future held.

After ten days in Salvador, it was time to depart. We refueled, heading out into the shipping lanes only for the engine to fail again. Thankfully we'd made a local friend, Marcelo, a big man with energy and an eye for a deal. He's also a handy guy with the knowledge to fix most things. We turned back, calling Marcelo to arrange a mechanic.

During our earlier stay in Salvador, Marcelo had invited us with other crews to his house for lunch. We ate fine Brazilian dishes while the kids played in a magnificent tree house Marcelo had built, complete with a 20-foot fireman's pole. Willow loved climbing up and coming down the pole. After lunch we'd visited his mother—a talented artist with exhibits all over the world—every inch of the place filled with her artwork. We all purchased mementos of that lovely day.

We sailed back to Bahia Marina, getting towed in with the help of several friends in dinghies. True to his word, Marcelo had arranged for a mechanic who diagnosed and fixed the problem with our secondary fuel filters. We ran the engine on the dock for an hour and all seemed fine.

We stayed in Brazil for another day and then headed north to the tropical islands of Fernando de Noronha. The first 48 hours were bouncy with the wind on the nose—Nichola and Columbus were seasick—it took time to adjust to being back at sea. But then we had a calm evening, the crew settled, while a full moon lit the sea around us. We were 25 miles off the coast, with *Hugur* and *Ayama* a few miles away for company, with all the hatches open sending the breeze down through the boat. This was the first time we'd had just the five of us aboard since Max joined us in the Cocos, so we had to adjust again to our routines without help to channel the energy of three lively kids.

Message from Max, January 11, 2016

As I read the new incoming blogs, it does make me very sad not to be there with you or be part of it on another boat sailing alongside you.

I am slightly homesick for a brief stint. *Aretha* was also my home and I miss her. I also miss the 24/7 company. Knowing that someone is always around the corner to chat to, jump on me, play with me or talk to me was a lovely thing. Rather than a distant-uncle Max I have hopefully been a not-so-distant uncle Max who the kids might have learned something from and hopefully not just picked up my bad habits.

I like to think we as a boat made a good team. I learned a huge amount and for me the only low was leaving you all behind. Each day for me had something that made me super happy to be there and not one day did I wish I was somewhere else.

The downs, such as our Réunion to South Africa crossing for me was a highlight—I don't think I have ever learned so much on a boat. Sailing when things are easy is nice but you don't really get to learn much. Dealing with drama is a skill that needs experience, and it was great to be there to help.

I think I finally got sailing in a slightly different way and began to get the joy of being at sea with a purpose to go somewhere in a different way.

Since coming back I am already in conversation with a company to start work on getting my day skipper and coastal [license]. Apparently I need four hours of night watch and 100 miles. I think I have 8,000 miles in total over two boats and just a few night watches… While I thought the course looked daunting before I left, reading through it again 90 percent of it looks like a piece of cake as I have now done it all a million times.

Before I came on the boat I didn't think you were bonkers, just a little brave. Seeing the change in the kids as well as you both it has been nothing short of a transformation in my eyes. The kids' confidence has naturally grown, Caspar has become far more relaxed than I ever thought possible and Nichola, well looks fabulous as she was always fabulous.

Now I am home, I wish I wasn't. It has been one of the most productive mental breaks I have ever had. A holiday is one thing, but holidaying with a true purpose is something else. I feel this is a key milestone in my life.

Sailing the Venezuelan Coast

 Captain's Log, 09°56'N 056°57'W, March 11, 2016

It's 2.37am. I've been sitting up on deck—the sky is incredibly clear and cloudless with a sliver of moon. The stars are so bright they come all the way down to the horizon and merge with the sea. It's hard to tell where the sky ends and the sea begins—it all blurs into one, making it nigh on impossible to distinguish ship lights from stars.

For the past three nights it's been like this and I've spent hours on deck with Bluebell and Columbus staring up at the stars and using the stargazing app, we have been identifying constellations, galaxies, planets, and stars. Favorites have been Jupiter, which is very bright to our starboard side, the Leo constellation next to Jupiter, Sirius, Orion, all of which Columbus is becoming expert at spotting. For an hour on deck tonight Columbus was utterly absorbed reading out to me

248

description after description of different things he was learning of the night sky. Learning by immersion definitely works for him and you realize that the night sky is available to every one of us every night to appreciate and enjoy.

Bluebell and I reflected on whether there was a little girl and her Dad sailing around their world some millions of miles away on another planet looking out at the dots in their sky and wondering if there were others like her out there. We spoke of how the world had been here for millions of years before us and how the world would be here millions of years after us and just how vast it was out there and the different galaxies and solar systems of which we knew so little. Food indeed for thought, and time to appreciate that we really are here in this world for just a heartbeat in the context of the universe and that it's for each of us to make the most of the time we are given here—to enjoy life and to contribute to others.

Three nights previously, I was on deck and in similarly flat calm conditions off the French Guiana coast when I spotted what I thought was a flare. My immediate thought was someone was in trouble, making sure the radio was turned up to listen for a call for help. The light, though, intensified and moved across the night sky with increasing intensity—more than you get from a flare. Ah, a shooting star—wow—this is a huge one. It kept going. After 20 seconds it was burning more brightly than ever in the shape of a large elliptical object. Maybe it's a comet, I wondered. It kept burning and was now flying over the top of *Aretha*.

The penny dropped. I remembered reading that Kourou in French Guiana is home to the European Space Center. It must be a rocket. It kept burning, moving fast until it disappeared behind a cloud. *Exody*, one of the other World ARC yachts, was 20 miles away from us; I called up Peter who'd been watching it too and had come to the same conclusion. Chatting with the other boats the following morning, some had seen it drop its afterburners into the sea as it continued skywards. I'm glad we weren't underneath that.

As we voyaged north to Grenada in the Caribbean we had flat calm seas, flat decks, and gentle trade wind sailing with the wind largely on the beam. It was civilized indeed—very enjoyable. We were due to finish the World ARC in St. Lucia. We only had two more nights of sailing in the company of our friends.

We sailed those last few miles of the ARC nearby our good friends, Luc, Sarah, and Kai aboard *Makena*. They sailed within 100 yards so we could take photos. As we closed we were surrounded by a large pod of common dolphins playing between the two sailboats as well as spinner dolphins with their characteristic twisting, spinning, airborne leaps. Luc launched his quadcopter—a flying drone with GoPro cameras on board—circling above the boats taking video as well as stills of us sailing surrounded by dolphins. All five of us were on deck, the children bouncing up and down, waving to Kai who was equally excited and wanted Sarah to launch their dinghy so he could come over to play. As the sun set, the clouds and skyline were intense—reds, oranges, blues, and grays with a vastness that a camera can only hint at—mesmerizing and enchanting.

After we watched the sun burn into the skyline, Sarah called us on VHF to look at their mainsail. They had turned their mainsail (and then their genoa) into an enormous cinema screen, projecting a video of Columbus's birthday party in South Africa. I challenge anyone else to say they have been to a drive through (sail through) cinema 250 miles off the Venezuela coast!

We now had just over 300 miles until we reached Port Louis in Grenada where we would cross our outbound track. We had cold drinks in the fridge ready to celebrate. That said, we were now in pirate waters and needed to be super-vigilant maintaining our offshore course. It was reassuring to sail in company with *Hugur* 50 miles ahead of us, *Makena* now 4 miles to port, and *Exody* 20 miles astern.

There was plenty of wildlife—unusual jellyfish with what looked like a pinky/red sail on top of the water; lots of dolphins; two bird visitors—even at 200 miles offshore—who simply hitched a lift overnight, using the aft deck as a poop deck then flying off in the morning.

Calm seas, glorious sunshine, happy children. We caught a small jack and a 20lb dorado—it took about 5 minutes for freshly filleted steaks to be sizzling away in the pan with olive oil and lime juice. Fresh food supplies were running low after a week at sea so it was a welcome addition. On the down side we snapped the stern bracket holding our Watt & Sea hydrogenerator—we were lucky to retrieve it before the whole thing fell off the boat.

Piracy

Before we left the UK we studied in great detail the areas of the world where there were pirate risks (one of the best resources was www.noonsite.com), planning our route from Day 1 to avoid piracy hot spots such as off the coast of Somalia in East Africa, in the Gulf of Aden, and the Straits of Malacca. It was something that we considered and took seriously. As we prepared to sail north from Brazil to Grenada we received reports of two separate pirate attacks off the north coast of Venezuela. The World ARC response and our opinion also was to sail 100 miles away from the coast, beyond the range of small fishing vessels used in the attacks, giving the area a wide berth.

Crossing Our Outbound Track

 Captain's Log, 1°58'N 61°02'W, March 3, 2016

We're now back in the Caribbean Sea and in 40 miles or so we will cross our outbound track as we enter the marina in St. George's in Grenada. It's hard to take in that in less than eight hours' time we will cross the line demarking that all five of us have sailed around the world. We had sundowners in the cockpit this evening and shared our favorite memories from what has been a remarkable experience.

We've come a long way since we left the UK in August 2014.

By the time we've moored up in Grenada we'll have stopped in 84 different locations around the world covering some 26 different countries and roughly 35,000 ocean miles. It'll take some time to sink in as we've been living at a fast pace and one experience has been layered on top of another on top of another. I'm certain we've all changed. Nichola and I are extremely privileged to be able to share so much time with our children, learning and experiencing the world on our way.

So, next stop Grenada, then we'll work our way north to St. Lucia where the World ARC finishes and we say goodbye to our World ARC family and head off for our next adventures. Details are still being fleshed out but I think we have a working plan.

I'm off to savor my last night watch—it's a glorious, starry night with the moon lighting up the sea, and I'm watching out for the lights on Grenada.

Team *Aretha* on the verge of circumnavigating the globe, Out.

Chapter 20

Working Together as a Team

"If you want to go fast, go alone. If you want to go far, go together."
—African Proverb

I think it's fair to say I didn't know my children very well before we embarked on our voyage. I'd spend only small amounts of time with them during the week, mostly when I was shattered—they didn't get the best of me. One of the reasons for our trip was that we wanted to get to know our children as people, sharing time and experiences together as a family. We wanted to teach them what we thought was important in life while experiencing the world with them. We hoped to teach them emotional resilience, and how to deal with adversity so that they could respond in the best way possible to whatever came up in their lives. We also wanted them to rub shoulders with, and learn from, some of the smartest and most inspiring people we knew.

The deepened relationship with our children is one of the enduring things that Nichola and I will carry for the rest of our lives—this experience makes the sacrifices that we made to get there worth every second.

I'll never forget the wonder of watching our children demonstrate their characters. Of three-year-old Willow utterly fearless walking among the Zulu warriors (at their welcome ceremony in South Africa) in full flow of war dance, then sitting down in the middle of the action to get a better view—she was simply curious and wanted to learn more. Of Columbus learning and sharing his knowledge all around the world; and of Bluebell courageously swimming into underwater caves in Tonga.

Teachers All Around

All along the way, the children learned from different teachers.

My mom has been a constant throughout my life—always there with advice and guidance. She taught sailing when she was younger and indeed taught me to sail in dinghies back in Devon on the south coast of the UK. Mom, a former teacher, emailed us questions and exercises for the children all around the world, urging the children to write back with creative and thoughtful responses. My mom loved being involved in our project and was a key part of the shore-based Team *Aretha*.

For several months the yacht *Makena* (owned by Sarah and Luc) was joined aboard by Sarah's dad, David, a brilliant mathematician. He taught Bluebell card tricks and how to play chess. He taught Columbus how to solve the Rubik's Cube by using mathematical formulas. David gave Columbus the space to figure things out for himself rather than just providing answers; within a month or so Columbus was confidently completing the Cube in under two minutes.

Sarah wrote her first best-selling mathematics book when she was 16, went on to become the Young European Scientist of the Year and then later enjoyed a diverse career in technology. Luc was a talented games designer who built and sold his own games companies in Silicon Valley. It's hard to convey the impact that this amazing couple and their two-year-old son, Kai, had on our children. They were so generous with their time. On the Indian Ocean, using the SSB net, Sarah taught Bluebell what a prime number was and how to work out all the prime numbers from 1 to 100 using a table. In Cocos (Keeling) Sarah bought a build-your-own combustion engine kit that she and Columbus completed in Cape Town over a couple of days. Afterward, Columbus proudly announced that he was now an engineer and showed their engine to the fleet, who would quiz him about the pistons, rockers, fuel tank, exhaust, etc. Luc discussed with the children the latest discovery that Pluto wasn't actually a planet.

Other sailors on the ARC included Pete, formerly in charge of running a fleet of US Navy warships in the Pacific, who shared knowledge on everything from tides to landing planes on aircraft carriers with our children. Another sailor was John, a fascinating character in his seventies, who spent hours talking with Columbus about different spiders and snakes in Australia. John had a diverse experience, from waterproofing the Sydney Opera House to owning and running a coffee plantation, as well as running a business catching fish and dangerous animals for sale to zoos around the world. His knowledge was only matched by his ability to tell a story and engage his listener. Many months after waving goodbye, Columbus still talked about him as the most interesting person he knew.

Having one-on-one conversations with so many talented and interesting people was the catalyst for the children learning so much; I'm not even scraping the surface of the people who spent time with them on *Aretha* and on land. Our unusual education and lifestyle presented vast opportunities for learning for our children—they thrived on it.

Cross-Cultural Experiences

Nichola and I were keen to instill in the children an appreciation of how fortunate they were and to help them live their lives with an understanding of humanity and other cultures. The sailing trip provided many different ways to expose them to cross-cultural experiences. They became innately familiar with having to adapt to languages and accents in different countries. The variety of food provided another perspective, ranging from the feasts of root vegetables, coconuts, and suckling pig in the South Pacific to the fire-baked fish in central Panama. We visited schools in different countries and let the children appreciate firsthand how schooling differed. We all carry strong memories of the school under the tamarind tree in Indonesia and the French school in Fakarava deep in the South Pacific. The traditions in each country involving singing, dance, and local musical instruments gave strong insights into how different cultures interact and enjoy time with each other.

Perhaps the simplest cultural experience was the children making friends and playing wherever we went. Seeing Willow play with a Panamanian girl of similar age in the Emberra village said it all for me. One fair-haired and with fair skin. One with dark hair and dark skin. No language was needed. Curiosity, a smile, and playfulness. Seeing humanity at its simplest shows us all we need to know. The human soul is happy to connect and play and be curious. Irrespective of race, religion, and background, at our core we are all humans and share that same innate warmth and desire to connect.

The Magic of Time Aboard

In my years following the BT Global Challenge, the friendships and the shared emotional highs and lows of that experience have been far more memorable than sailing any stretch of ocean. The shared situations became the anchor points for friendships that have lasted my lifetime. The same was true with our circumnavigation as a family.

The togetherness and camaraderie forged in time spent at sea is hard to convey. We were there in the same storms, the same anchorages with incredible sunsets. We'd shared our boat problems and worked together to solve them. Whenever possible, we'd been there willing and available to help other sailors when we could. It's just part of what you do at sea—going the extra mile for others. It's not just sailboats, but all mariners understand this, like the captain of an oil tanker sailing to Galveston (US) from Saudi Arabia who radio called us because he was concerned that we might not have enough food on board, to ask if we needed anything.

The crews from the ARC boats we sailed with became lifelong friends. We have spent far more time with these people than we'd spent with people back home. In port, we moored next to each other and saw them daily. We went on tours together, experiencing different cultures, whether climbing volcanoes or providing humanitarian aid to cyclone-hit regions. We shared meals. We'd talk late into the night, sharing stories from the past and hopes and dreams for the future. When at sea we were in constant contact, twice daily on the long-range SSB roll call to check in and provide help for those who needed it. When in VHF range, we also chattered away on the airwaves, swapping notes on sea conditions, fishing lures, and meals for the day.

No One Does This Alone

Taking on a project this size was no small thing. It was impossible to achieve what we wanted working alone. We simply couldn't have done this without the support of our friends and family. Throughout everything—getting the money together, building new businesses, making our plans, and especially while sailing around the world—we had to work as a team.

Lasting Change

The magnitude of our plan to sail around the world forced all of us to grow in ways we couldn't have even begun to imagine before we cast off.

I ask myself what I am certain that we have learned. I'm certain that the children have grown and learned much—not just school subjects, but about life and people and the world we live in. I'm certain we have all developed new levels of resourcefulness—no matter the situation, to stop, think, and figure things out using the materials at our disposal. I'm certain that we have all grown immeasurably in confidence. I'm certain we are more relaxed and happier with the world and ourselves. I'm certain that our relationships have grown and we understand each other a lot better. I think our growth on a deeper level began many years before we slipped lines from Southampton.

Our world has changed forever and our horizons are broader than ever. I look to the future and am excited to see how our children develop and grow with the real-world education we've been fortunate enough to give them. Understanding is one of our values. I'd like to think our understanding has grown—of us as people, of each other, of different cultures around the world, of the natural world.

If there is anything that I'd consider myself proud of, it is to have taught my children to understand emotions and how to react to whatever comes up, how they show up in the world, to focus on what they can give, not what they can take. I know our children are developing a global view of the world, understanding other cultures. I consciously don't ask them what they want to do when they are older. Instead I ask them what problems they want to solve, and how they can make the world a better place.

What Next?

We celebrated our circumnavigation with our friends in Port Louis, Grenada (see plate section, image 38). Port Louis was one of the finest marinas we'd been to with first-class docks, excellent Wi-Fi, a pool, a friendly bar, and restaurants. We had a bottle of champagne on board, special drinks for the children—we celebrated after we had tied up securely. It was an incredible feeling and it was lovely to rejoice in a place like Grenada with all our now-close friends.

The most common topic of conversation among our friends, as well as whenever we spoke to family and friends back home, was what we were going to do next.

One of the principles we set up when we planned our vision seven years earlier was that this was just part of our journey, a stepping stone that would lead on to new exciting things.

The Children's Perspective

Bluebell

What have you learned about yourself?
I have learned that I am very understanding about other people and their lives and I think that I have come more independent and more responsible and just helping out and being free at hand to whoever needs it. So I think that I have changed a lot.

What have your parents taught you?
My parents taught me lots of things like how to sail and schoolwork but most importantly they taught me how to be relaxed and happy and how to live my life.

What did you enjoy most?
The thing I mostly enjoyed was swimming with whale sharks it was so amazing and brilliant. I was just amazed how big they were.

What was it like having your parents as teachers?
It was interesting and it was fun and cool as they always made me laugh and so did Columbus and Willow.

Were you ever scared?
I was scared when there was a big storm and the rigging had broken and Willow cut her head.

Can you describe two really memorable experiences that you will remember all your life?
One of them is swimming with the whale sharks and also crossing the equator and enjoying the stars as we crossed it I had a pink milk. It was amazing.

Columbus
What have you learned about the world?
A shrimp's heart is in its head. Cape Town is voted the world's favorite city. That the big 5 are rhino, elephant, lion, buffalo, and the leopard.

What did your parents teach you?
Mathematics, spelling, how to earn money in life.

What did you enjoy most?
I really liked holding on to the fin of a nurse shark. I liked climbing Mount Yasur and seeing the lava splashing on the crater at the top. I really liked going on safari and seeing the animals. I liked snorkeling in the Caribbean. I liked going on a quad bike around Porto Santo.

Can you describe two really memorable experiences that you will remember all your life?
Diving with the nurse shark and holding on to its fin in a meter of water with the guide. The nurse shark would come along, grab its fin and he would pull me down and I would grab on to the fin. It felt very rough (the fin) and it was going along underwater with me holding on to its fin. I'd lose my grip.

Sailing round the world. Every day in the Indian Ocean we'd find flying fish on the boat. Going to the capital cities of countries, Lisbon, St. George's (Grenada), Panama City, Papeete (French Polynesia), St Denis (Réunion), Port Louis (Mauritius), Cape Town.

Re-entry Lessons from the BT Global Challenge

As I have mentioned, sailing the world on the BT Global Challenge Yacht Race had been a remarkable, life-changing experience. In my eight months of preparation I developed my sailing skills, raised a large amount of money, and attended to my relationship with Nichola. The focus was on preparing for and then experiencing the adventure. The one thing I didn't even consider was what would happen afterward. A life-changing experience would surely lead to amazing things and great stuff would happen, I thought.

Several months after I returned I was at a birthday party for my dad in Hope Cove in Devon. We'd had a lovely evening and much to celebrate. Despite all that I felt incredibly lonely. It was as though my world had just stopped. Imagine you are running along on an escalator and the world is fast moving. Then the escalator suddenly stops and you are wading in treacle. I'd had all these amazing experiences and life had suddenly gone back the way it had been before. Same apartment, same job, same routines. It was as though I had grown and I was now trying to fit back into my old world, which felt like it had shrunk. I'd moved on, yet everything at home had stayed the same.

I remember sitting at the bottom of my dad's garden at 2am feeling pretty low. One part of it is that what you've done is so extreme, no one can relate to it. Hundred-foot waves and icebergs and mayday situations back at home are all just words and it's hard to convey what you've experienced. When you have an amazing high like sailing around the world, the big danger is that you hit a big low.

So I had learned my lesson and knew that planning what came next was fundamentally important.

Reintegration—Adjusting to Life on Land

The Time After Our Circumnavigation

This time around we knew that our circumnavigation would be a springboard for something different. Right from the start, in our vision statement, there was space for what we were going to do next—to allow us to focus on what would follow. What we hadn't figured out until now was what exactly it would be.

We knew that whatever it was, it would be different and exciting. I knew that going back to our old home routine and getting on the daily commuter train was not an option. Our world had changed forever and we had the opportunity now to embark on new adventures. This was just the start.

Many people who have taken time out of the normal routines of life say that reintegration can be the hardest part. We've certainly met plenty of other people who've been on adventures and have fallen into a tough place afterward as they have struggled to adapt back to normal life.

We made certain that our time sailing around the world was only one part of our story. To the outside world I'm absolutely certain that it looked like the whole story but to us, right from the first idea, this was always more than sailing around the world. This was about changing our lives fundamentally in every way you could imagine.

What were we going to change? Our relationship with each other as husband and wife. Our relationships with our children, our perspective on life, our finances, the way we lived, what we were all about, and how we could contribute to the world.

We sailed around the world, but the fact was that it could have been anything that we could have done: a bike or camper van adventure, running an orphanage, living on a deserted island. The point was that we chose a burning focus and set a date when it had to happen by. That single decision catalyzed us to change our lives, to work together as a team, and to follow our Reason Why—to create life-changing experiences for us and our children.

And we did change everything in our lives. Having truly lived, worked, and enjoyed life together as a family, we are stronger, happier, healthier, and have far more to offer to the world than we did before.

While sailing, we made a decision that we didn't want to live in just one place. We had our home in England, just outside London. We decided that we also wanted to spend a good part of our time living in exciting, vibrant places around the world. We came up with a short list: Cape Town, Sydney, San Francisco, Boston, San Diego.

As we crossed the Atlantic the second time to arrive in Brazil, we debated this question at length among all five of us. We all had a view. We ended up choosing San Francisco as one place we wanted to spend more time in. We were drawn by the buzz and it helped that we knew a good few people there, and it was the center of the technology world. It's also known as the most European of US cities, and it has an amazing natural harbor. We decided to make plans to base ourselves there, at least for part of the time, and we made the decision to sail *Aretha* there so we could have a base.

Over the course of April and May 2016 we sailed *Aretha* back across the Caribbean Sea from Grenada, through the Panama Canal and the long upwind voyage on the Pacific Coast to San Francisco. Nichola, Bluebell, and Willow sensibly decided not to sail the upwind voyage so Columbus and I built a new crew to take on what is probably one of the toughest sailing passages in the world. A month of hard upwind sailing into big seas and big winds. Brutal is the best word for it.

At the end of May 2016 on a beautiful sunny morning we sailed underneath the iconic Golden Gate Bridge, entering San Francisco ready for the next chapter of our lives. We'd been fortunate to secure a place in one of the best marinas in the Bay area in Sausalito.

Since we landed there, we've been spending our time between London and San Francisco, planning the next stage of our lives using exactly the same process I've shared in these pages. We're sitting down most weekends, cutting out pictures, talking and imagining the next stage of our lives. We're pushing ourselves out of our comfort zone. We don't have the answers yet to how we are going to achieve this. We know that it will fall into place once we are clear on what we want for our lives and when the story we create about our future is so compelling that it is literally pulling us into the future. It's a continual conversation and it's exciting.

Where are we up to? We have our home in the UK and our boat home in San Francisco. We have created a new vision of the future that we are working toward—rather than having a traveling focus, our lifestyle is much more about the way in which we live our lives. We have created a vision of what we call "First Class World," which we now have as a handwritten family vision statement on our kitchen wall in full view of everyone who visits our home. In this vision we talk about living our lives focusing on the experiences we share together and how we manage life. We have again set wealth targets and a set of principles about how we will achieve our next goals. It's exciting and it's energizing us as a family to live every day and make the most of every moment.

While I travel the world delivering keynote talks on building teams and leadership, as a couple we have together launched programs called "The Brave You" and "Design Your Life," sharing with others the specific steps that we have used to consciously, deliberately, and specifically design exactly what we want in our lives. The most rewarding part of this is seeing the impact when other people apply the same tools and techniques in their lives that we have used and move their existence to a much fuller, intentional place, stepping beyond their comfort zone where the magic happens.

We continue to have sailing adventures and in the summer of 2017 we sailed *Aretha* on a month-long expedition from San Francisco to Canada, exploring the British Columbia coastline. We have many adventures ahead of us as well as a list of exciting things we are planning for the future using our vision of living in First Class World.

The Children's Reintegration—Back to School

When we first came up with our idea I had contacted Brian and Sheila, who'd circumnavigated with their three children three years before us. Their oldest daughter, then 13, was so confident and full of questions, it was remarkable. While on their trip they hadn't followed any formal schooling and just let their children experience the world. When they returned the children hadn't skipped any progress, rejoining their schools.

By the start of 2017 our children were attending schools near our London home. It took several months for them to adjust back to traditional schooling. Since then, they are embracing it and are thriving. They are in the same year as if they hadn't taken any time out—with their old friends.

Bluebell, Columbus, and Willow enjoy being back with friends and are making the most of every opportunity they have. We all travel together when schooling allows and we are continually shaping our plans for the future as we split our time between the UK and US.

We recall the fears that friends and family shared when we had our vision seven years earlier: you'll never settle, you won't get school places, the children will lose out, they won't be able to catch up what they miss in school, you'll find life really hard.

None of that came to pass.

What's really interesting is the reaction of their school friends. There have been several comments along the lines of "Gosh I'm really amazed that you are doing so well and coming top of the class, and I'm having to work hard to keep up with you."

They seem happy to be learning, growing, and enjoying life. They are extremely socially confident and nothing seems to faze them. There are times when things don't work out and they get a poor test result. Their resilience and their reaction at these times is telling: they put their energy to figuring out what they don't know and get on with it.

I'm certain that if our plans were just an adventure rather than the start of a lifelong journey, then things would be different. We're not trying to fit back into an old life, which I know would be hard and cause more adjustment difficulties. Nor are we travelers who just have to keep moving. Right now, we are involved in multiple early-stage businesses and are thriving on creating things and making an impact on the world. We relish every minute of every day and are still absolutely driven by making the most of every moment.

Reintegration of Our Children by Nichola

Many thought we were cavalier with regard to taking our children out of the school system for two years. Pre departure we received critical reactions from some parents about our decision.

On the contrary, the safety, happiness, and education of our children was uppermost in our minds. I was the parent who always made sure the children got to school on time, every day. I believe teachers do an amazing job and don't need that job made harder by difficult parents.

The timing of our adventure was deliberately planned to coincide with Bluebell coming back in time for secondary school, for Willow starting school, and for Columbus finishing primary school. As mentioned earlier, when planning our trip I talked often with Bluebell's and Columbus's teachers. I also spoke to friends of mine who were primary school teachers and, importantly, knew our children. I told them about our plans, asking for advice on how to ensure that the children would be able to settle back after two years away.

The advice we heard was that because the two oldest children were good students they would find it easy to reintegrate and would thrive from their global experiences. We had been advised that we should continue with regular mathematics and encourage the children to read as much as possible to broaden their literacy. We did both of these things. In addition we followed the experiential method that Bluebell's junior school was already using: rather than teaching different subjects, we gave the children projects that encompassed geography, history, literacy, etc. We selected projects related to the places we traveled. Instead of learning about World War II, we taught the children about explorers. Rather than learning about the Egyptians, they learned about the Incas when we went to South America, and learned about the building of the Panama Canal, etc. The only discrete subject taught separately was math.

Plus for four months, our additional crew member Caroline, a former middle school teacher, worked with the children every day.

When we returned Willow started kindergarten in September along with all her classmates. We secured a place for Bluebell in a London secondary school at the end of September. Columbus had to wait a bit longer until a place became available, but by the beginning of the spring term in January, he had a place at the junior school. Both Bluebell and Columbus were back in classes with their friends. The schools were extremely welcoming and helpful in seeing that the children settled in. They are now doing well, excelling in the subjects they always loved, disliking the same subjects that they found difficult beforehand.

They have also returned to school with something very important: an appreciation of the wider world—they are citizens of the world. They love life and want to explore the world they live in. They love spending time with their friends, but they also know that when we make our next plans they can spend time somewhere else while still maintaining those friendships, and that they will still have their home as a secure base to come back to. They feel their roots, a base from where they can have further adventures and a loving close family. That's a great foundation for life.

We did everything we could to ensure that the children could settle as much as possible when they returned home. We took into account their personalities, their ages, and their abilities. Our choices were right for our family.

We have spent a lot of time as a family since our return discussing what we did. The children talk to their friends about life away. Columbus's friends (typical 10-year-olds) love to hear stories of the places we visited and the animals we saw. I help in Willow's class and I have taken in photographs to give the children a taster of what Willow experienced with her family. We also spend time together planning what's next.

For our return I carried out some research on the effects of reintegration on children. Most of the information is on children who have been excluded from school or who are from gypsy families and traveling communities with other issues to deal with. However, the research seemed to suggest that people who travel are more able to gain perspective on life, making them less emotionally reactive to day-to-day changes, which in turn increases emotional stability. It also makes them more creative and more adaptable.

What I can attest to are the advantages of what we did. In particular, we broke from the digital environment and introduced our children to new things, teaching them about the wide world we live in, the richer learning environment, well beyond a classroom's four walls. These experiences made our children more social and bonded our family into a wholly new, strong team.

My Wish for You—Where the Magic Happens

My wish is that our story has both inspired you and provided practical steps you can take to shape your world. Live your life by making conscious choices about what you and your family truly want. Where does the magic happen? The magic happens when you step outside your comfort zone, when you dare to imagine what you truly want for your life and create a compelling vision of that future. When you take action bravely, pushing beyond into uncertainty. Not recklessly, but with steely determination and discipline, and thorough thought and planning to create the vision you imagined. That is Where the Magic Happens.

All of us have a brave part inside of us. If we allow that courage to come to the fore it will be the catalyst for creating magic. No matter where you are in the world—or how big or small your dream—it's your time to seize your moment, to make your Magic Happen, to make your life everything you wish it to be.

Consider your life as a blank sheet of paper. Imagine what you want together, create a story that excites all of you, then go ahead and create that vision for your lives and what lies beyond it. Start now. That's the first step. Life is a continuous journey and it's in your grasp, right now, to shape the future you want.

Appendix I

Resources

There are many important issues to consider when undertaking a project like this. This section provides an insight into the levels of planning we did in different areas. This is by no means comprehensive. Wherever you decide you want to make your magic happen, you'll have to undertake your own planning and research to get comfortable with the risks and rewards that you face.

There are many fabulous books that we used to address these questions in much more detail. You'll find these listed at the end of this section.

By the Numbers

These are the monetary resources we needed to sail around the world. There are less expensive ways to do it, and there are more expensive ways. These were simply our costs and I would expect them to be mid-range costs. For a deeper examination of voyaging costs, see *The Voyager's Handbook* by Beth A. Leonard.

Boat Purchase Costs:
Our boat purchase budget: $500,000–$750,000 (£380,000–£570,000)

Monthly Living Costs:
We allowed approximately $6,000 (£4,500) per month for eating out, trips, provisioning, and boat maintenance (a total of $72,000, or £54,000, for the year). This was probably a mid-range amount. It could be reduced further by carrying out more of your own maintenance and eating

wherever possible on the boat. We know friends who've sailed the world on a budget of some $2,000–$3,000 (£1,500–£2,300) a month.

Approximate Additional Costs—Training Courses Per Person:
Medical training courses—approximately $1,500 (£1,100)
Radio operator's licence course—$1,000 (£750)
Weather course—$500 (£380)
Diesel maintenance course—$500 (£380)
Sea survival course—$200 (£150)
Competent crew—$800 (£600)
Day skipper—$800 (£600)
Coastal skipper—$2,000 (£1,500)
Yachtmaster—$2,000 (£1,500)
Offshore safety—$200 (£150)

Approximate Additional Other Costs:
Medical supplies—$5,000 (£3,800)
Vaccinations—$1,500 (£1,100)
Annual storage costs—$2,000 (£1,500)
Buying and installing our secondhand SSB radio kit—$5,000 (£3,800)
Buying our satellite phone (Iridium pilot)—$5,000 (+$1,000 for installation) (£3,800 + £750)
The cost of the World ARC from Panama to Australia—$15,000 (£11,400)
The cost of the World ARC from Australia to St. Lucia—$15,000 (£11,400)

Sailing Training

Although I'd circumnavigated with the BT Global Challenge in 2000–01, I never underestimate the sea and the need to undertake continual training, and to be on top of the latest thinking and developments is essential. Nichola, who'd sailed less, had a lot of training to go through to get her in a place where we were safe to go.

Here's the list of training courses (all RYA approved) we attended in the buildup to departure:

- Competent crew (Nichola)
- Day skipper (theory and practical) (Nichola)
- Coastal skipper course (theory) (Nichola)
- Coastal skipper practical (Nichola)
- Yachtmaster course (theory and practical) (Caspar)
- Offshore safety course (both)
- Sea survival course (both)
- First aid course (both)
- Ship's doctor's course (parts 1 and 2) (both)
- Diesel engine course (Caspar)
- Weather course (Caspar)
- Radio course (VHF) (Caspar)
- Radio course (Long wave) (Nichola)
- Optional extras—rigging course (Nichola)

Systems to Consider when Searching for an Offshore Boat

Autopilot (either wind or electronic)
Power generation systems:
- Generator (fixed or portable)
- Wind power
- Solar power
- Hydrogenerator
- Charging from the engine
Watermaker
Electronic navigation systems (and backup systems on handheld devices)
Satellite communication systems
SSB Radio/VHF Radio
Washing machine
Entertainment systems (stereo & TV)
Fridge and Freezer
Air conditioning
Fresh water system
The number of fuel and water tanks you have

Boat Preparation

When we bought *Aretha,* we had a significant amount of work to do in order to get her ready for ocean passages. This involved refit work and we also developed a series of regular maintenance routines. Oyster was helpful in providing schedules detailing the routine work that we needed to undertake on a regular basis.

Immediate Modifications Made to Aretha

Here is a list of the steps we took or adaptations that we made ahead of our journey. We did this after we had a full survey of the boat and worked with specialist suppliers to get *Aretha* ready for our departure. This is not a full list—it's simply indicative of the amount of detail needed:

- Added a third reefing line to the mainsail
- Main dealer service of the engine, generator, and watermaker
- Installed a new TV, music system, and computer
- Installed satellite communications—phone and email
- Replaced the deck hatches
- Fitted jackstays as clipping-on points, which ran the full length of the boat
- Fitted new running rigging
- Added a second radar reflector to the mast
- Purchased second EPIRB and additional handheld GPS
- Fitted a new spray hood (dodger) and bimini
- Overhauled both the main and the headsail
- Serviced all the winches and backstay
- Serviced the gas (propane) alarm
- Fitted a new liferaft, lifejackets, and fire extinguishers
- Serviced all bilge pumps
- Serviced the steering gear
- Serviced the fridge, freezer, and heater
- Serviced all the heads
- Serviced all the seacocks
- Repaired the dinghy
- Serviced the outboard

- Placed netting around lifelines due to having children on board
- Treated the decking
- Deep cleaned under all sole boards
- Adapted the reefing lines so that they went back to the cockpit

Aretha *Schematics*

Sail plan

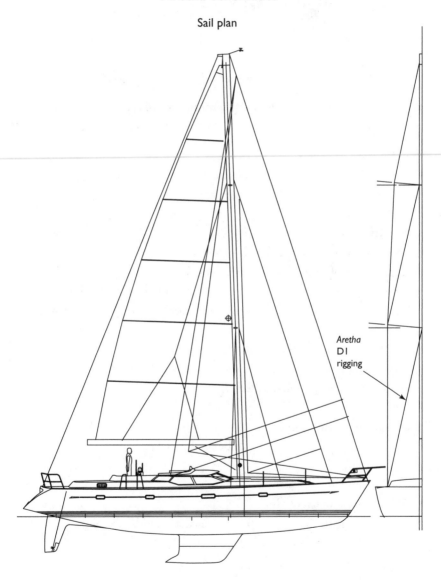

Aretha
D1
rigging

Interior layout

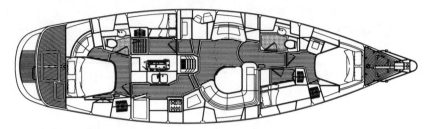

Safety Equipment

We made sure that our safety equipment was in date, in good working order and that crew knew how to use them. The safety equipment that we carried was:

- Liferaft (with hydrostatic release fitted)
- Lifejackets (with spares) and storm hoods
- Harnesses/clip points (D rings), jackstays
- EPIRB (x 2)
- PLB (Personal Locator Beacon) (inserted in lifejackets for adults or attached on outside of children's Personal Flotation Devices)
- Grab bag (including emergency water, first aid kit, extra GPS, sat phone, sunburn prevention, dehydration prevention), yacht name and lanyard attached
- MOB (Man Overboard) (Jonbuoy dan buoy)
- VHF (handheld in addition to the main one)
- Radar (with passive radar reflector)
- AIS
- Flares (heavy duty gloves as well)
- Lifebuoy or life sling, which can be used in a MOB situation
- Bilge pumps
- Navigation lights
- High-powered searchlight
- Bolt croppers or similar equipment (hacksaw and blades/angle grinder with case and backup batteries)

- Emergency tiller
- Paper log and charts in the event of power loss
- Handheld GPS
- Foghorn (x 2)
- Fire extinguishers and fire blankets
- Smoke detectors

Emergency Systems to Practice

Having safety equipment is one thing. Knowing how to use it when you need to in an emergency is another thing entirely. I made sure we took the time as full crew to talk through different emergency procedures and what we would all do in certain situations. Talking these through made us more aware of the risks and appreciated the gear that we had on board. Whenever we had new crew on board, I took the time to walk through equipment and procedures. I'd usually involve the children as it helped to reinforce the learning for them. Some of the procedures we talked through were:

- Man Overboard
- Fire
- Losing the mast/rigging
- Losing steering
- Flooding/water ingress
- Dark boat (no power)
- Setting up a tow
- Heavy weather routine, boat handling, heaving-to and using drogues
- Medical emergencies
- Abandon Ship

Boat Checks—Daily Routines

There were lots of boat areas that needed continuous management and maintenance. Just as an insight, some of the daily routines we used were:

Rigging and Sails

We checked our rig every day at sea, both at deck level and checking aloft with binoculars. We were constantly looking for chafe and general wear and tear so that we could make repairs in advance of things going wrong. In addition, we went all the way up the mast and checked everything before every ocean or long sail departure (going aloft). We used liberal amounts of silicone spray to ensure everything moved smoothly, and we used amalgamating tape for rough edges. When going aloft we'd always wear a helmet (climbing helmet) and use a bosun's chair.

We also had professional rig checks as an extra precaution at four different points around the world.

Essential rigging tools:

- Teflon spray
- Silicone spray
- Selden rigging screw oil
- Blakes mast care
- Brass wire wash
- Ormiston Monel seizing wire

Power Management

Power management was a constant issue while at sea—both the generation of it and the management of what you have in your battery banks. We worked out our daily power needs compared to our capacity and monitored the use of power on board carefully using our battery management system. We added additional power sources as we went around to give us more options in the event of power failure!

Water Management

The management of our fresh water in both obtaining and consuming was crucial and very much like power management—a constant issue while sailing. We were carefully monitoring both the creation of water (through our watermaker) and the use of it.

Whenever we had the opportunity on land, we always topped up our one water tank. I also stipulated that we always carried over 200 liters of bottled water as an emergency supply should we ever have a problem with our water system. We never had to use this.

We were vigilant in our water consumption when cooking, cleaning, washing, and laundry, although compared to other smaller boats we were in a relatively luxurious position in that we had 900 liters of water in our tank as well as bottled water, and the means to make water.

We were able to and I allowed showers daily (although not hair washing daily). Some boats, primarily those with smaller capacity tanks and no watermaker, installed taps that provided sea water to be used for washing up. Others rigged makeshift showers on deck, which collected the rainwater and then enabled a shower with the collected water.

Medical Considerations

We needed to be as self-sufficient as feasibly possible when it came to medical matters. We'd be on our own for long stretches of time and after much research we decided to thoroughly explore every avenue available to us to minimize risks around this. We decided that we both needed to be as fully trained as possible and to have the very best equipment and resources on board *Aretha*.

Medical Training

We both attended the initial first aid one-day course and then two further courses for our ship's doctor's qualification. The total ship's doctor's course in the UK is 9 days long (a four-day and a five-day course). We had to have attended the one-day course to qualify for the next stage and then the second stage course in order to qualify for the final stage course. The certificate, once awarded, lasts for five years. For the latest courses available in America, you can go to the US Sailing Organization at www.ussailing.org or the Wilderness Medical

Society at www.wms.org who provide a Diploma in Dive and Marine Medicine.

Medical Equipment

We had three levels of first aid kit—a small daily kit, which is instantly accessible and probably resembles one you may have in your home containing a thermometer, Band-Aids, alcohol-free moist wipes, antiseptic cream and so on.

The next level of first aid kit contained more complex items and was still easily accessible.

Finally, the large ocean medical kit, which contained a more involved level of equipment for more serious situations, probably where on land you would be seeking medical assistance. It was stowed and less accessible (although still accessible quickly), containing sterile syringes, suture kits and so on. In addition we always kept burn gel in the galley beside the stove in the case of burns to the skin.

With our medical kit, we tailored what we needed for our specific circumstances and made sure we had access to medical experts.

We looked practically at the ages of our crew and any requirements—on the one hand, with children on board we took greater care with medical training and put the needs of the children above ourselves and so we had lots of pediatric supplies (for example, pediatric needles). On the other hand, with a younger crew we made the choice not to take a defibrillator in the case of heart attack, which boats with older crew did carry.

We carried a list of our medical supplies with us and left a matching list with a GP friend at home. That way, in case of emergency we could contact our friend (via email or sat phone—depending on the emergency) and they would know what we were carrying and what could be used in each situation. Remember the medical courses give you a very basic knowledge and wherever possible you should always seek professional assistance and never administer medication without medical advice.

We also had access to the trainer from our medical course who we could contact by email and was helpful regarding advice.

Next to our satellite phone, we had a laminated card with the phone number of Falmouth Coastguard in the UK who we knew we could always call 24 hours a day for emergency medical advice while at sea.

Any crew who traveled with us provided a complete medical history (confidentially) and we ensured that they had any spare medication that they needed.

Basic First Aid Equipment

This is the list of basic first aid equipment that we carried within easy reach in the main living area:

- Alcohol-free moist wipes
- Gauze sterile swabs
- Assorted Band-Aids, including child-friendly Band-Aids for minor cuts and scrapes
- Surgical tape
- Large adhesive wound dressings
- Sterile dressings for variety of wounds
- Adhesive suture strips
- Sterile eye pads
- Eyewash
- Variety of bandages (finger, triangular, elasticated crepe)
- Burn gel and gel burn dressings
- Non-latex gloves
- Scissors, tweezers, safety pins, etc.
- Foil blanket
- Thermometer
- Instant ice and heating packs
- Splints
- Emergency dentistry kit
- Pre-threaded suture kit

- Arnica
- Essential oils
- Painkillers
- Diarrhea relief
- Laxatives
- Antacids
- Rehydration salts
- Antihistamines
- Seasickness medication
- Common cold remedies
- Preparations for thrush and vaginal infections
- Antiseptic preparations
- Antibiotic ointment
- Hydrocortisone ointment
- Eye drops (both antibiotic and anti-inflammatory)
- Ear drops (see notes on ear infections and the prevention of, on p. 282)
- Anti-inflammatory gel
- Local anaesthetic gel
- Antifungal preparation.

More Complex Ocean-Ready Medical Equipment

These complete kits can be purchased ready to use in the UK; however, without the extensive medical training course we would not have purchased this.

Common Medical Issues

There is always potential for major medical emergencies. However, more common are the everyday ailments typical to tropical waters.

Seasickness

Nichola experienced this every time we set sail. She learned steps to manage it and ensure she made a speedy recovery. We found the best solution was to have a good night's sleep beforehand, and avoid fatty foods and alcohol. Be well rested, dress warmly, and eat something simple that lines the stomach before setting sail. Nichola tried many products, plasters you stick behind the ears, bands, a variety of medication, ginger... the most effective plan was for Nichola to help set sail then once we were underway she would take a heavy-duty anti-sickness tablet, which knocked her out for several hours. Then she would wake in time for the night watch. The bouts of seasickness reduced from four days to one by following this procedure.

Sunscreen—Dealing with Heat and Sun

We stocked up on the highest strength sunscreen before we left (it's very expensive in many countries). We restocked in Australia. Zinc sticks were also great for noses! Polarized sunglasses were essential for eye protection and we had wide-brimmed hats for everyone.

A bimini (covering the cockpit) was essential. We considered but didn't get a larger one that covers the entire deck for when you are moored for long periods of time. It is important to stay as cool as possible whether or not you have the luxury of air conditioning, which we did not have.

Mosquitoes

We carried lots of very strong mosquito repellent. We took lots of calamine lotion for the mosquito and sand fly bites (very high incidence of both in the Caribbean). We also took mosquito nets to cover our bunks, even though our hatches came with mosquito net covers. Mosquitoes were a real concern when moored. We took long, loose clothing for sunset and after dark, and in some areas for during the day as well.

We researched if we needed malaria tablets. We just needed them in Vanuatu. We also checked as we sailed that we were up-to-date with the latest advice for places where we were headed.

Common Ailments

Calpol and similar paracetamol-type medicines for the children were invaluable.

Tropical ear infections are very common, especially in children. All three of ours experienced them. A good tip we learned is after they have been swimming in the sea to apply a special treatment in their ears which dries up the sea water and makes ear infections less likely. (N.B. Our product was purchased in Tonga but in the US a similar product would be Earol Swim Tea Tree Oil spray.)

We learned that any cuts will get infected if they get wet in tropical seas. We discovered how easily mosquito bites can get infected as well. Fucidin was excellent for treating this.

Other Medical Considerations

Vaccinations
These were expensive and time-consuming but are vital. We discussed the countries and regions we would be visiting with our local medical doctor and followed their advice on the vaccinations we'd all need.

Medical Insurance
Absolutely vital and in some countries (for example St. Helena) we could not disembark without evidence of this. We also made sure all crew who joined us had comprehensive offshore medical insurance. This is a specialized type of medical insurance, rather than your regular type, which would only really provide for coastal sailing.

Obtaining Medical Supplies En-route
We had the details of a registered pharmacist, who had a copy of our ship's doctor's certificates and therefore was happy to ship us medical supplies on request. We would get them sent to the address of a friend or family member at home, who then brought them out to us. We always made sure we had plentiful stocks of the broad-based, most useful antibiotics, for example.

Medical Documentation
We traveled with the children's medical records as well as their birth certificates. We also made sure that dental and optician appointments were up-to-date before departure.

Provision of Medical Services Generally

We found excellent medical provision all round the world. In Australia we found we could access reciprocal medical treatment so that on providing our British passports, our medical treatment was free. In many countries medical treatment was both excellent and cheap. For example, in Tonga we had a wonderful New Zealand doctor to treat Columbus for an ear infection at a negligible cost. In French Polynesia the doctors were often from France.

Other Ways of Accessing Medical Advice

There are services that you can pay for that will provide different levels of medical advice and assistance while at sea. Effectively, the greater the cost, the more advice and assistance provided. We did not use any of these services.

Boat Hygiene

Another part of medical management was most definitely boat hygiene. We continually kept on top of cleanliness, stopping the spread of germs and avoiding any bugs getting on board. This was vitally important to maintain a healthy boat. Washing hands after using toilets and before any food preparation and the use of disinfectant sprays with paper towels on surfaces, floors, door handles and other places that hands come into contact with were good habits to maintain. Personal hygiene was also vital, even with a possibly limited water supply for washing one's body. The management of effective storage and disposal of rubbish was also important.

Communications at Sea

The communication systems we had on board were satellite phone (providing both email and internet access) and the Yellow Brick satellite tracking system. We carried both VHF radio and SSB radio. The VHF signal also provided the information for the AIS system to digitally recognize other boats at sea.

SSB radio was essential for the Pacific Ocean so we could easily communicate with other boats. We did need to have a long wave radio license in order to be able to operate the SSB. SSB can also be used to send and receive text emails. However, they are expensive. (I would estimate that the total cost of our secondhand equipment and installation was approximately $5,000. It would be closer to $8,000 if installing new equipment.)

Good installation was essential to getting good reception. We didn't have a ground plate so we used something called the "Kiss" system. It would be advisable to get advice from a reputable installer as to the best system suitable for your boat as it is a fiddly and complicated system to get right.

We went for a midrange satellite phone system from the start. Excellent fitting is essential for this to operate well. If there are any kinks at all in the cabling or if it is pulled too tight in the fitting you will damage the cable and the signal will not travel through the cabling. Our sat phone was an iridium pilot for $5,000, which was the cost without installation (a further $1,000). Ongoing usage cost of the sat phone just for sending and receiving text emails was approximately $750 per calendar month.

We also took two good-quality handheld VHF radios.

We considered how we wanted to document and share our adventure. We kept a blog and actively used Facebook to share photos, videos, and blogs. This enabled family and friends to follow our journey.

Weather at Sea

Getting regular up-to-date weather information at sea was essential for us. It enabled us to be prepared—both boat-wise and crew-wise—for what lay ahead of us and if necessary to adjust our routing accordingly.

We used our satellite system to email our provider (in our case we used mailasail.com) to obtain GRIB files. This was emailed back to us as a text file. We had already downloaded the specific weather program on to our computer. This program was then used to open the GRIB file we had been sent so that we could read it.

Apps and programs are changing all the time. We downloaded and regularly used the latest weather app recommended by fellow sailors at the time (Weather 4D Pro).

We attended a good weather course before we left that focused on the specific areas of the world that we were going to sail to.

Life at Sea

Crew Preparation

Taking on board additional crew is a big commitment. This is a checklist that we used for each additional crew member we considered:

- How do we know them? Have they sailed with us or people we know before?
- Will we get on with them?
- What are their gaps in sail training?
- What clothing and equipment do they need, what will we supply?
- Have they completed a sea survival course?
- Explain to them the watch system, mother watch, and domestic chores and what is expected of them
- The need for cleaning, boat maintenance and boat hygiene
- The importance of free time but also the rules on drinking and smoking on the boat and/or at sea
- Allocating responsibility, keeping crew involved and busy
- The vaccinations the crew have or may need
- Their personal medication and medical history
- Money issues
- How to keep in touch with family and friends—available communications
- Immigration matters, including any visas, passports
- What happens in the event of a range of emergency situations
- The importance of maintaining security
- What to pack—clothing and equipment
- Boat rules, including the protocol on wearing lifejackets, leaving the cockpit at night when alone on deck, watch rules

- Harness procedure—when to clip on (maybe heavy weather, at night, MOB, on watch alone, fog, crew ill, reefing)
- Familiarity with safety equipment on board, such as fire extinguishers, their lifejacket, liferaft and other on-deck safety gear, gas shutoff valves, EPIRBs, communications equipment and the location of the grab bag

Clothing

The clothing we chose for time both at sea and on land was important. We looked at our routing and planned our clothing accordingly. Foul-weather gear was absolutely essential wherever in the world as squalls and wet weather happen the world over.

- Foul-weather gear
- Midlayers
- Thermals
- Summer gear
- Footwear
- Headgear
- Gloves—lightweight and heavier duty
- Polarized sunglasses

Useful Equipment for Paperwork

- Small compact printer together with lots of paper and ink cartridges
- Laminator together with spare sheets (invaluable for laminating lists, etc.)
- Heavy-duty, clear plastic sheeting to put over table in saloon (under this you can keep the latest chart you are following as well as any essential lists, etc.)
- Small label-making device with extra cartridges

Electronic Essentials

- Computer that can be used to download GRIB files for the weather (we used a MacBook Pro)

- Good large camera with extra memory cards
- Small underwater camera
- Batteries of all sizes that you will need (look at everything you intend to bring that needs batteries)
- iPad (with inbuilt Wi-Fi) for additional navigation charts
- Cellphones

Watch Systems and Boat Routines

Which watch system will work best given the number of crew and their experience? Will it always be two crew at any one time? Will everyone participate in the watch system or will the skipper be left out, ready on standby when needed?

Consider having laminated sheets on which you can write with a chinagraph pencil. These might include a list of the routine each day at sea, the to-do list before setting sail, or the watch schedule.

Domestic Routines

We appointed one person to be responsible for the boat provisioning in each port (it was usually me). We found it helpful to create a weekly meal plan to work out what to buy. We didn't always stick to the plan but it gave a structure. When morale is low, remember that the meals provided are often the key to lifting spirits. Share the cooking, although on our boat I undertook the majority of cooking, while Nichola preferred to undertake the majority of the cleaning.

Connected in some way to provisioning is the subject of storage. Storage is at a premium on a boat, as well as finding locations that will remain dry, whatever the sailing conditions.

As we have already mentioned, boat hygiene is vital. You will probably find the need for vast quantities of paper towels to keep the boat clean. Wherever possible, use eco-friendly cleaning and laundry products. As much as I would have loved one, we did not have a washing machine. Even with three children we managed without. A mixture of handwashing, using machines when on land, and the children wearing swimwear 99 percent of the time helped in no small part. We found the following items essential:

- Vacuum cleaner (handheld Dyson)
- Plastic clothespins and washing lines
- Mosquito-repellent coils and plug-ins
- Laundry handwash materials (even if you have a washing machine)
- Laundry bags
- Plastic rather than glass "glasses"
- A kettle

Galley Essentials

- Individual named water bottles
- Treats and comfort food, for special occasions
- How to best pack and store food in the case of bugs, water, heat etc.
- Favorite recipes
- Galley equipment
- Crockery that feels like china but is durable (we used a make called Corelle)
- Any particular gadgets
- Coffee press or coffee maker

Entertainment for Children and Adults

- Toys—one small box for each child
- Great games include jigsaws, board games, and Lego
- Audiobooks
- Art materials
- Fishing equipment
- Cooking
- Dressing-up clothes
- TV/films/music
- Snorkeling gear
- Paddleboards and other water toys
- "Happy hour" treats (for every time clock moves forward one hour)
- Treasure hunts

- Birthday traditions (for example, the birthday flags)
- Christmas (mini Christmas tree/Christmas stockings)
- Other occasions, for example Halloween and Easter
- Skipper's cupboards
- Snack cupboard
- Toasted marshmallows
- Afternoon tea
- Movie afternoon
- Homemade popcorn
- Land ahoy (first one to spot this)
- Values prizes

Ideas to Familiarize the Children with the Boat

- Regular fun time on the water
- Swimming courses for the older children
- Learning musical instruments capable of being brought on the boat (e.g. guitar)
- Winners' Bible with collages, pictures of what the children imagined life would be like
- Familiar bedding, cushions from home
- Nice-quality bedding
- Photograph collages of friends and family

Paperwork and Certificates Needed

- Birth certificates
- Marriage certificate
- Sailing certificates
- Radio certificates
- Boat insurance
- Medical insurance
- Travel insurance
- EPIRB certificates
- Boat ownership certificates

- Boat paperwork
- Passports
- Visas
- Logbooks
- Paperwork for each individual country
- Courtesy flags for each individual country as well as a "Q" flag
- Driver's license

Homeschooling

Homeschooling was a key part of how we had to manage our time. To give an insight into what we did, here are some details as to how we prepared for this, what essential equipment we took with us, and the subjects we covered.

Homeschool Preparation

- Talk to the children's teachers in advance.
- Obtain the national curriculum for the years you will be away.
- We were advised to continue with math (especially multiplication) and read as much as possible.
- We decided that other subjects would be covered in topics based on the countries we were visiting. We also joined a home education society. (For us this was the Home Education Advisory Service in the UK.)

Homeschooling Essentials

- Whiteboards and pens
- Multitude of notebooks, paper (white and colored), scrapbooks
- Pens, pencils, erasers, sharpeners, rulers, sticky tape, glue, coloring pens and pencils, stapler and staples, scissors
- Blank cards and envelopes
- Gift wrap paper
- Small gifts for those unexpected birthdays, etc. as you travel
- Thank you cards (fairly neutral to cover all sorts of occasions)

- Clear plastic zip envelopes (A4 size is best) to file papers (better than A4 files), which keeps papers dry and takes up less room
- Books (see separate book section)
- Chemistry set
- Daily journal
- Educational DVDs
- Audiobooks
- Individual cameras
- Wall calendar
- Math materials: playing cards, calculator, measuring jugs, tape measure, scales, fridge magnets, dominoes, Guess Who, thermometer (inside and outside variety), number fan, 100 square, number lines, pack of digit cards, variety of dice and counters, clock, protractor, plastic coins
- Essential words for spelling

Subjects Covered

We covered the following topics:

- Spelling, literacy (creative writing, grammar)
- Math
- Geography
- History
- Science
- Religious studies
- Art and Design
- French
- Music
- Sailing
- Philosophy
- Communications and Technology
- Pre-school topics with Willow (Kumon books were excellent for this)

Online Teaching Resources

We used the following; however, I am sure that these are being updated all the time:

- primaryresources.co.uk
- bbc.co.uk/bitesize
- topmarks.co.uk
- woodlands-junior.kent.sch.uk
- ictgames.com
- iboard.co.uk
- ahomeeducation.co.uk
- bbc.co.uk/schools
- bbc.co.uk/learning.schoolradio/
- theschoolrun.com
- educationotherwise.net

The World ARC

The World Cruising Club runs both the ARC (Atlantic Rally for Cruisers) and the WARC (World Rally), both of which we participated in. Currently these are both run annually. In addition they run other rallies and this list continues to evolve. At the time of writing these include ARC Europe and ARC Baltic, among others.

The benefits of joining a rally are numerous. By joining up with the WCC, for a fee, you have an experienced team who provide you with information that acts as a starting point for issues to consider before embarking on your sailing adventure.

You are introduced to other boats and sailors who will be sailing the same route as you, which provides safety as well as the opportunity for making lifelong friends with other cruisers.

Then when you are underway, the WCC have someone to meet you at each new location as you arrive and to help you take care of the paperwork involved in clearing in and out of new countries, which allows you more time for exploring or boat work!

Initially our intention was to join the ARC and then continue on our route on our own. However, once we had experienced the ARC and could see the benefits to us, especially sailing shorthanded with three young children, we felt that continuing with the WARC added additional safety and support around the world.

The ARC was made up of about 200 sailboats. The WARC was a smaller fleet of approximately 15 core boats, with some boats joining from the Caribbean to Australia and then other boats joining from Australia back to the Caribbean. (See Appendix of Boats who we sailed with on the WARC.)

Bibliography

The potential list of books is endless—these are the books that we used.

Medical Books

BMA new guide to medicine and drugs, DK Publishing (Dorling Kindersley), 1st edition, 2015 (really excellent and easy to follow)

BNF (British National Formulary) for children, Pharmaceutical Press, 2016 (guide to the pediatric dosage—really important if taking children)

The Ship's Captain Medical Guide, Stationery Office Books, 22nd edition, 4th impression, 2005 (quite complex to read and understand)

St. John's First Aid Manual, DK Publishing, 10th edition, 2014

Stoppard, Dr. Miriam, *Baby and Child Healthcare*, DK Publishing (Dorling Kindersley), Updated edition, 2001 (an old classic but excellent)

The course notes from the medical course we attended.

Engine Books

Calder, Nigel, *Marine Diesel Engines: Maintenance, Troubleshooting, and Repair (International Marine–RMP)* 3rd edition, International Marine/Ragged Mountain Press, 2006

Seddon, Don, *Diesel Trouble Shooter*, Fernhurst Books Ltd., 2001

RYA Diesel Engine Course book

Boat Maintenance/Electrics

Calder, Nigel, *Boatowner's Mechanical and Electrical Manual: Repair and Improve Your Boat's Essential Systems*, Adlard Coles, 2017

Manley, Pat, *Essential Boat Electrics*, Fernhurst Books Ltd., 2014

Manley, Pat, *Simple Boat Maintenance*, Fernhurst Books Ltd., 2014

Books on Weather

Houghton, David, *Weather at Sea*, Fernhurst Books Ltd., 2006

Rousmaniere, John, *Captain's Quick Guides—Heavy Weather Sailing* (laminated edition), International Marine/Ragged Mountain Press, 2005

Sea Survival

Bartlett, Tim, *RYA Navigation Handbook*, Royal Yachting Association, 2nd edition, 2014

Colwell, Keith, *RYA Sea Survival Handbook*, Royal Yachting Association, 2017

Sailing Books/Charts

Bauhaus, Eric, *The Panama Cruising Guide*, Sailors Publications, 4th edition, 2010

Blewitt, Mary, *Celestial Navigation for Yachtsmen*, Adlard Coles, 13th edition, 2017

Carnegie and RCC Pilotage Foundation, *Channel Islands, Cherbourg Peninsula, North Brittany*, Imray, Laurie, Norie & Wilson Ltd, 2015

Clarke, James, *Atlantic Pilot Atlas*, Adlard Coles, 5th revised edition, 2011

Cornell, Jimmy, *World Cruising Routes*, Adlard Coles, 7th Revised edition, 2014

Chris Doyle's Sailors Guides, Imray Laurie Norie & Wilson, Various

Ford, J.W.W., *A Seaman's Guide to the Rule of the Road*, Morgan's Technical Books Limited, 7th Revised edition, 2003

Guide to Navigation and Tourism in French Polynesia, Editions A. Barthélemy, 2003

Hammick and Keatinge, *Atlantic Islands*, Imray, Laurie, Norie & Wilson Ltd, 6th revised edition, 2016

Heikell, Rod, *Indian Ocean Cruising Guide*, Imray, Laurie, Norie & Wilson Ltd, 2nd revised edition, 2007

Heikell, Rod and O'Grady, Andy, *Ocean Passages and Landfall*, Imray, Laurie, Norie & Wilson Ltd, 2nd revised & enlarged edition, 2009

Lucas, Alan, *Cruising the Coral Coast*, Alan Lucas Cruising Guides, 7th revised edition, 1996

Pacific Coasts of Central America and United States Pilot, United Kingdom Hydrographic Office, 13th revised edition, 2013

Patuelli, Jacques, *Grenada to the Virgin Islands*, Imray, Laurie, Norie & Wilson Ltd, 3rd revised edition, 2015

Pavlidis, Stephen J., *A Cruising Guide to the Windward Islands*, Seaworthy Publications, Inc. 2nd edition, 2013

RCC Pilotage Foundation, *Atlantic Spain and Portugal*, Imray, Laurie, Norie & Wilson Ltd, 7th edition, 2015

RCC Pilotage Foundation, *The Atlantic Crossing Guide*, Adlard Coles, 6th revised edition, 2010

Reeds Astro Navigation Tables, Featherstone Education (annual astro navigation tables)

Scott, Holly, *Charlie's Charts: Western Coast of Mexico and Baja*, Charlie's Charts, 2015

van Hagen, Kitty, *The Pacific Crossing Guide*, Adlard Coles, 3rd revised edition, 2016

Wood, Charles and Margo, *Charlie's Charts: Polynesia*, Imray, Laurie, Norie & Wilson, 2015

Books on Cruising

Copeland, Liza and Andy, *Cruising for Cowards: A Practical A-Z for Coastal and Offshore Cruisers*, Romany Publishing, 2nd edition, 2014

Copeland, Liza, *Just Cruising: Europe to Australia, via the Mediterranean and Caribbean: Europe to Australia—A Family Travels the World*, Romany, 1st edition, 2014

Copeland, Liza, *Still Cruising: A Family Travels the World, Australia to Asia, Africa and America,*, Romany, new edition, 2003

Rodriguez, Nicola, *Sail Away: How to Escape the Rat Race and Live the Dream*, Fernhurst Books Ltd, 3rd edition, 2011

Travel Books

We found the Lonely Planet series of books to be excellent.

Sailing with Children

Myatt, Claudia, *RYA Go Cruising Activity Book*, Royal Yachting Association, 2007

Myatt, Claudia, *RYA Go Sailing: A Practical Guide for Young People*, Royal Yachting Association, 2005

Myatt, Claudia, *RYA Go Cruising: A Young Crew's Guide to Sailing and Motor Cruisers*, Royal Yachting Association, 2006

Schinas, Jill, *Kids in the Cockpit: A Pilot Book to Safe and Happy Sailing with Children*, Adlard Coles, 2005

Cookbooks

Irons, Jan and Sherlock, Carolyn, *The Boat Galley Cookbook: 800 Everyday Recipes and Essential Tips for Cooking Aboard*, International Marine/Ragged Mountain Press, 2012

Sims, Fiona, *The Boat Cookbook: Real Food for Hungry Sailors*, Adlard Coles, 2014

Homeschool Books

Danks, Fiona and Schofield, Jo, *Make it Wild! 101 Things to Make and Do Outdoors*, Frances Lincoln, flexibind edition, 2010

My First Book of World Flags, Collins, 1st edition, 2013

Oxlade, Chris, *Nature: Explore the Natural World with 50 Great Experiments and Projects* (Hands on Science), Southwater, 2008

Rey, H.A., *Find the Constellations*, HMH Books for Young Readers, 2017

Slavinski, Nadine, *Lesson Plans Ahoy: Hands-on Learning for Sailing Children and Home Schooling Sailors*, Slavinski-Schweitzer Press, 3rd edition, 2014

Stars and Planets, Collins Pocket Guide, 3rd edition, 2001

This list includes lots of books available in the UK—similar titles are available in the US:

- DK Eyewitness books
- Usborne books
- Lots of fiction (especially Roald Dahl and many other classics)
- Horrible History books
- Encyclopedias
- Atlas/world map
- Dictionary
- Nonfiction books
- Schofield and Sims arithmetic books
- Collins Primary Focus books

- Bond range of books (English, math, verbal and nonverbal reasoning)
- Various Key Stage learning books
- Rising Stars science books
- Schonell's spelling books
- 100 Ideas for Teachers series
- What On Earth? books
- Make and do type books

Appendix 2

World ARC Boats 2015/16

Boat Name	Make and Length	Country of Origin	Crew	Legs Sailed
Aretha	Oyster 53	UK	Craven family	ARC, Panama–St. Lucia
Allegro	Trintella 45	Portugal	Couple plus a friend	ARC WARC
Aplus 2	Amel 54	Switzerland	Couple	ARC WARC
Afar VI	Moody 47	UK	Couple	ARC St. Lucia–Fiji
Ayama	Ocean Cruiser 42	Sweden	Couple	ARC WARC
Aquilon III	Lagoon 440	Australia	Couple	St. Lucia–Australia
Exocet Strike	Beneteau First 47.7	UK	Couple and friend	St. Lucia–Fiji
Exody	Starlight 39	UK	Couple	ARC WARC
Garlix	XP-44	Germany	Couple	ARC WARC
Hugur	Najad 520	Iceland	Couple	ARC WARC
Juno	Oyster 575	UK	Couple and friend	ARC St. Lucia–Australia
Karma Wins	Fountaine Pajot Orana 44	Australia	Couple	St. Lucia– Australia
Luna Quest	Rival 38	UK	Couple	WARC
Makena	Lagoon 620	US	Family	ARC WARC

Boat Name	Make and Length	Country of Origin	Crew	Legs Sailed
Pentagram	Oyster 41	UK	Couple	St. Lucia–Australia
Wayward Wind	Hans Christian 43	US	Father and daughter	WARC
Chat Eau Bleu	Lagoon 41	Australia	Couple	Australia–St. Lucia
Circe	Hallberg-Rassy 48	Germany	Couple	Australia–St. Lucia
Starblazer	Hallberg-Rassy 42	UK	Couple	Fiji–St. Lucia
Tulasi	Amel 64	Switzerland	Couple	Australia–St. Lucia

Acknowledgments

The essence of everything we as a family achieved is all about "We, Not Me."

None of this would have been possible without an exceptional team where every single person brought their own unique energy, skills, experience and contribution.

The team reaches far and wide. It starts with Nichola, my wife and the center of my world. Our children, our parents, our siblings, and our extended family. The army of friends and colleagues who were part of our story before, during, and as we continue on our journey of making magic happen by stepping beyond our comfort zone.

And last but by no means least, to all those who dream of more and are emboldened by some of the ideas here to make your own magic happen.

Index